Prestel Museum Guide

Wilhelm Lehmbruck Museum

International Centre of Sculpture

Duisburg

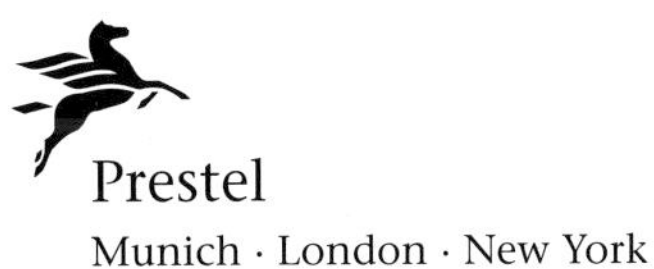

Prestel
Munich · London · New York

Front cover: Wilhelm Lehmbruck, *Loving Heads*, see p. 19
Back cover: Alberto Giacometti, *Woman on a Carriage I*, see p. 97

Edited by Christoph Brockhaus
Editorial direction: Gottlieb Leinz
Sponsored by the Sparkasse Duisburg
Authors of the texts on the works and their initials:
Christoph Brockhaus ChB; Söke Dinkla SD; Gottlieb Leinz GL; Katharina Lepper KL; Renate Heindt Heller RHH; Hubertus Schlenke HS

Photos by Octavian Beldiman, Thomas Durchschlag, Britta Lauer, Bernd Kirtz, KVR Essen and from the museum archives

Die Deutsche Bibliothek – CIP-Einheitsaufnahme:
Wilhelm Lehmbruck Museum. – Munich : Prestel, 2000
(Prestel Museum Guide) English edition
ISBN 3-7913-2111-0

Translated from the German by Elizabeth Clegg, London
Designed by Rainald Schwarz, Munich
Printed and bound by Passavia Druckservice GmbH, Passau

Printed in Germany on acid-free paper
ISBN 3-7913-2115-3

The Wilhelm Lehmbruck Museum
Director: Dr. Christoph Brockhaus
Friedrich-Wilhelm-Strasse 40
47051 Duisburg
Tel. +49 (0203) 283-2630 or 3294
Fax +49 (0203) 283-3892
e-mail: lehmbruckmuseum@stadt-duisburg.de
website: http://www.duisburg.de/lehmbruck

The Museum is located in the city centre in Kant Park, five minutes from the main station. It can be reached by any tram or bus operating within the inner city area.

Opening hours:
Tues – Sat 11 a.m. – 5 p.m.
Sun 10 a.m. – 6 p.m.
(closed on Mondays)

Children's museum
Bookings for all paedagogical activities under
Tel. +49 (0203) 283-2195

Artothek
Every first and third Tuesday of the month
5 – 7 p.m., entrance 'New Building'

Picture consultancy
Every first Wednesday of the month
2 – 4 p.m.

All exhibitions and events, as well as the prices for all publications and fees for the museum, guided tours, courses and workshops are listed in the Museum's own publication released every 3 months.

Museum café and restaurant
'Café Art' welcomes all visitors
Tues and Sat 11 a.m. – 5 p.m., Sun 10 a.m. to 6 p.m.
Groups are kindly asked to make a reservation

Contents

2005: A Museum of Modern Sculpture Marks its Centenary

The December Uprising of 1905: At the end of 1905 twelve Duisburg citizens, well-known figures in public life, issued an 'Appeal'. To complement the Duisburg Museum Association, founded in 1902 in support of the erection of a museum building and up to this point focusing its interest on local cultural history, there were now moves to establish a separate group. In the future this was to work, together with the collector Karl Ernst Osthaus and his Folkwang Museum in Hagen and with the Union of Art Lovers in the Regions bordering the Rhine, towards achieving and funding the installation of permanent exhibitions of paintings, sculpture and in particular objects of applied art. Only a year later it was not this new group but, rather, the Duisburg Museum Association itself that was to be found establishing 'a new department of our collection' for acquisitions of contemporary art, albeit principally painting with a local connection. It was for this new department that, in 1912, the Duisburg sculptor Wilhelm Lehmbruck was commissioned to make a marble copy of his *Standing Female Figure* of 1910. 1915 Lehmbruck refused to participate in a competition for a war memorial in Duisburg, but worked on the theme in private. For three decades it was the family of the industrialist Eduard Böninger who were the principal patrons of the planned museum collection.

From the Duisburg Museum Association to a Museum of Art (1924–1933): Inspired by the ideas embodied in the Folkwang Museum, August Hoff, from the time of his appointment as Secretary of the Duisburg Museum Association in December 1924 until his politically motivated discharge at the end of 1933, evolved the idea of a living museum. In the house of a Duisburg building society (at Tonhallenstrasse 11a), he installed galleries for a permanent display and for temporary exhibitions. The museum was to embrace a collection of the work of Wilhelm Lehmbruck and German sculpture and art from Duisburg and the surrounding region. In addition, Hoff acquired sculptures by Aristide Maillol, George Minne, Ernst Barlach, Käthe Kollwitz, Ewald Mataré and Gerhard Marcks. Temporary exhibitions that changed every month were intended not so much to promote individual artists as to focus on contemporary themes in both national and local art, on architecture and the applied arts. By 1930 the Association building was generally regarded as the 'Duisburg Museum'. In 1931, as part of the implementation of new municipal regulations and the restructuring of local institutions, the city officially established the Museum of Art. This was Hoff's last triumph before his fall from power. In October 1933 the Commission for Culture decreed that the museum should move into the late nineteenth-century, neo-Renaissance villa of a former mayor in the city's main street (Königstrasse 21). This was to remain its home until 1958.

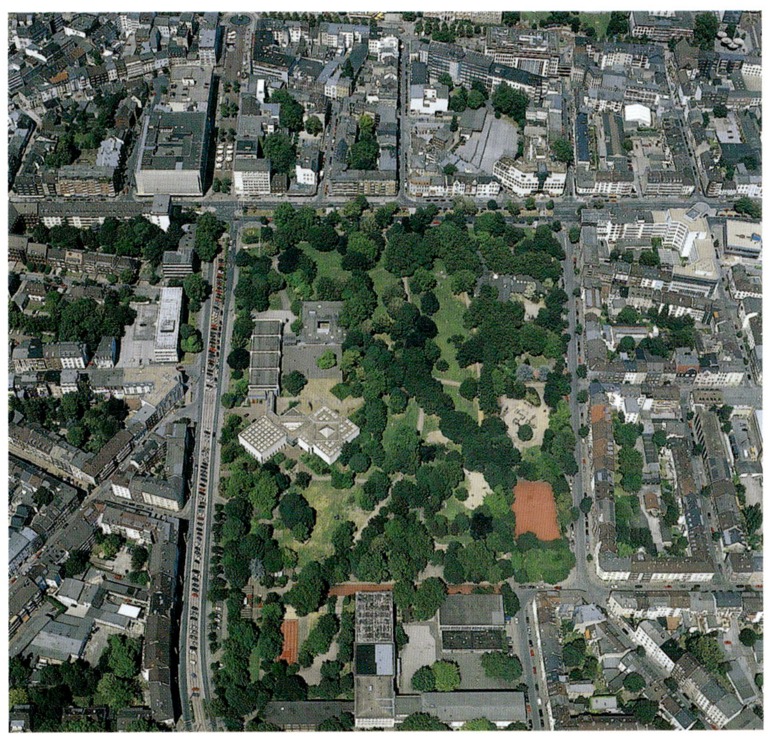

The Wilhelm Lehmbruck Museum with the Sculpture Park (Kant Park) and Fountain Mile (Königstrasse). June 1999 (Photo: KVR, Essen)

The City Art Collection during the Third Reich (1934–1945): The initiatives in private patronage, which had been financially underpinned by state expenditures, now gave way to political dictatorship. There was little room for the new director of the museum, the Leipzig art critic Herbert Griebitzsch (1934–45), appointed in 1934, to manœuvre. He continued his career after the war as Head of the Museum of Art in Oberhausen. The Duisburg museum, now perforce run as the City Art Collection, was constrained to mount ever more exhibitions serving largely as propaganda for the régime. Far worse, the work from the estate of Wilhelm Lehmbruck, painstakingly acquired for the city, had to be returned to the family. As a result of works from the museum collection (all acquired by Hoff) being loaned to the infamous exhibition of 1937/38, 'Degenerate Art', the institution lost over a hundred items, most of these paintings and works on paper, by artists including Wilhelm Lehmbruck, Ernst Barlach, Erich Heckel, Oskar Kokoschka, Ewald Mataré, Max Pechstein, Christian Rohlfs and even by Arno Breker, a sculptor favoured by the National Socialist régime. From November 1938 the museum was requird to display at its entrance a notice reading: 'No entry for Jews'.

The City Art Collection and the Era of Reparation (1945–1954): In 1945

Ernst D'ham, the Head of the Cultural and Legal Department, and himself a collector, became director of what now assumed the title of City Art Collection, remaining in this post until 1954. His principal contribution lay in the reconstruction of the badly war-damaged building, a new inventory of the holdings (which now included all the acquisitions made by the Museum Association), a lively programme of exhibitions and, above all, the acquisition of Expressionist paintings and works on paper, which was perceived as a form of 'reparation'.

A New Building for the Wilhelm Lehmbruck Museum and Its International Collection of Sculpture (1954–1970): With the appointment of Gerhard Händler as director in 1954 (he was to remain in this post until 1970), the second, and so far most decisive, phase in the development of the Duisburg Museum of Art got underway. Händler again secured the work in the Wilhelm Lehmbruck estate for the city. He was able to acquire outstanding examples of international sculpture (thanks to a grant from the B. D. I. [Federal Guild of German Industry]) as well as 20th-century German paintings and an international range of works on paper. In 1964 the museum building designed by Manfred Lehmbruck, the sculptor's son, was opened in Kant Park – a piece of land formerly owned by the Böninger family – as the Wilhelm Lehmbruck Museum. In 1966, with a decisive orientation towards international sculpture, the Wilhelm Lehmbruck Prize was awarded for the first time, to Eduardo Chillida. (It was thereafter to be awarded every five years, later recipients including Norbert Kricke, Jean Tinguely, Claes Oldenburg, Joseph Beuys, Richard Serra and Richard Long). From the mid-1950s greater financial support from industry was forthcoming and the regional government of Nordrhein-Westfalen itself started to provide support for acquisitions and exhibitions. In 1968 a Museum Supporters' Circle was founded to focus more intensively on acquisitions. Every three to five years the Supporters' Circle has awarded the August Seeling Supporters' Prize to sculptors of outstanding talent. The international reputation of the Wilhelm Lehmbruck Museum as a centre for modern and contemporary sculpture was now assured.

The 'Democratization' of the Wilhelm Lehmbruck Museum (1970–1984): In view of the founding of ever more art museums in the region around Duisburg – most focusing on contemporary painting – the new director, Siegfried Salzmann (who was in this post from 1970 to 1984) decided not to acquire further paintings (in 1999 these became the core of the Hans Grothe Collection housed in the Küppersmühle Museum). Salzmann sought to make the museum intellectually accessible to new target groups, established international Object Art as the focus of the collection and focused on mounting exhibitions based on the museum's holdings, in particular in Central and Eastern European art. Since 1977 a two-year grant, the Wilhelm Lehmbruck Stipend, has been awarded anually to three or four young sculptors, one of these always a non-German national.

The Extension of the Wilhelm Lehmbruck Museum (from 1985): From 1985 to 1987 the museum doubled in size through an extension created after the plans of Manfred Lehmbruck and Klaus Hänsch, while the 'Old Building' was renovated between 1987 and 1991. For the first time it was possible to display the collection of modern sculpture in an aesthetically acceptable manner, and a museum education programme appealing to an increasingly diverse public (and fully embracing children) was developed. From 1990 the museum extended its display area for the sculpture collection to include the surrounding Kant Park and also took part in art programmes in urban spaces in the spirit of a new 'culture for industry'. These embraced the erection of large-scale sculptures within the city, the Königstrasse 'fountain mile', Art for the Underground, *Rhine Orange* created by Lutz Fritsch for a site at the meeting of the Rhine and the Ruhr, Dani Karavan's 'Garden of Memories' for the inner harbour and several art projects in the landscape park in the Duisburg-Nord district. The museum has continued to mount numerous exhibitions of modern and contemporary art in former East Germany and in the countries of the former Soviet Union. Within Western Europe, there have been exhibitions mounted in Great Britain and France. Financial support from the Peter Klöckner-Stiftung (1985–94) and the Duisburg Sparkasse (from 1990) has made it possible to make outstanding acquisitions. With further support (from 1990) from the regional foundation *Kunst und Kultur des Landes Nordrhein-Westfalen*, the collection has been substantially enriched and extended to sculpture in photography and in New Media. The museum will in future be developed through the support of a foundation drawing on the capital gains of Duisburg industry and of the Rhineland Association for Landscape. *Christoph Brockhaus*

The Museum Architecture of Manfred Lehmbruck

The building of the Wilhelm Lehmbruck Museum, erected between 1959 and 1964 to designs by the sculptor's son Manfred Lehmbruck (1913–92), had hardly been completed when it became the object of international discussion in the context of the search for the 'ideal' museum architecture. It drew such attention on account of a number of striking features, in particular the emphatically contrasting design for the two parts of the building: in one case the use of concrete and glass (for the section intended to house the Wilhelm Lehmbruck Collection, with a 'floating' roof and a central courtyard open to the sky), in the other the 'neutral' presence of glass and steel (for the large multi-functional hall with its innovative use of movable walls and its virtually all-round glazing, permitting a maximum of natural light).

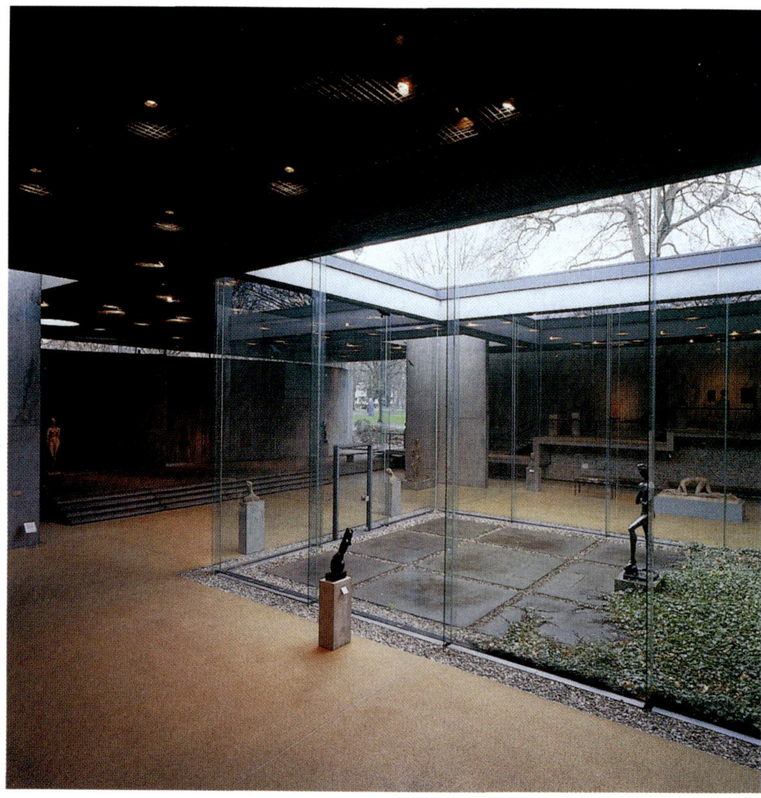

The Lehmbruck Wing with glazed central courtyard

As an architect, Manfred Lehmbruck was an artistically gifted draughtsman in the tradition of the Bauhaus, especially influenced by the style of Oskar Schlemmer. After his first attempts at a career as a sculptor, he evinced a constant dedication to the architecture of museums, in both the theoretical and the practical sense.

Between designing the Reuchlin House for Pforzheim (opened in 1961 as a cultural centre and museum of jewellery) and the Federsee Museum in Bad Buchau (oriented towards Natural History and completed in 1968), Manfred Lehmnbruck oversaw the completion of the first two sections of the Wilhelm Lehmbruck Museum. A third was originally planned to house a lecture theatre but could not be realized because of insufficient funds.

In spite of the different functions of the three museum buildings designed by Manfred Lehmbruck, they share a common architectural language and consistent structural principles. Among the shared stylistic characteristics are the embedding of the main block of the building in the ground in such a fashion that the visitor is drawn up, at his or her own pace, through a number of storeys and intermediary levels and is finally prompted to a deeper experience of

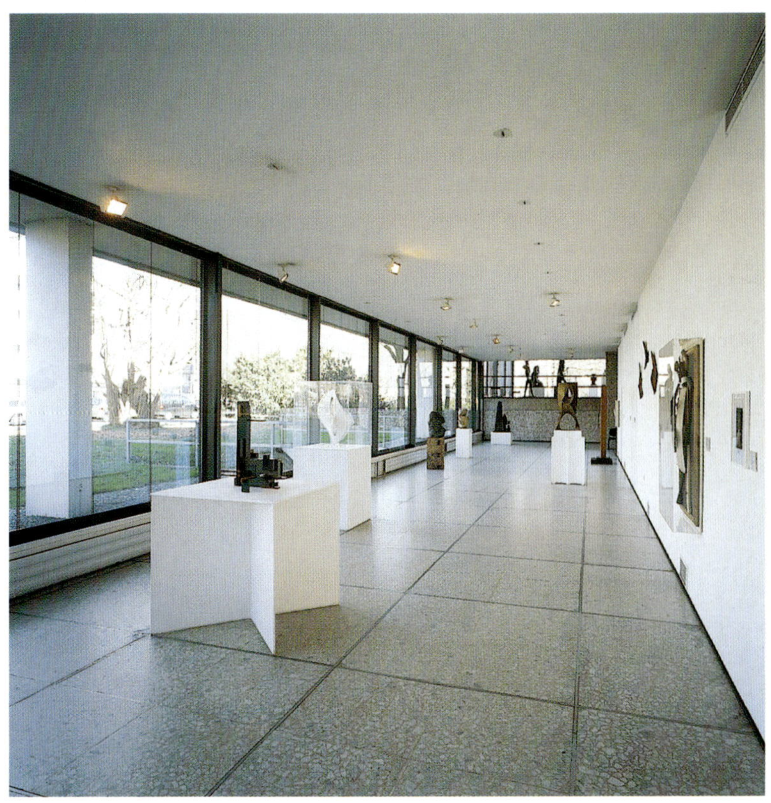

The 'street gallery' of the large hall with Cubist and Constructivist sculptures

the trees around the buildings as an embodiment of nature. The language of architectonic forms aims at a sense of tension between the static and the dynamic, with the individual sections of the buildings arranged, according to the principle of the windmill, around a central free plane – in the case of Duisburg around the sculpture court. The interaction of outer and inner space is here emphasized not only through wall-high glass panels but also through massed panels that convey the impression of spatial flow. Finally, Manfred Lehmbruck always set himself the task of designing every detail of the interiors of his buildings just as carefully as he determined the combination and reciprocity of building materials (fair-faced concrete, pebble-dash, brick, glass, sand and panels in concrete or artificial stone in a variety of colours).

A scheme of 1977–79 for extending the building in order to remedy the lack of space below the sculpture court had to be abandoned for financial reasons (the drawings survive). It was only the pledge in 1985–87 of a long-term loan of a collection of Expressionist paintings and works on paper (a pledge ultimately withdrawn) that made possible this enlargement. This now houses publically accessible galleries for both the permanent collection and temporary exhibitions, in addition to previously lacking spaces and facilities such as a lecture hall, library, administrative offices, workshops and storage areas. The two cubic buildings, placed at an angle of 45 degrees to the hall and with an ornamental and relatively compact facade in glass and concrete – this notably permitting views through the window of the foyer into the sculpture court and out into the park – were realized by Manfred Lehmbruck in collaboration with his long-term partner from the Braunschweig Technical College, Klaus Hänsch.

Thanks to its various extensions, the Wilhelm Lehmbruck Museum (although again confronting the problem of space) now occupies a park area of ten hectares, an interior display area for the permanent collection of 5,150 square metres and a temporary exhibition area of 750 square metres. When this last is not sufficient, the exhibition area can be extended to include the upper triangular-shaped rooms of the New Building, usually reserved for the permanent collection of sculpture after 1970. While no possibilities for further extension are at hand, parts of the collection will alternate with studio exhibitions in all three buildings to meet the needs and wishes of visitors.

Christoph Brockhaus

Hall for temporary exhibitions with paper sculptures by A. D. Christian (right) and two-storey collective gallery in the extension wing (below, right)

Large hall with Christo's oil drums and the *Spielstadt* by Navarro

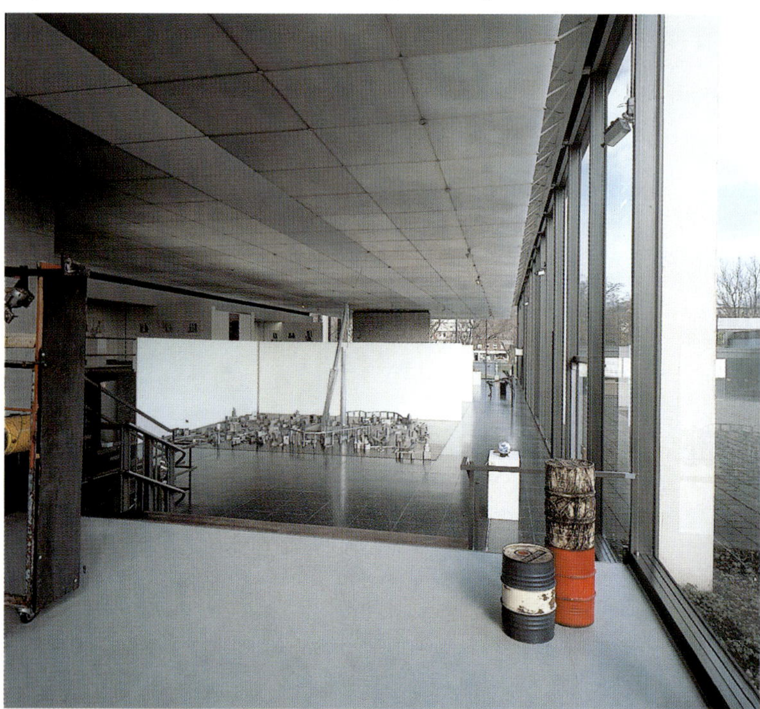

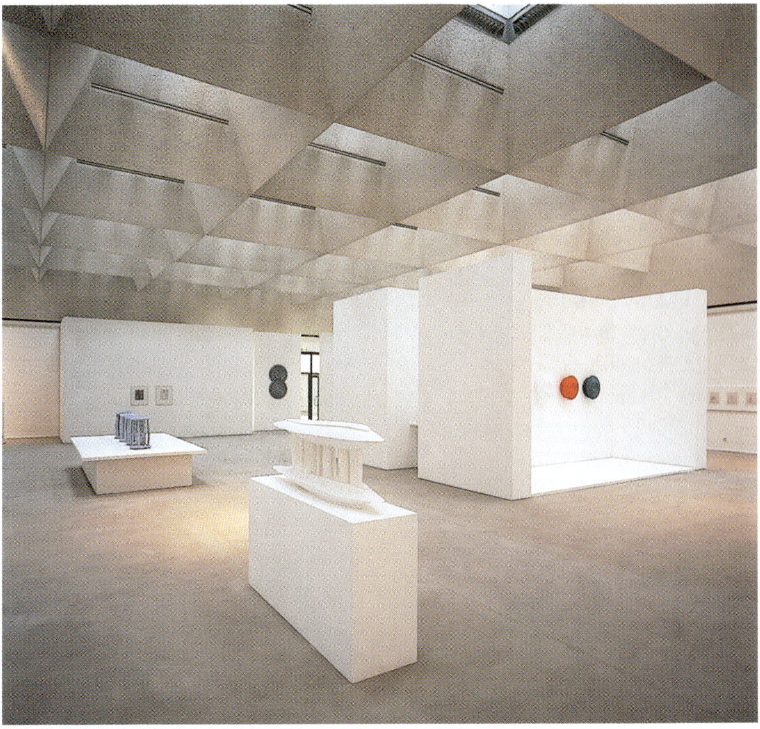

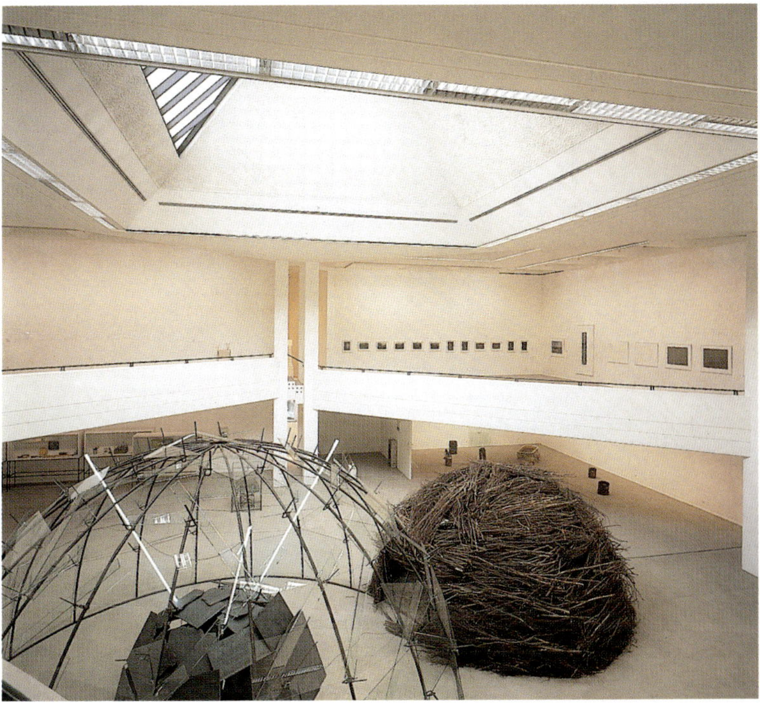

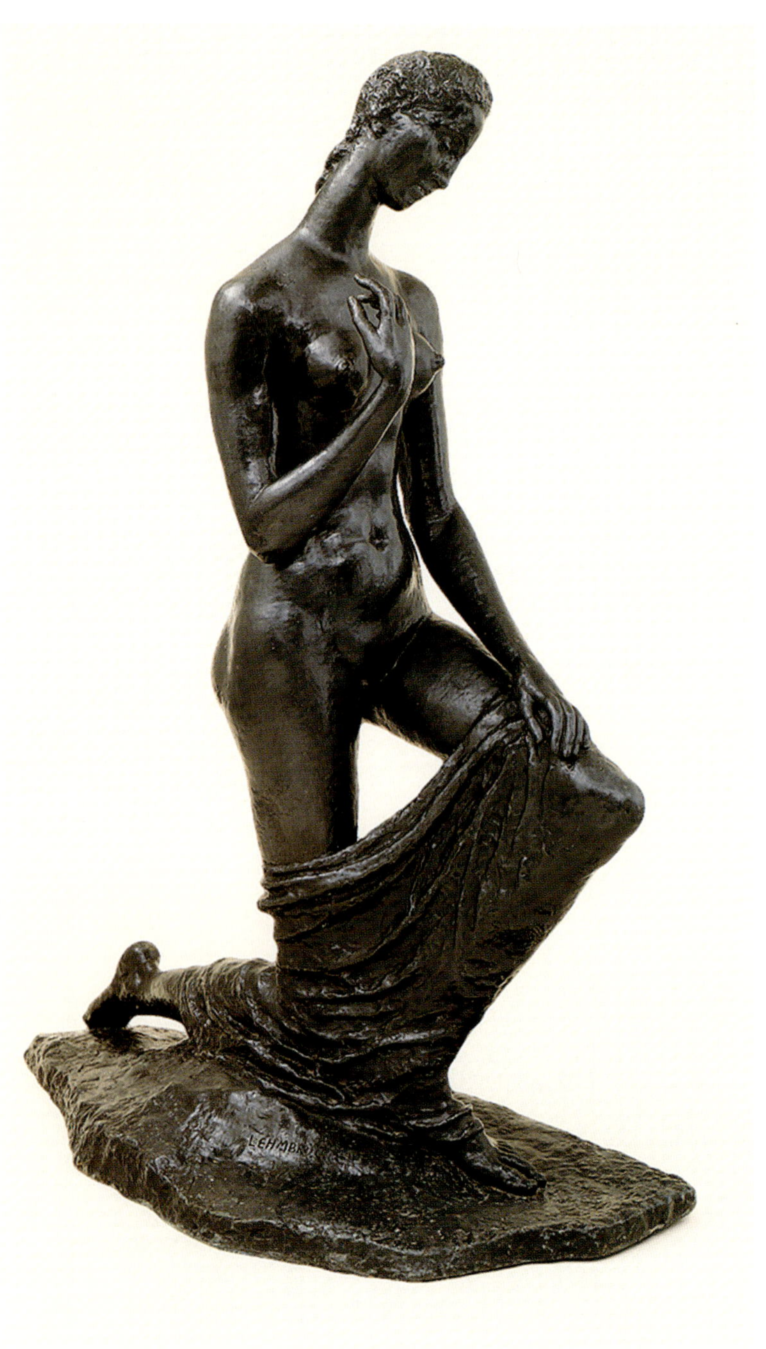

The Work of Wilhelm Lehmbruck

Wilhelm Lehmbruck was born in 1881 in Duisburg-Meiderich. He was the fourth of eight children in the family of a miner who also owned and ran a small farm. Both parents originally came from the surrounding farming region, and their move away from the land, in this case eased through the possession of a small property, was characteristic of the period. In 1895, thanks to a grant from the local community, Wilhelm Lehmbruck, aged 14, embarked on studies at the Düsseldorf School of Applied Arts, where in those days the teaching was focused on craft skills. However, the foundations of his artistic career were more truly laid during his years at the Düsseldorf Academy of Fine Arts, although his beginnings here were conventional enough.

Between 1910 and the outbreak of war in the summer of 1914, Lehmbruck lived in Paris. It was there that, with his *Kneeling Woman* of 1911, he achieved a break with everything that he had so far accomplished. This long-limbed, over-life-size female figure, who offers an image of the purely spiritual with a gesture of contemplation or perhaps even of prayer, was compared by contemporaries, on account of its language of form, with the shafts of the arched buttresses of Nôtre Dame in Paris. This work marks the emergence of Lehmbruck's highly expressionistic figure type, which was widely perceived as 'Gothic'.

Kneeling Woman, 1911, bronze, h 178 cm

The architectonic quality embodied in *Kneeling Woman* was to set the tone for the artist's subsequent over-life-size figures. The *Ascending Youth*, a towering figure of 1913, is posed on its trapezoidal base as if simultaneously resting and climbing. (Much the same quality is to be found in other works by Lehmbruck, for example *Defeat* of 1915/16). The upright torso of *Ascending Youth*, with its sharply bent arms, assumes a rigid, box-like quality, which is extended into the plane, a planarity that is already present, albeit in a 'Gothic' variant, in *Kneeling Woman*.

On account of the insistent pointing gesture of his right hand – present in a gentler and more restrained form in the female figure – the corporeal structure is relatively tight. While Lehmbruck had by this point ostensibly shaken off the influence of Rodin, *Ascending Youth* recalls aspects of the French master's *Burgers of Calais*. Lehmbruck here appears to grasp the concrete possibilities of the shaping of an 'inner self-portrait'; at the same time a potential element of discord lurks in the ambiguity as to the direction of the implicit movement.

An effective female counterpart to *Ascending Youth* is to be found in *Contemplation*, a figure with an extremely compact pose, a very slight distinction between the supporting and the free leg and with the head turned slightly to one side. Also recurring

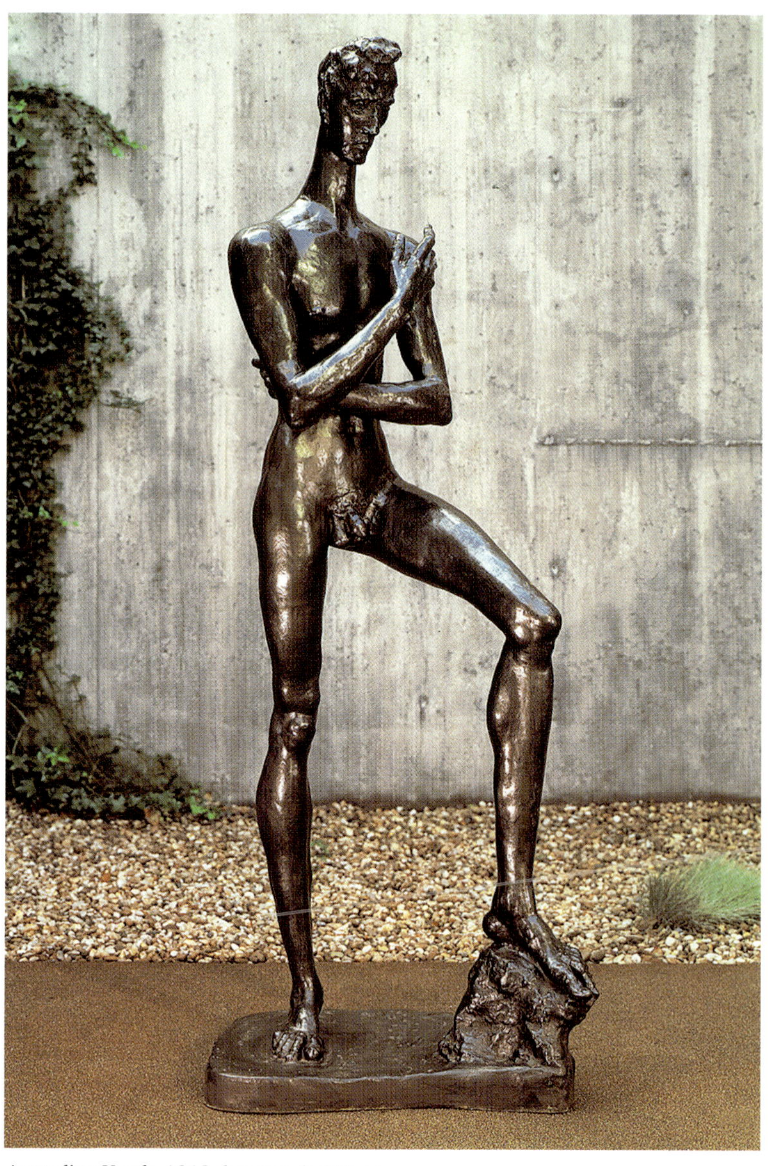

Ascending Youth, 1913, bronze, h 228 cm

here is the motif of the bent arm, in this case with the left hand clasping the right arm behind the figure. This gesture appears to 'open' the figure to the spectator and also, perhaps, to set it in a 'dialogue' with *Ascending Youth*. The implicit pairing of these

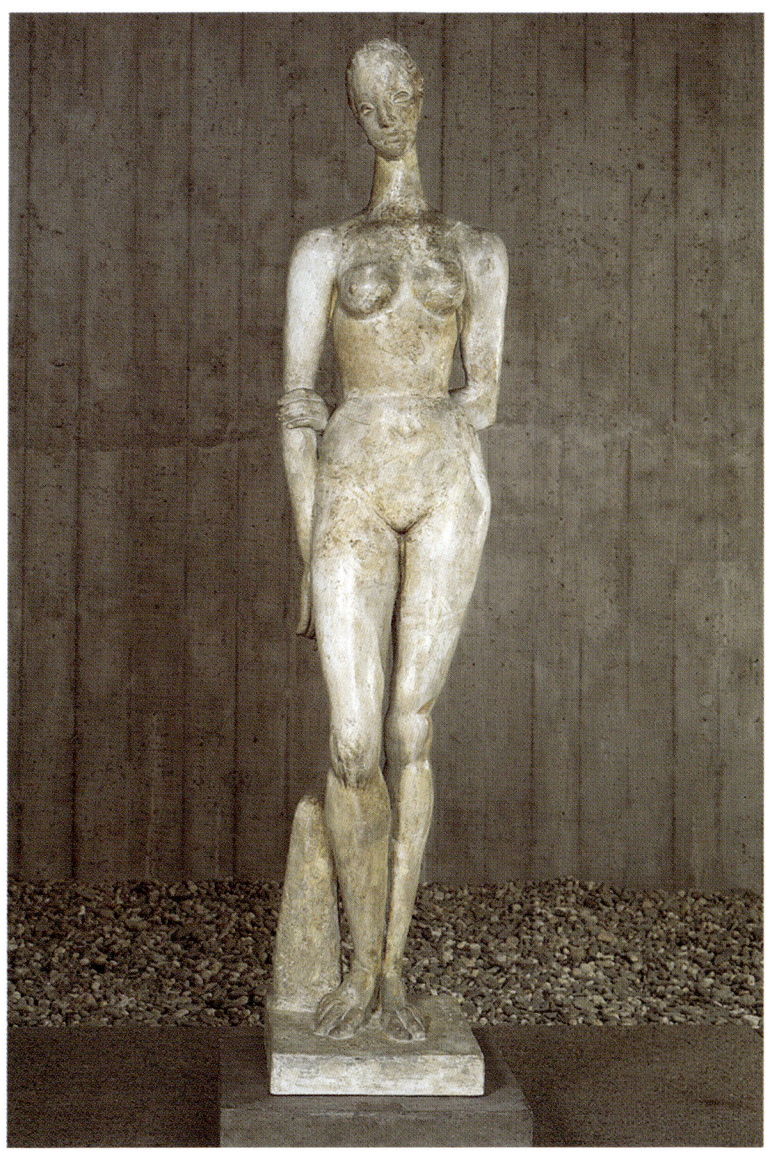

Contemplation, 1913, plaster, h 208 cm

still essentially self-contained figures establishes a timeless formula for what was soon to become Lehmbruck's central theme: the interrelation of man and woman. The absence of any element of exaggerated emotion is supported by the lack

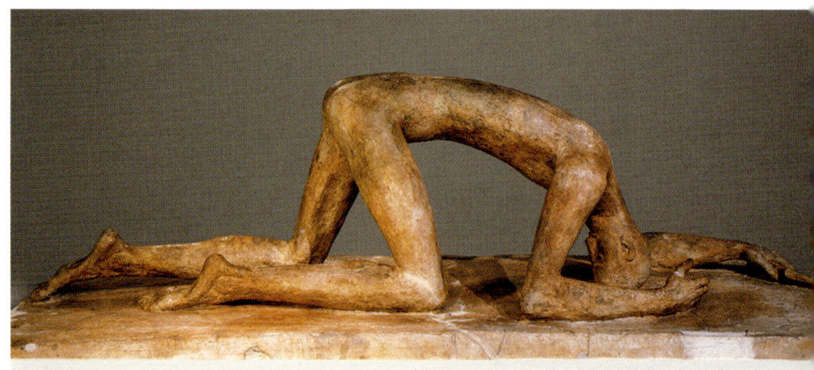

Defeat, 1915/16, plaster, l 240 cm

of indications of movement or action. It is also significant that Lehmbruck was now experimenting with other, simpler materials, notably plaster, which he would cast in a mould. Plaster and earthenware, in turn, brought distinct aesthetic values to the fore in Lehmbruck's work.

On his return to Germany on the outbreak of war, Lehmbruck was called up, only to be released from further military duties shortly thereafter. He initially settled in Berlin, but in the winter of 1916/17 he had the chance to move to Zurich. Until his suicide in the spring of 1919 he divided his time between Zurich and Berlin, by this point having established good contacts in the latter with a number of gallery owners, artists and other people in the city's art world.

Lehmbruck's work of the war years was influenced by both the larger military and political events of the period and also by a sense of crisis in his personal life. His sublime and timeless *Defeat* of 1915/16 and *Seated Youth* of 1916/17 are compelling treatments of the themes of death and sorrow. It has been assumed that *Defeat* emerged from Lehmbruck's preoccupation with the subject of Siegfried, hero of Teutonic legend. The figure, rendered in its elemental nakedness and with elongated limbs, crawls on all fours apparently on the point of physical and mental collapse, as if vainly making one last attempt to raise itself. The body encloses a space that is effectively sealed off by the head, which has sunk to the ground, thereby also concealing the face from the spectator. The swordless pommel in the right hand would appear to allude to the iconography of Siegfried, but, in his reluctance to identify this figure more precisely, Lehmbruck led the way among German sculptors in transforming the soldiers currently fighting and dying for the German Empire into 'unknown', and hence universal, human individuals.

The *Portrait of Elsa Oeltjen* of 1915/17, in coloured plaster, is among the autonomous portraits that were not made as part of a larger series. Lehmbruck employs a simple and traditional bust format but renders detail in summary fashion. The shawl or broad collar is present only as a hint. Attention is focused on the head, its slight sideways turn enlivening the sitter, who appears as if about to engage in conversation with the spectator. Ultimately, however, this image of a fellow artist remains as calm as do those of Lehmbruck's other subjects.

Lehmbruck originally made *Seated Youth* of 1916/17 in cement. The work's other title, *The Friend*, alludes to the artist's several friends who died during the war, preserving the notion of remembrance. In this case Lehmbruck adopted the figural form used in *Defeat*. In the case of the later work, however, we find a deeply hunched seated figure, his head bowed, his arms loosely crossed and resting on the knees of his trousered and spread legs. In showing the right leg more outwardly inclined, a slight right-hand turn of the torso, and the distinct positioning of each of the hands, Lehmbruck creates that subtle suggestion of movement that is characteristic of all his figures.

Seated Youth draws on late Medieval representations of the Wretched Christ or the Outcast Job, both images of intense misery, but the bowed head, allowing a view only of the bald crown, is a badge of anonymity. The work's tectonic structure, with its vulnerable and yet humbling attitude, underlines the general expression of sorrow.

The bronzes by Lehmbruck in the Wilhelm Lehmbruck Museum were cast in the early 1920s in order to be erected in a new Duisburg War Cemetery. In fact, they remained there both during the National Socialist régime (from 1933) and

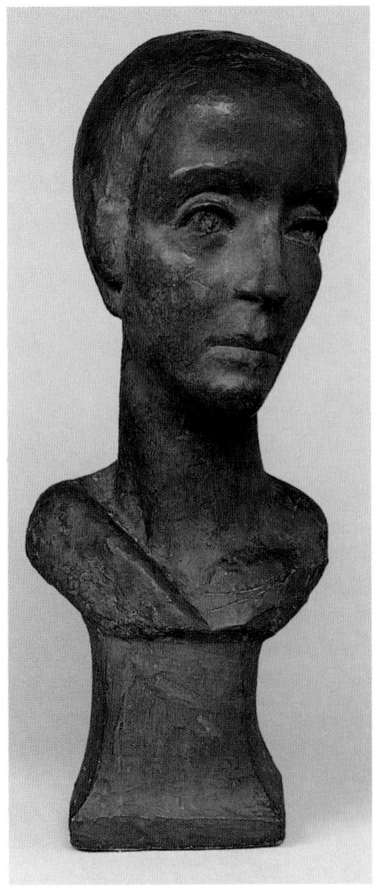

Portrait of Elsa Oeltjen, 1915/16, red-stained plaster, h 67 cm

during the Second World War. This was perhaps the most advanced war memorial of an era that denied the exaggerated expression of feelings. In 1940 it was earmarked to be melted down as a contribution to the war effort; it survived, however, because, on the written orders of Hermann Goebbels, it was designated as 'intended for sale' and was thus spared destruction.

The two late sculptures *Female Torso* and *Loving Heads*, both of 1918, demonstrate that Lehmbruck started

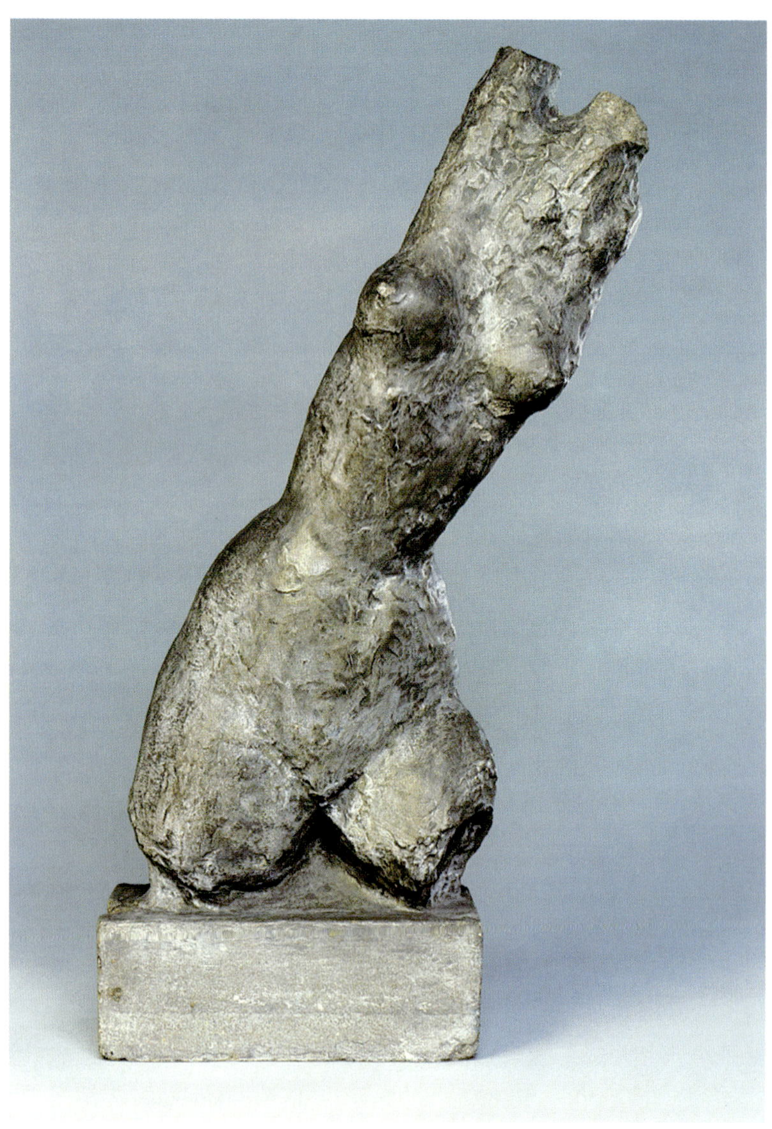

Female Torso, 1918, cement, h 77.5 cm

by seeking a formula for the whole figure but was drawn increasingly to forms focused on the torso – a development unique in sculpture of the Classical Modern period. In the stretched and doubly truncated *Female Torso*, a slight turn towards the side achieves an extraordinary dynamism. The material too, a dark grey English cement, absorbs the light, ensuring that the primary emphasis is on form.

Loving Heads is a work that represents the extreme of this approach in as far as two torsos are reduced to little more than two heads turned towards each other. The sharply receding upper torso attached to the right-hand 'figure', with its inclined neck, thus has a formal significance while simultaneously serving as a thematic 'conclusion'. Just as the flowing hair serves as that of both figures, this is also true of the single, unattached arm. Despite the spiritual proximity conveyed by the two heads, there is no real sense of an embrace.

In Lehmbruck's paintings, too, one finds an increasing formal simplification and its application to a few, essential elements. In *Crucifixion* of 1917/18 Lehmbruck paints on a pale grey ground, which is itself incorporated as an element of colour within the image. Following the account provided in Matthew 27:45, Lehmbruck renders the event in outlines with cursory, dry brushstrokes. Yet he allows the paint from the head and body of Christ to run down the surface of the canvas as if this itself 'wept', sharing in the general mourning – a truly shocking notion for an artist to employ by the standards of the period. The principal lines of the composition meet in the sunken head of Christ, which itself signals that the moment of death has passed. The proximity of the face to Lehmbruck's 'inner self-portraits' cannot be overlooked. The character of this painting offers a vivid reflection of the monstrous pressure under which Lehmbruck then felt himself to be, a pressure that was indeed soon to defeat him. KL

Loving Heads, 1918, cement, w 49 cm

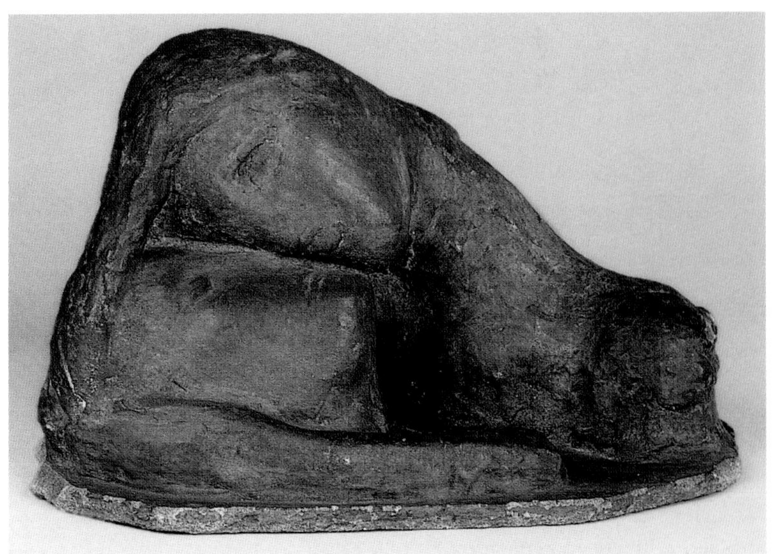

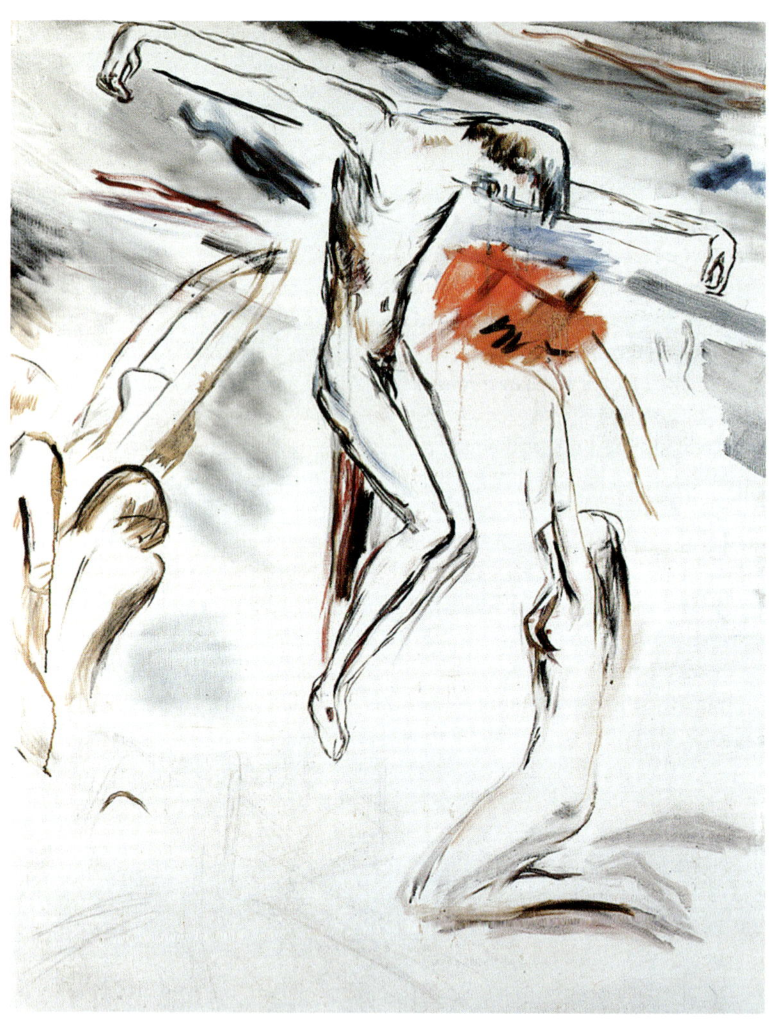

The Crucifixion, 1917/18, oil/distemper and chalk on canvas, 119 x 90.8 cm

Painting: From *Die Brücke* to Informal Art

The display of paintings gets underway with variants of Expressionism. While the Austrian Kokoschka was interested above all by facial and gestural expression, and in penetrating to the core of his subjects, for the artists of the group *Die Brücke* [The Bridge] vibrant colour was of much greater significance. They wanted to give 'direct and sincere' expression to subjective experience. Their favoured themes were unadulterated nature and humanity unencumbered by convention. Established in Dresden in 1905, the group broke up in Berlin in 1913, as its members began to pursue their own preoccupations more than their shared artistic goals. In Munich, Jawlensky, who was a key member of the circle around the almanac *Der Blaue Reiter* [The Blue Rider], evolved a mystically informed variant of Expressionism. While he focused his attention on the face, the 'Rhineland Expressionists' Macke and Campendonk produced images that conveyed the harmony of nature.

The artists represented by the next group of works are linked by a shared tendency towards Constructivism: all of these derived fruitful impulses from Cubism. While it was the regularity of Cubism that was important for Schlemmer, other artists found their starting points in its broken forms, even though each treated these in a distinctive manner. A more rigorous form of Constructivism is to be found in the work of Dexel and Vordemberge-Gildewart. With the exception of these two, all these Constructivists were associated in some measure with the Bauhaus in Weimar, and later Dessau, the centre of Constructivist art and related trends in Germany.

Beckmann's work of the 1920s is usually classified as an example of *Neue Sachlichkeit* [New Objectivity]. This is only partly true, for he strove not only to represent a reality that was free of illusions but also to render 'visible the invisible'. Beckmann himself described the principle informing his approach as 'transcendental objectivity'. While there were many painters in Germany working in a realistic style, a German-based variant of Surrealism was almost non-existent. Max Ernst was the only German artist to venture into the world of dreams and the pre-conscious and to devise a meaningful equivalent for the element of irrational coincidence.

As a realistic style was open to ideological exploitation during the National Socialist era in Germany (1933–1945), many German artists saw abstract painting as a form of liberation, be it from inherited concepts and models (permitting them to use pure form to establish new fields of association and emotion) or from pre-established formal principles and aesthetic hierarchies (freeing them to make the act of painting or the material itself their subject and so to emphasize the unique character of their pictures). RHH

Oskar Kokoschka (1886–1980)
Children at Play, 1909
Oil on canvas, 72 x 108 cm

We see here the children of the Viennese bookseller Richard Stein, who are shown lying on an indeterminate, but apparently soft, surface. Their childishly relaxed demeanour ensures that the scene does not in any way seem posed. While the boy turns to the girl, looks at her and takes hold of her arm, she withdraws from this approach and looks vaguely, almost absently, at the spectator. Equally indeterminate here is the setting. The intermingling reddish browns that surround the children steep the scene in a distinctly unchildlike atmosphere that is dark and subdued.

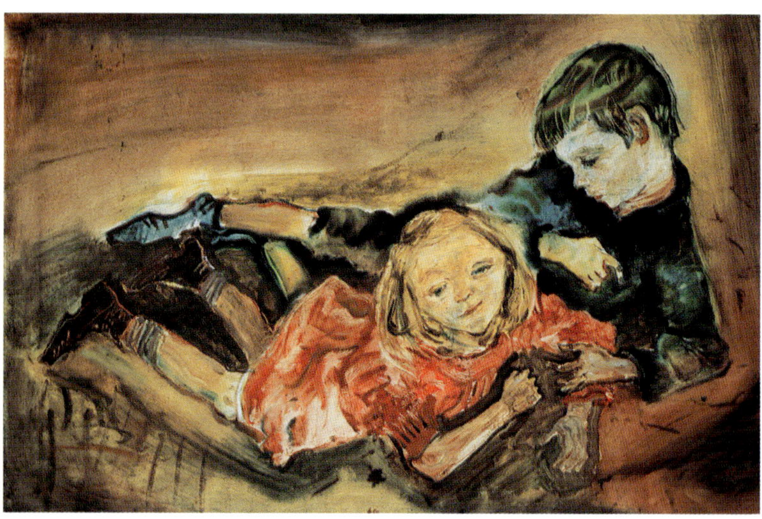

Between 1908 and 1910 Kokoschka painted numerous portraits, many of individuals who were mentally disturbed and whose psychic or intellectual degeneration he conveyed through the suggestion of physical deformity. He sought to penetrate the surface of things and people by probing appearances like a psychoanalyst in order to discover what lay within. Employing broken outlines, agitated, undulating brushstrokes and thinly applied and seemingly transparent paint, he effectively deprived his sitters of their protective skin and exposed them to his analytical gaze, which was always capable of perceiving what was amiss within. One of his central themes, and one also recurring in his works for the stage, was the eternal dilemma posed by the simultaneous and alternating attraction and antagonism between male and female. As this picture reveals, Kokoschka recognized that this was a dilemma present in childhood.

RHH

Erich Heckel (1883–1970)
Windmill in Dangast, 1909
Oil on canvas, 71 x 80.5 cm

This picture was painted in Dangast, a small Baltic fishing village, where Heckel went to paint each summer between 1907 and 1911. In this broad landscape with its clear, coastal light Heckel was able to free himself from his great model, van Gogh, transforming the impulses derived from the Dutch artist's work into images that were distinctively his own. His colouring became purer and his compositions clearer. It was in Dangast that Heckel painted the pictures that were later seen to mark the beginning of his maturity as an artist. In the *Windmill in Dangast*, however, one of the highpoints of Heckel's early work, an echo of the influence of van Gogh is still detectable in the swift and emphatic brushwork, in the development of the image out of coloured lines and in the treatment of space (which, as in the work of van Gogh, combines several points of view). Nonetheless, Heckel's unbroken colours are already clearer and more glowing, the paint no longer pastose in its application but thinly and lightly distributed. The broad brushstrokes are not tautly parallel like those of van Gogh, but seem to preserve the free, loose movement of the artist's hand. They leave patches of the palely grounded canvas uncovered, which itself underscores both the spontaneity of the painting process and the vitality with which the subject is imbued. This landscape image thus becomes a form of expression for a creatively inspired appropriation of nature. There are, in fact, very few pictures in which the *Brücke* ideal of the unity of art and the experience of nature appear to be so directly and intimately realized. RHH

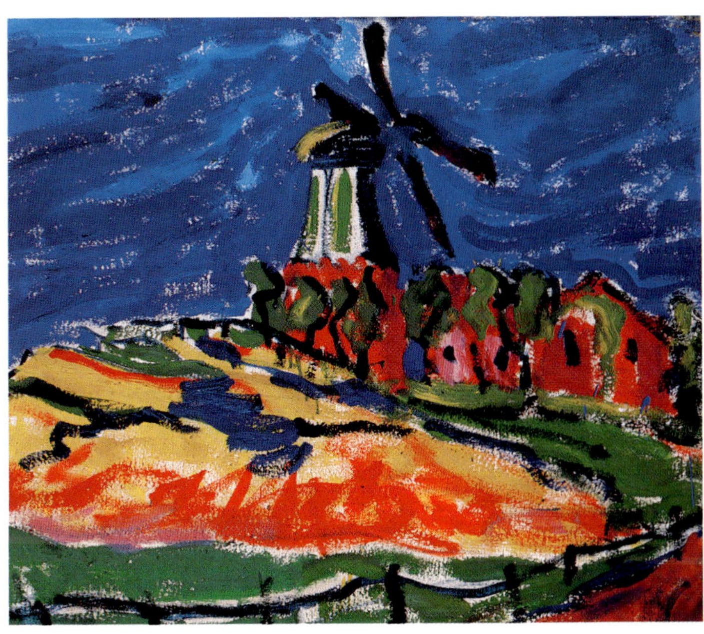

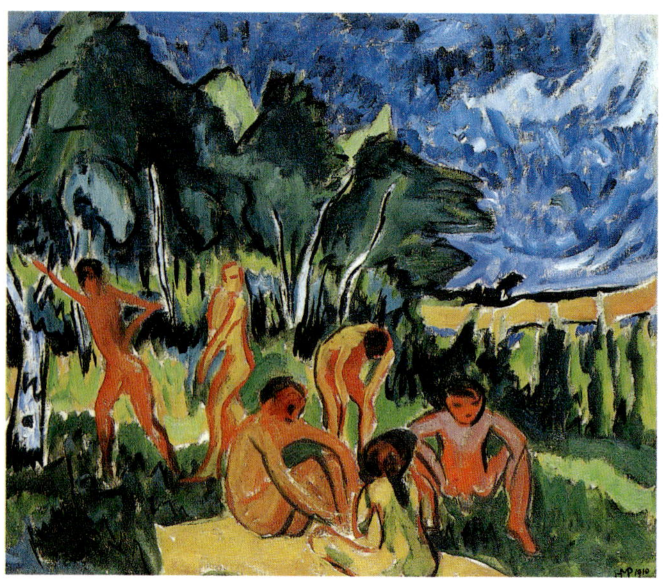

(Hermann) Max Pechstein
(1881–1955)
In the Open Air (Moritzburg), 1910
Oil on canvas, 70 x 80 cm

Pechstein became an enthusiastic member of *Die Brücke* in 1906; he believed that he would find 'a complete unanimity in the yearning for liberation, for a forward-striving art that was not inhibited by convention'. The significance of working alongside artists who shared such convictions is, however, only rarely reflected in Pechstein's work as clearly as it is here. It was painted at the Moritzburg lakes, where Pechstein spent a summer with Kirchner and Heckel drawing and painting nudes. Common to the work produced here by all three friends are the recurrence of slim figures, an interest in forms suggestive of movement, an apparent indifference to facial features and an overwhelming sense of figures totally integrated in their landscape. Pechstein's picture is distinguished by its greater proximity to a naturalistic rendering of the scene. The nudes are precisely and thoroughly drawn; the colours appear largely natural and, where they are less so, their intensity is relatively restrained; and the treatment of space employs an essentially conventional perspective. Also characteristic of Pechstein's approach is his particular use of line: shunning every element of aggression, and circumscribing the motifs in gentle, alternating, rhythmically interrelated curves, his contours unite all the elements in the picture into a decorative linear structure. Intrinsic to this is a relatively detached approach towards the individual and his or her relationship to nature. Nonetheless, by 1911 Pechstein claimed 'to grasp man and nature in their entirety, more powerfully and more from within than [I did] in Moritzburg in 1910.' RHH

Ernst Ludwig Kirchner
(1880–1938)
Two Female Nudes, Fehmarn, 1913/20
Oil on canvas, 125.5 x 90.5 cm

From 1911 Kirchner spent his summers on the island of Fehmarn. Although he was there able to conjure up a painterly world to counter that of the metropolis, the earlier, self-evident unity of man and nature here appears in many respects to have broken down. The harmony of green and ochre is disturbed by the element of artifice represented by the pale violet form. Chromatically, this stands in opposition to nature, but as an expressive element of restlessness, it is comparable in its effect to the vehement, short brushstrokes with which Kirchner intimates the abundance and movement of the vegetation. At the centre of the image we find two elongated female nudes standing in front of a calm, high plot of land that serves to define them as both formally and chromatically removed from the 'savage' green environment. Although surrounded by nature, they are not at one with it – in this resembling quintessential urbanites at the seaside. RHH

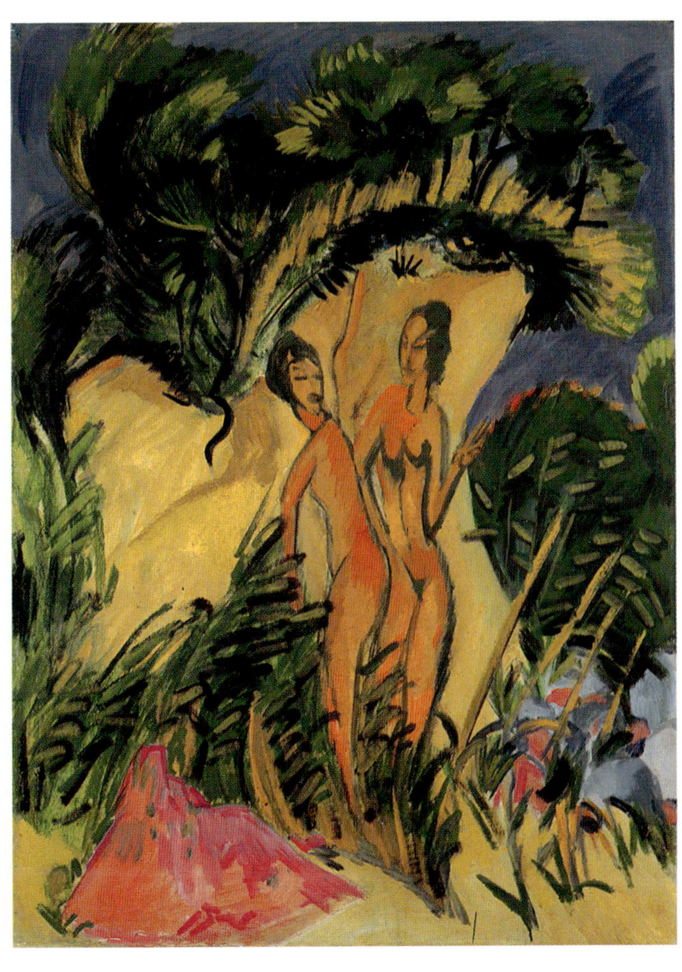

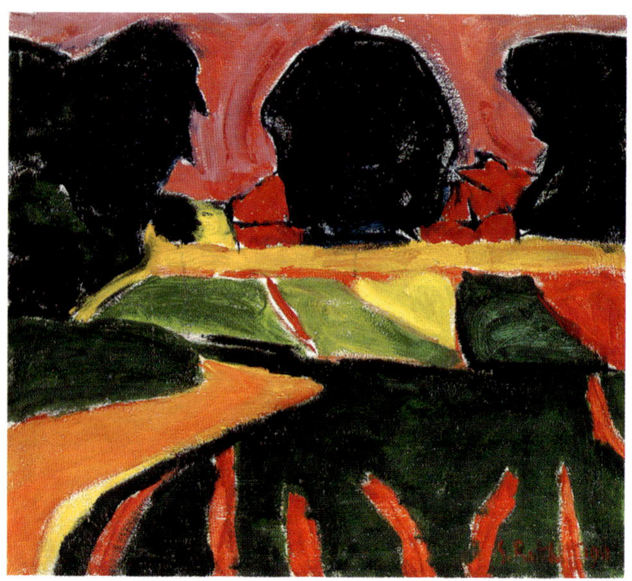

Karl Schmidt-Rottluff (1884–1976)
Landscape with Fields, 1911
Oil on canvas, 80 x 96 cm

Silent monumentality is the prime characteristic of the unpeopled landscapes painted by Schmidt-Rottluff during a summer stay at Lofthus in Norway. Here he produced a number of paintings that were more abstract, two-dimensional, architectonic and full of tension than anything that he had done before. In his monograph on Schmidt-Rottluff (Stuttgart 1956, p. 62) Will Grohmann writes: 'Here every externally visible element of dynamism is suppressed in favour of a grandiose calm and festive solemnity. [...] His pictures are firmly constructed through the juxtaposition of broad coloured planes and in no respect go beyond the boundaries of the pictorial. They are silent, describing nothing and only give an account of the painter's conception through the expressive power of their colouring.' In *Landscape with Fields* the dominating contrast between red and green is pushed to its greatest intensity, but the result is not the shocking effect or the orgy of colour that is to be found in so many of the pictures by the *Brücke* painters. Rather, it is the expression of an almost overwhelming emotionality held in check, but by no means neutralized, by the rigorous pictorial construction. The composition is organized around the opposition of forms that both strive inwards from the corners and at the same time push outwards into each of the vertically stacked pictorial 'strips' and beyond. The result is that architectonic stability makes itself felt as a state of extreme tension resulting from the opposition of two equally powerful forces. The tenseness of the image reiterates the emotionally charged contrast of colours on a formal, indeed intellectual, level, with a resulting impact that might well be termed 'monumental'. RHH

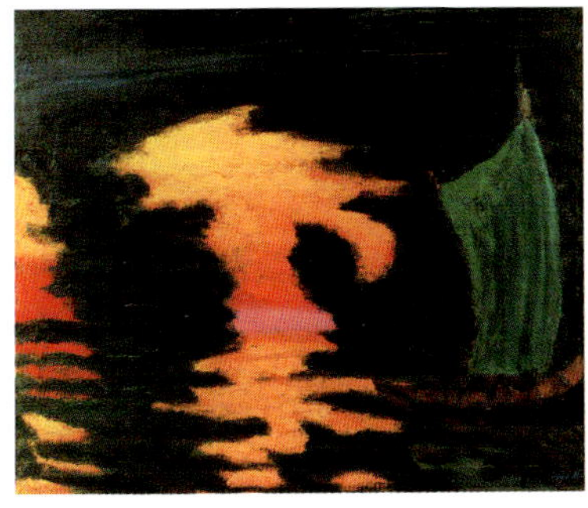

Emil Nolde (1867–1956)
The Sea at Evening, 1919
Oil on canvas, 86 x 100 cm

For Nolde the sea is a phenomenon that he found to embrace all the forces of nature and to embody creation and death, destructive power and the certainty of duration and eternity. This particular image shows the sea at sunset: the sun has already sunk below the horizon but is still reflected in the clouds that are themselves reflected in the water. The picture is made up entirely of colour. A glowing orange shimmers against the almost black background of the sky, which takes on a pink-violet tone near the horizon that recurs in the form of broken reflections in the calm water. The green of the sail, on the other hand, is a colour one would not be surprised to find in nature, and it here holds its own serenely against the burning orange. It is found again in the water and in the sky, linking the world of humanity with the chromatic harmony of nature that remains untouched by the dramatic restlessness of the passing illumination. This painting thus assumes the character of a vision, a fantastical apparition from a supernatural realm beyond earthly reality while still being a part of it. RHH

Otto Mueller (1874–1930)
Couple in a Low Dive, c 1921/22
Distemper on burlap, 110 x 85.5 cm

This image has a vigorously geometric construction. It is dominated by a large diagonal formed by the outline of the back of the nude that demarcates this in relation to the figure of the man. Numerous shorter lines, running parallel or in opposition to this, intensify the dynamism of the diagonal planar structure. As a counterforce, we find a system of orthogonal lines that bestow stability on the composition and simultaneously testify to the artist's intention to draw the couple closer together. The chromatic contrast underlines this expressive power. It would appear that the man seeks to include the woman within his own sphere, while she tries to evade this fate. The juxtaposition of naked and clothed figures underlines the division between these individuals. RHH

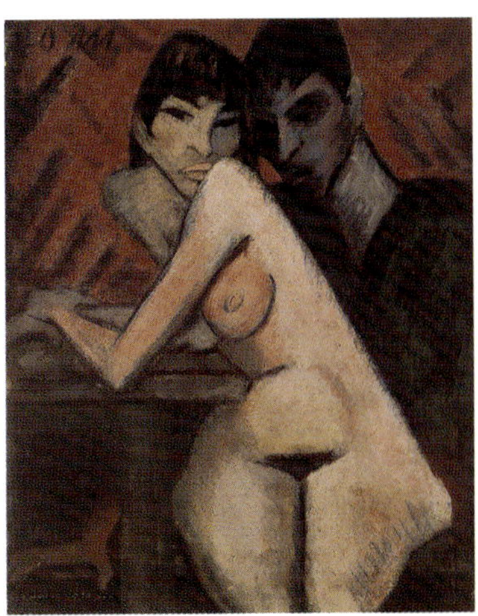

Alexej von Jawlensky (1864–1941)
Large Female Head (Marble Head), 1917
Oil on cardboard, 50 x 40 cm

In 1914, at the start of the First World War, the Russian Jawlensky (as an enemy alien) was ordered to leave Germany, where he had lived in Munich since 1896; therefore, he emigrated to Switzerland. He later wrote of this period in a letter: 'I wanted to go on painting my powerfully colourful pictures, but I simply couldn't. [...] I sensed that I had to find another language, a more spiritual language.' In the 'Variations on a Landscape Theme', painted beside Lake Geneva, he evolved a new abstract pictorial language. Its subsequent modification was issued in the series 'Mystical Heads', painted from 1917 in Zurich. These heads so fill out the available painting surface that both hair and throat are cropped by the frame. Yet the faces, brought unusually close to the spectator, appear as if not projecting at all from their backgrounds and so remain removed, as if lost in thought. While most of the heads of this period were in fact portraits, *Large Female Head* is anonymous, appearing to derive from no observed model. It is distinguished from others in the series by the fact that the eyes are closed, signalling an absence of visual contact with the outside world. De-individualization and spiritualization here combine with a rigorous structuring of the face into basic geometrical shapes and subdued colours based on red/green and yellow/violet contrasts. RHH

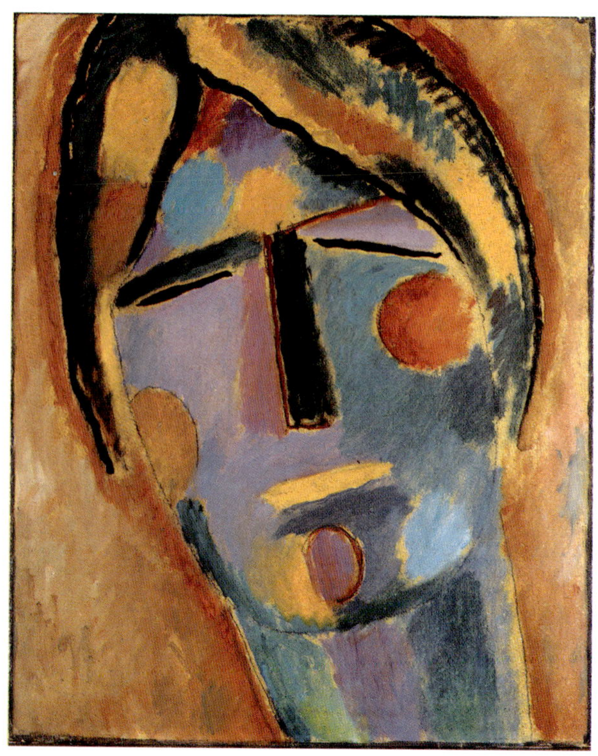

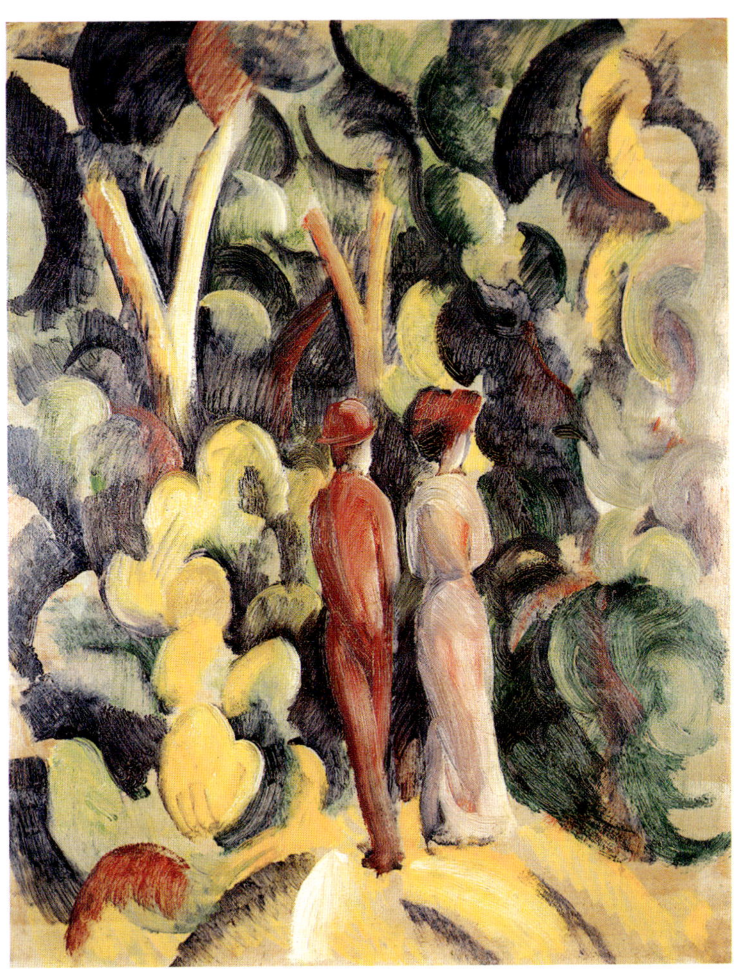

August Macke (1887–1914)
Couple on a Path in the Forest, 1913
Oil on cardboard, 81.5 x 61.5 cm

The positioning of the limbs of the couple out walking suggests that they are about to make a turn to the left, but their upper torsos and faces go right. They find themselves at the edge of a forest and are peering into it, but they are also near another path curving off from the first but not leading into the trees. With this motif Macke succeeds in capturing the characteristics of motion while translating the energy of movement into a suggestion of contemplation. He integrates the couple into the rhythm of the natural setting. He achieves this in formal terms – through reiterating indications of direction and rendering all the objects in terms of planar values – so that the suggestion of actual movement into depth is preserved. At the same time he employs light and colour values as 'space-constructing energies' that activate the inner movement. RHH

Heinrich Campendonk
(1889–1957)
The Sixth Day, 1914
Oil on canvas, 100 x 130 cm

The title relates to the Sixth Day of Creation, during which God made the animals before creating man and woman. On the left we can make out a large wild cat and to the right a smaller goat. In the upper part of the picture a curving dark blue line is evocative of the back of a horse. Here it is not only the animals that are treated with a variety of degrees of abstraction, but also their setting. Several formal abbreviations suggest fir trees and encourage us to read the vertical, coloured strokes as tree trunks. Within the associative context of the forest, the pale, white-yellow passages towards the upper edge of the picture convey the impression of a daytime sky, while the orange-coloured segment of a circle above the cat's head is suggestive, rather, of a crescent moon.

Campendonk is not concerned here with presenting a scene with animals or a forest landscape, but instead he seeks a symbolic representation of the unity of nature. He achieves this through coloured shapes that interpenetrate and thus interlink all the elements in the picture into the structure of its coloured planes. While the crystalline colour beams enter into the images of the animals, the organically rounded internal forms of the latter also impinge on their surroundings. The inner and outer worlds of the animals are interwoven. Formal principles derived from Cubism are applied to an expansive and intensely coloured formal vocabulary, with the result that the faceting of the individual objects does not really open them out but ensures that these are harmoniously integrated into the picture surface. RHH

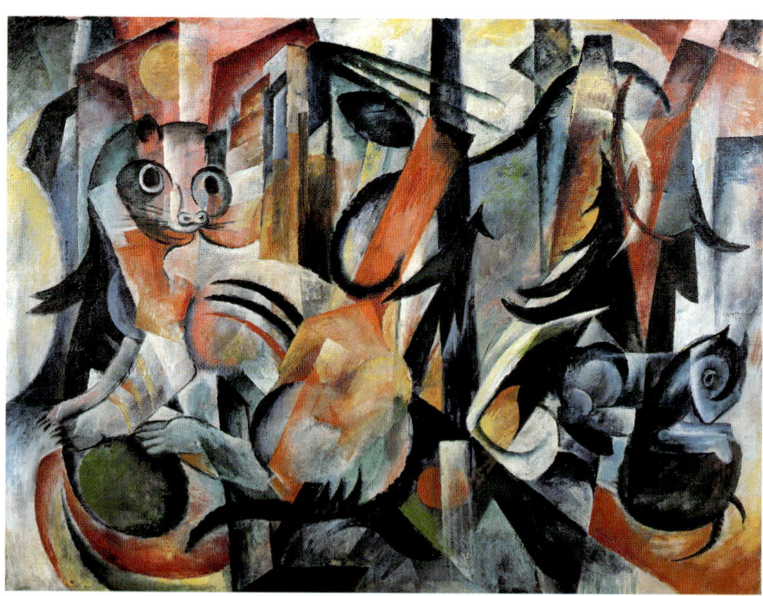

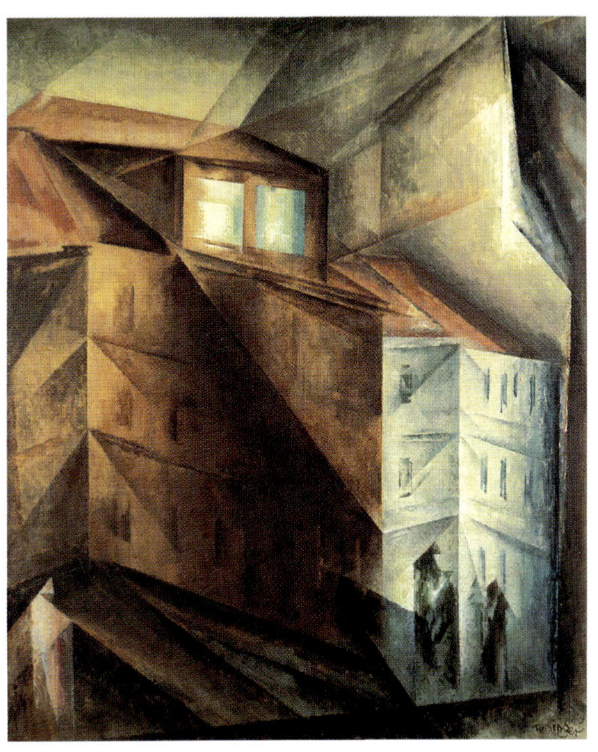

Lyonel Feininger
(1871–1956)
The Studio Window, 1919
Oil on canvas, 100 x 80 cm

The starting point for this picture was Feininger's delight in his new studio at the Bauhaus in Weimar. What we see here is, however, the view from outside the building with the illuminated studio window just below the roof. The image unites exterior and interior and is in effect a symbol, in the iconographic tradition of Romanticism, for the presence of man, for his sense of being at home in the world.

Feininger's formal language bears witness to his engagement in both Cubism and Futurism, as is especially evident in the prismatic refraction of his forms, the 'cloudy' application of paint, the toning down of the layers of colour, the combination of several points of view and the radial compositional structure. At the same time Feininger does not proceed with the angular rigour of Cubism; he seeks, rather, for large forms, for a 'closed harmony'. Diagonal lines connect the window lit from within and sections of the facade lit from without so that these become complementary visual phenomena. Their glassy blue-green colouring is set in contrast to the warm brown that generates an area of shadow evocative of an interior while the counter-form of the passage of sky appears to push outwards, its greenish tone recapitulating the chromatic contrast of cold and warm. The image unites architecture and sky, external and internal space into an 'experienced' unity. RHH

Johannes Molzahn

(1892–1965)

The Battle between Ideas and Movement (To You, Karl Liebknecht), 1919

Oil on canvas, 149 x 139 cm

Three months after the murders of Rosa Luxemburg and Karl Liebknecht, Molzahn painted this picture and dedicated it to the latter. However, in 1933 he over-painted the dedication (added below the picture's title), not in order to distance himself from his original intention but, rather, to protect himself – the Gestapo having several times arrived to check through the contents of his studio. In 1919 the short-lived era of revolution in post-war Germany inspired Molzahn to paint a picture that is not only unique in his œuvre but that has also been recognized as the most important contribution to German Futurism. The art historian Herbert Schade has compared the dynamic composition with an 'exploding rock'. The centre of this 'explosion' is placed asymmetrically in relation to the composition as a whole. Its force smashes the shapes and forces them apart. At the same time it sets off a rotating movement that seizes each element in the picture and sets it circling around the centre. This appears to be accelerated on account of the effect of diagonal lines, segments of circles and staggered groups of shapes in which the movement of one element is taken up by that of another. It is the power

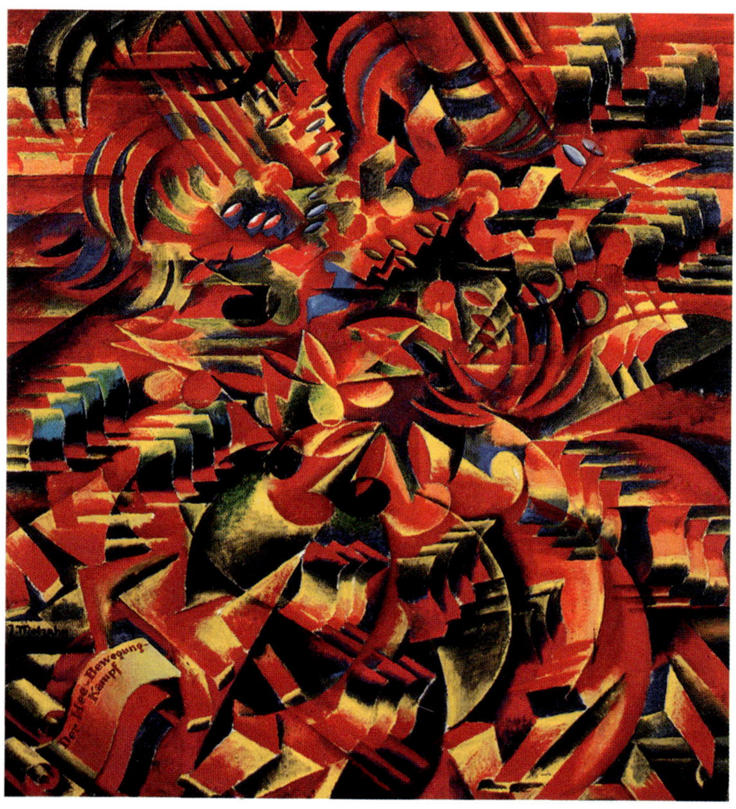

of this ordely rotational movement that holds the visual drama together within the almost square surface. RHH

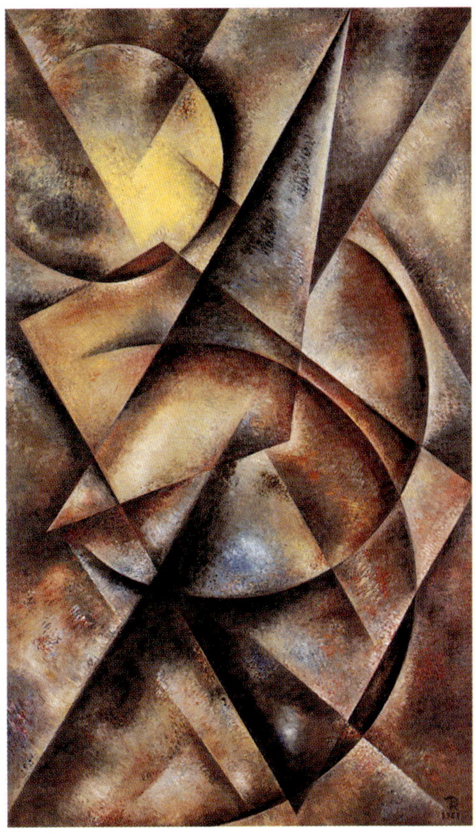

Thomas Ring
(1892–1983)
Breakthrough/Three and Four, 1921
Oil on canvas,
209 x 120.9 cm

The concept of counterpoint became the leitmotif of Ring's work when, around 1920, the artist fully embraced abstraction, working with geometric, Constructivist forms. The principal formal elments in this picture are a large, irregular downward-pointing quadrilateral, an upward-pointing triangle and three open arcs of circles, in addition to four triangles extending from the upper and lower edges towards the centre. As the colours belong within the same range and are applied in thin, almost transparent layers, there is in fact almost no suggestion of a superimposition of forms. Rather, these appear to interpenetrate, establishing countless further shapes – both contrary and corresponding, internal and external – which extend diagonally over the entire planar composition. The result is a degree of calm that does not remove the inner rhythmic vitality of the image. Hence, for example, straight and curved lines and pointed and rounded planes are here united into a harmonic balance that, to Ring's mind, stood for the 'universal'. Also of metaphysical significance for him were the numbers 'three' and 'four', which he associated with the notions, respectively, of male and female, the spiritual and the earthly. RHH

Georg Muche (1895–1987)
Space-Plane Construction/Space-Plane I, 1916
Oil on canvas, 59.5 x 52.5 cm

Muche started to evolve his own abstract painterly language of form in 1915. What concerned him was the rhythmic interplay of the colours that he began employing in the form of large planes. The picture shown here marks a turning point in his work in as far as it is characterized by a more intricate structure. Within a system that is, as a whole, established in relation to the horizontal and the vertical, colour planes are juxtaposed. Through their varying size and chromatic intensity they establish a rhythmic alternation of denser and more open passages that is enlivened by the presence of a few arch-shaped and diagonal forms. As the colour planes are separated from each other by dark outlines, there emerges a lattice structure that recalls leaded stained glass windows, and this underscores the planarity of the composition. The larger lines used to establish autonomous forms counter this impression. Together with the varying luminosity of the colours, they give rise to an indeterminate sense of space. This produces the impression of a layer of space vibrating with colour and rhythm. RHH

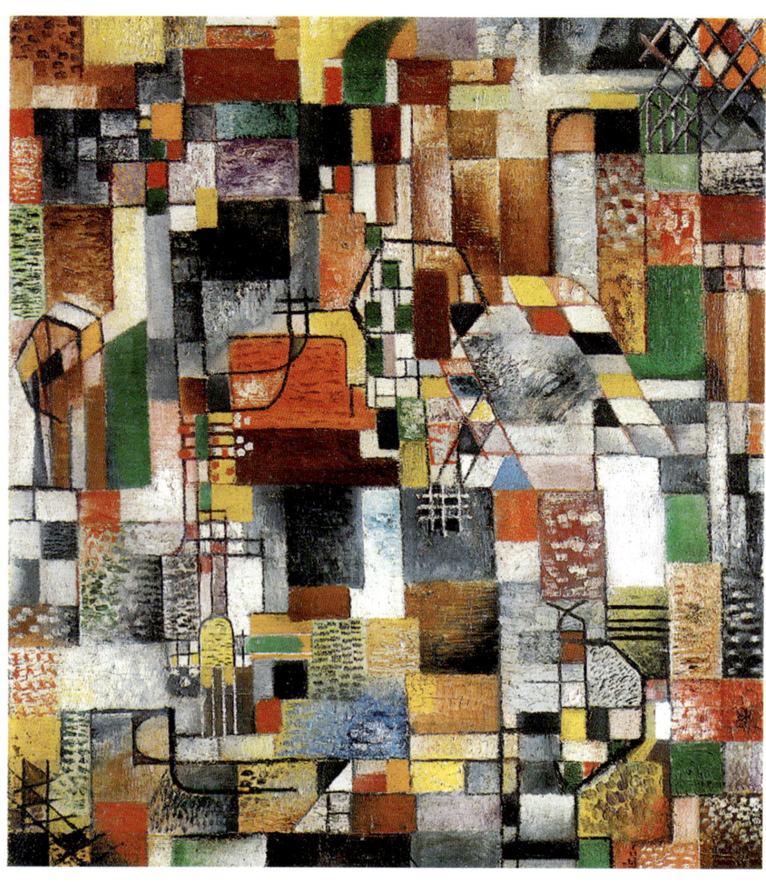

Oskar Schlemmer (1888–1943)
Group of Fifteen, 1929
Oil and distemper on canvas,
178 x 100 cm

This multi-figural composition shows nudes on a steep stairway engaged in gymnastic and balletic movements. They are largely free of individual characteristics and are transformed into architectonically and functionally articulated types. They are frozen in exemplary states of movement that confirm the rectangularity of the space they occupy as a group. Schlemmer speaks of the 'mechanics inherent to the human body' corresponding to the 'laws of Cubist space'. Here, however, the bodies do not appear to be suited to occupying abstract space and, rather, represent its regularity as a quality intrinsic to themselves. The mathematical rigour of the composition is enlivened through a few figures whose movements are organic, apparently determined by emotion and thus 'imponderable'. RHH

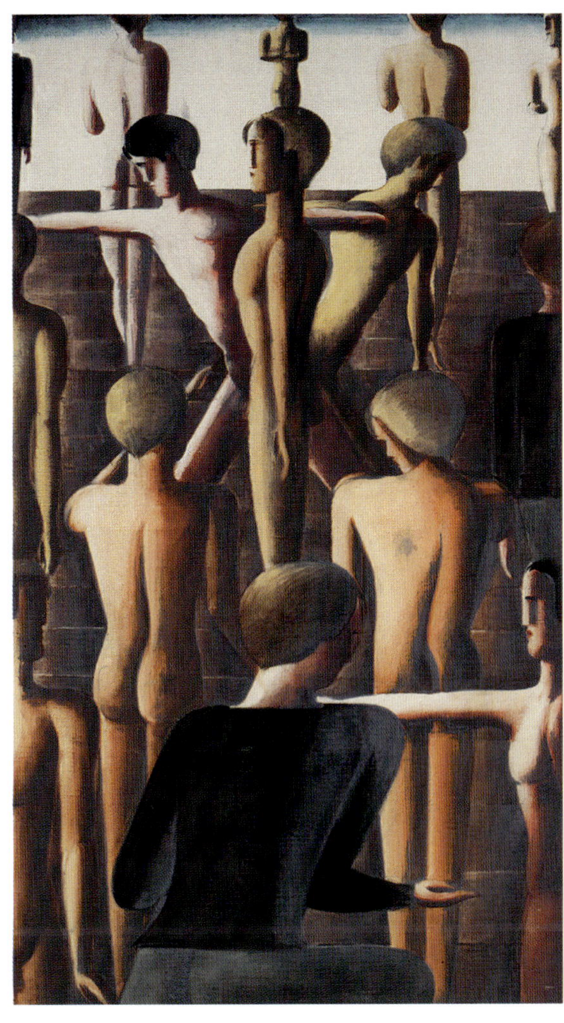

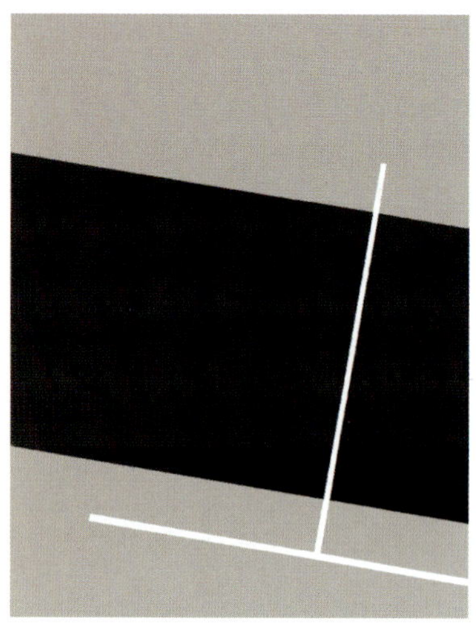

Friedrich Vordemberge-Gildewart (1899–1962)
Composition No. 54, 1929
Oil on canvas, 80.5 x 60.5 cm

From 1924 Vordemberge-Gildewart belonged to the *De Stijl* group and shared its Purist and Constructivist approach to form. In his tensely asymmetrical painting in white, grey and black, the two white lines meeting at right angles link the three overlapping zones by, respectively, cutting and running parallel to the black parallelogram in the right corner. The areas painted in black have matte and shiny parts that taper in opposed directions, with the end of one visible at the left picture edge but that of the other left for us to imagine at a point lying beyond the picture plane. While the dynamic directional structures of the black area imaginatively extend the pictorial space, the white lines draw the eye to the formal internal structure of the concrete planes. RHH

Walter Dexel (1890–1973)
Figuration 1923/IX, 1923
Oil on canvas, 82 x 71 cm

This Constructivist painting is made up of vertically and horizontally limited rectangles. These extend as narrow strips upwards and downwards from the centre of the image but become larger towards the left and right edges so that the two dark grey planes correspond with the pale grey planes of the background. As a result of this close connection between form and background, the image appears to be organized into four zones of equal 'value', to each of which two reciprocal diagonals are assigned. The arrangement of the diagonals is energized through the intensive colouring and the emphatically opposed movement of the central rectangle, so that there emerges a sense of centrifugue. As the energy radiating from the centre is, nonetheless, calmed in the larger lateral planes, the orthogonal structure remains fundamental for the harmonic balance of the planar construction. RHH

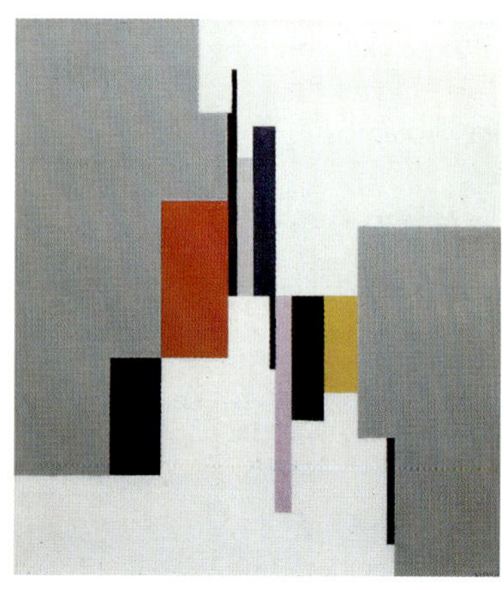

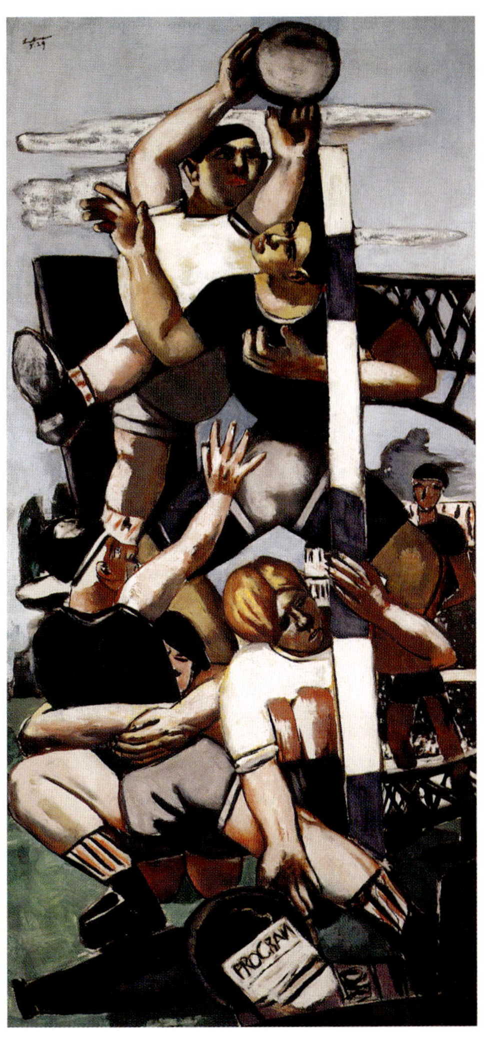

Max Beckmann (1884–1950)
Rugby Players, 1929
Oil on canvas, 213 x 100 cm

Beckmann shows us the crucial moment before the ball is thrown up over the bar. The goal-post marks a borderline situation and at the same time indicates the direction in which the movement of the players tends. Through the clamping together of the contending forces of movement, Beckmann freezes a series of poses that embrace both victory and defeat. The picture thus becomes a metaphor of the vanity of violent engagement. The wind instrument, programme and book stand for the spectator as well as the painter, but are both spatially and thematically connected with the playing field. The artist here sees himself as a spectator, watching both a real and a metaphorical world championship in which he feels himself to be involved. RHH

Max Ernst (1891–1976)
The Temptation of Saint Anthony, 1945
Oil on canvas, 108 x 128 cm

This picture, with which Max Ernst won first prize in a competition of 1945 to provide a painting to be used on the set of the American film of the Guy de Maupassant novel *Bel Ami*, is one of the most idiosyncratic works in the artist's œuvre. From a formal point of view, Ernst takes his starting point in the conventional interpretation of this subject established in the late Middle Ages. The figure of the saint, whom we here see reclining or pursued by monsters, derives from a picture type associated with the Upper Rhine in the late 15th and 16th centuries; there, however, the figure is invariably prostrate in prayer. Ernst moves the dividing rocks into the immediate foreground, which swarms with further monsters. The fantastical creatures lunge at the saint, preparing to tear him apart, or they have already settled around him and between his legs. The lateral framing incorporated within the picture gives way on the left to a rocky structure with more monsters, and on the right we see a tree like those found in pictures by Altdorfer; between these lies a landscape of lakes like those painted by a follower of the Danube School. Within the rocky formations of the background we find the motif traditionally assigned to this particular saint: a naked woman, here wound about with a snake, and on the right, as an idol placed at the top of a narrow column. The saint's rust-brown habit has led a contemporary commentator to describe Saint Anthony as a half-cooked lobster. The blue, brown and green tones of the landscape are yet another indication of the proxim-

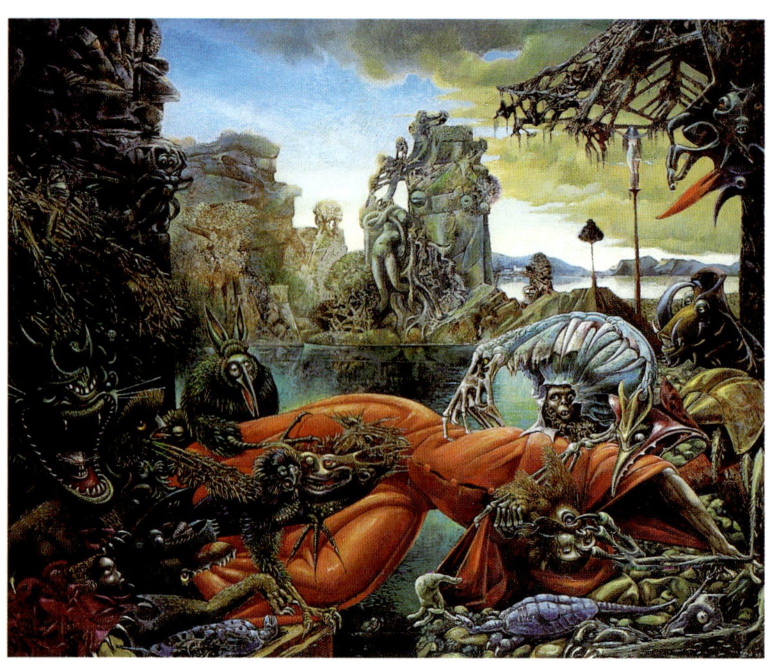

ity to the Danube School. Alongside the already mentioned tree, Ernst depicts fabulous creatures taken from the work of other artists, from Hieronymus Bosch to Picasso. By means of this assembly of 'wax-works', he adds substance to a vividly imagined world that he evoked as follows: 'Sprawled diagonally over the still pools of his dark, sick soul, screaming for help and light, Saint Anthony receives, as answer, the echo of his own dread: the laughter of the monsters that are the creatures of his own vision.' KL

Max Ernst (1891–1976)
Small Bird Monument, 1928
Oil on canvas, 91 x 74 cm

This is one of a group of bird 'monuments' made between 1927 and the early 1930s. In front of a diffuse light-blue background, a 'mother bird' embraces embryonic bird-like twins, while holding a fully formed young bird by a rudimentary tail feather. Despite the small scale of the composition, the use of colour achieves an effect that is truly monumental in combination with the tight formal structure (with the young birds clasped within the outline of the body of the parent). Starting with primary colours – the blue of the background and the yellow of the mother-bird's back – Ernst mixes these two tones until a pale green and a soft brown are achieved. We find this last in the feathers of the belly and the neck of the mother-bird, while the covering of the young birds ranges from light blue to pale green. The pale blue appears to be that of the cloak traditionally worn by the Virgin, and the figure of a mother with twins itself draws on representations of Roman Charity. Here, however, this is travestied and trivialized through the transformation of woman into bird – one of the creatures most favoured by the Surrealists. KL

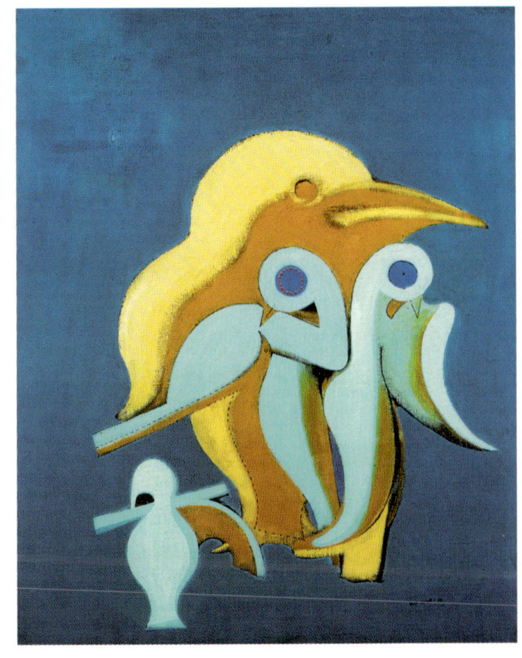

Willy Baumeister (1889–1955)
Atlantis, 1947
Oil and putty on hardboard,
80.5 x 99.6 cm

In 1945 Baumeister became a leading figure among exponents of non-objective painting in Germany. He considered art to be a mythical process that brought forth ideas and concepts that could only exist on the picture plane. *Atlantis*, from the series 'Metaphysical Landscapes', prompts associations with a map or a mythical island. The image conveys the impression of spatial depth, an impression that functions both optically (through the chromatically varying, juxtaposed planar forms) and haptically (through the irregularly applied putty, which gives the image real relief). In colouring the raised passages brown and setting these in contrast with the blue of the background, Baumeister opens up associations with the jagged earth, immense age and water. RHH

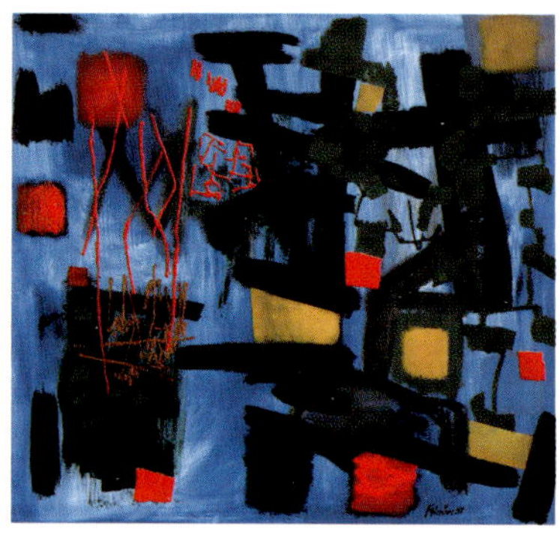

Fritz Winter (1905–1976)
The Great Summer, 1957
Oil on canvas, 135 x 145 cm

This painting was produced over several sessions and in several layers. To begin with, a thin, luminous blue was applied as a background colour. Dense coloured shapes and black beams, resembling a sort of script, were then placed upon this with a bristle brush and a palette knife. The upper layer of painting consists of red paint squeezed directly from the tube. Although this type of painting, which is in fact as controlled in reality as it is

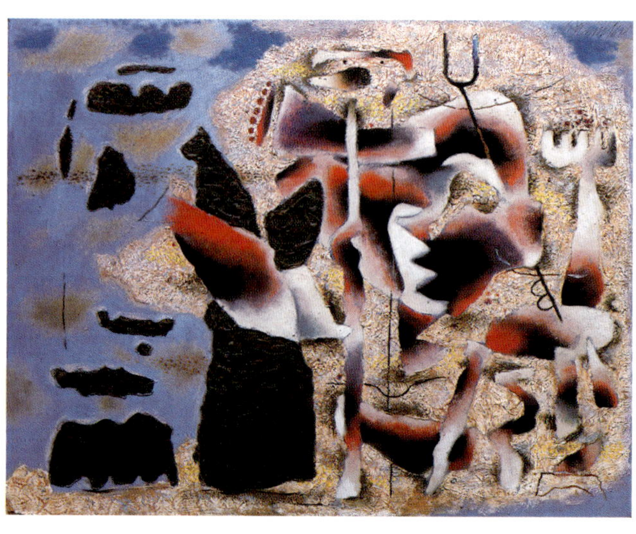

spontaneous in appearance, is abstract in its result, recalling the forms assumed by growth in nature, while the colouring evokes the mood of summer. RHH

Ernst Wilhelm Nay (1902–1968)
Star Balance, 1956
Oil on canvas, 125 x 200 cm

This painting is one of the 'Disc Paintings' that brought Nay international fame in the mid-1950s. In 1955 he published his text *Vom Gestaltwert der Farbe* [On Colour as Form], in which he declared himself unambiguously in favour of an autonomous, absolute painting beyond imitation or psychology. Its only 'commitments', according to Nay, were to 'planes, colours, and consciously arranged complexes of form'. It takes nothing as its subject, seeks to establish no relation to reality, nor even to the personality of the artist. Here, then, we cannot even understand the picture's title as a reference to a representation of the sky or to a concept of cosmic order. The title, rather, posits an analogy between visual form and a universal space, of which Nay writes: '[...] it is known that every single point in the universe is its centre and that it is possible to think about space but not to imagine it, and to think about it [only] as extending endlessly – from each and every point.'

In Nay's work the disc is a coloured point extending in a plane that has its own centre and no outer boundary. It is neither a form of subjective expression nor a body geometrically defined; rather, it unfurls freely to form a plane of varying size in which it releases and radiates its energy in the form of light and colour. Out of the co-existence of these fields of energy a coloured space spreads beyond the canvas. This has no perspective and it permits no illusion. Nonetheless, the overlapping of the discs gives rise to a spatially pulsating movement. This extends the picture plane to form an open space that is filled by a chromatic harmony with dark undertones. RHH

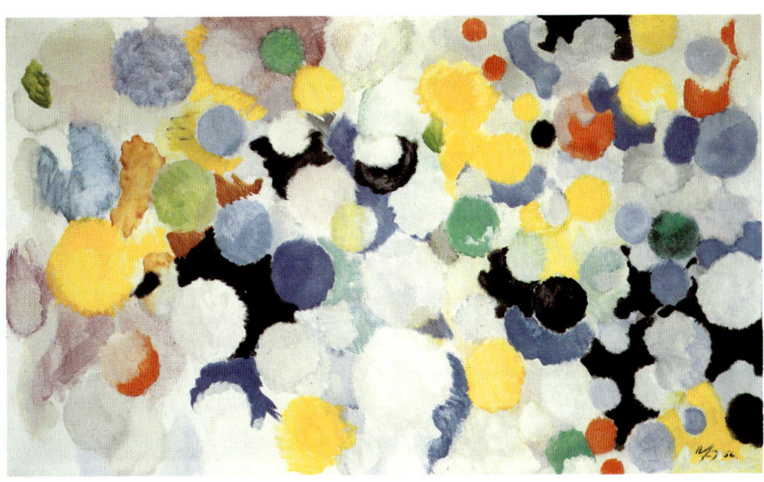

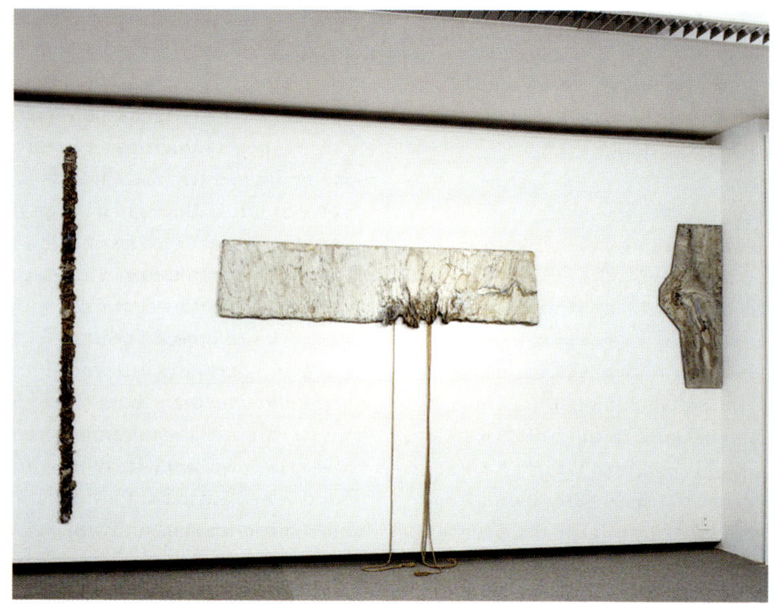

Gerhard Hoehme (1920–1989)
S'amje, 1957
Polyester, lime mortar and hemp rope on canvas, mounted on specially constructed frames;
186 x 183 x 7 cm as installed
Colour Stake, 1957
Polyester on wood,
Space Bulge, 1957
Oil on canvas (shaped canvas),
100 x 41.7 x 1.8 cm

In 1957 Hoehme wrote: 'It's always been only against my will that I've followed the law of the plane. I've been far more interested in the regularity of colours, their flow and their growth, their material qualities and their structure.' In the tradition of Informal Art, Hoehme thereby underlined the basic requirements of his own pictures, the process of their evolution and their materiality. The notion of art as process was based, for Hoehme, not in the subjective gesture, but in the behaviour and reactions of the material, with which the artists necessarily complied. In the case of the *Colour Stake*, the coloured polyester is so thickly moulded on its slat that it rejects the geometrical form in favour of the demands of the material itself. The other works emphasize, in particular, the spatial resonance of colour. In the case of the *Space Bulge*, the grainy colour, applied in several layers, flows to the middle of the left edge, where it begins to swell. While there are here still unambiguous limits to the image, *S'amje* is nonetheless unbounded: on the one hand through its unsmoothed edges, on the other through the ropes that literally link the painted rectangular form with real space. This process starts from a place in which paint darkly thickens, overlapping and bulging in a sculptural fashion. Unboundedness is here embodied in the energy of an aesthetic violation.

RHH

Emil Schumacher (1912–1999)
Touch Object/Object for Touching 57/12, 1957
Black-stained insulating panel, 105 x 82 cm

In 1957 Schumacher wrote: 'In 1951 I embarked on my first attempts to deal with the material and structural characteristics of painting. I started to become interested in paint as material, as something palpable [...] As a result of pursuing this new notion I hit directly upon what have now become my "objects". These creations, made out of easily maleable materials are to such a degree identical with the stuff of which they are made that their power of expression follows spontaneously. None of them is a picture of something, but [a picture] through something. [...] Their effectiveness also extends, purely optically, beyond their boundaries; space invades them, and their quality as objects breaks through. It surges from the core to the edges and enters into true communication with space as soon as it meets with it. I call my objects "touch objects" because the spectator is able physically to feel them in their entirety, both psychic and physical.' In the following years Schumacher worked with more compact, coloured material to which he added scratches, thus unifying gesture and texture in a truly 'corporeal' form of painting. RHH

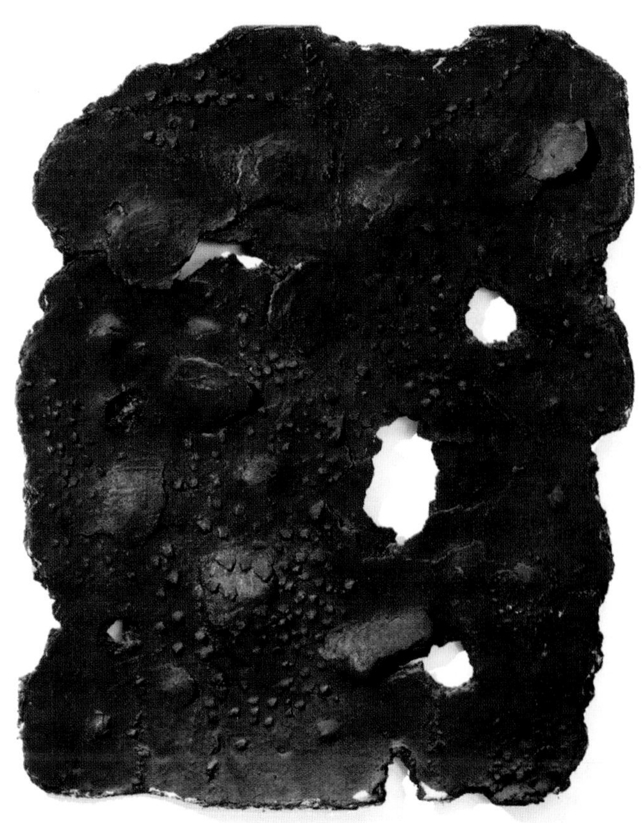

International Sculpture in the 20th Century

In the wake of the *assemblages* of Cubism, the entirety of Object Art may be said to have its real starting point in the 'accidental' gesture of Marcel Duchamp's 'readymades'. The 'aura' of the work of art and its status as a unique object made by hand is definitively eschewed in favour of the opinion that invention and the creative idea are in essence more important than originality and uniqueness.

With Duchamp we stand at the beginning of Conceptual Art. The creative idea is manifest in the selection of a trivial object that forfeits its originality and makes even the artist dispensible. Yet pieces such as Duchamp's *Glass Drying Rack* of 1914 have become among the most celebrated works of art of the twentieth century – this is an item, according to Duchamp, '[at which] one no longer really looks, while nonetheless knowing that it exists.' In 1964, as a protest against what he saw as a pointlessly ironic attitude, Joseph Beuys was to produce a manifesto-object entitled 'The silence of Marcel Duchamp is overrated'.

In the 1920s Kurt Schwitters and other Dadaists extended the realm of Object Art through the use of scrap materials. Schwitters, moreover, who simultaneously strove to adopt an ironic attitude towards the artist's vocation ('I'm a painter and I knock pictures together') created what we can still recognize as a true 'total work of art', which culminated in the *Merzbau* with the Cathedral of Erotic Misery. This first 'work in progress' by Schwitters, which grew to occupy every floor of his house in Hanover, was transformed by the artist into a cave-like, walk-in installation that served as the model for all later artists' 'environments'.

Architectonic sculpture, of which the *Merzbau* is in effect a variant, assumed a simultaneously monumental and dynamic quality in the work of the Russian Constructivists and the related Kinetic Constructivists (from Tatlin to Gabo), and also embraced an implicit blueprint for a new, and usually unrealized, social order. In works such as Tatlin's *Monument for the Third International*, the artist slips into the role of engineer and architect to produce a truly Utopian blend of functional architecture and sculpture.

Also informed by the achievements of Kineticism and Constructivism was the 'concrete' art that Max Bill first exhibited in Basle, in 1944, and Lucio Fontana's first manifesto piece, *Ambiente Nero* (1949). Fontana's conception of 'existence, nature and material' had a significant influence on the Informal Art of the 1950s and 1960s, and even more so on the kinetic sculpture of the *Zero* group (which made use of light) and the installations of the Op-Artists. While figurally oriented sculptors such as Alberto Giacometti, Henry Moore, Marino Marini and, in particular, Pablo Picasso became the models for post-war Modernism, this in no way weakened the dominance of Object Art, the 'exit from the picture' and the socially critical approach of those rebelling against consumer society.

For all that, the generation of artists emerging in the tone-setting 1960s also sought, through poetry, the 'preservation of evidence', machine art and performance art, to unite the realms of art and myth with the everyday reality of the present, reformulating the 'open concept of art'. This was increasingly evident in the reconciliation of 'higher' and 'lower' artistic genres. In place of the conclusiveness and unique qualities of a work of art, these artists emphasized the processes used to create it, even if – as in the case of many examples of Land Art or the spectacular, large-scale 'wrappings' by Christo – the realized ideas only remained visible for a short time.

The provision of easily comprehensible structures for sculptural objects is one of the fundamental principles of modern sculpture. The work of artists as diverse in origin and approach as Donald Judd, Sol LeWitt, Richard Serra or Ulrich Rückriem has embodied this notion. 'Primary structures' determine the formal rigour of the frugal cubes, boxes, and wall reliefs, their stereometry and modularity challenging the perception of the spectator. The geometrical, serially produced orderliness of Minimal Art was generally the result of industrial prefabrication and execution. It is thus to be understood as occupying a position opposite to that of Abstract Expressionism and, in particular, to 'vulgar' Pop Art. The transitions from idea to action, concept to realization, object to space become fluid. In the USA this led to the numerous variants of Conceptual Art, while in Europe a similar development issued in Process Art (Franz Erhard Walther) and *arte povera*. In this last in particular, the unadulterated 'poor' materials employed by the artist were intended to draw attention to society's loss of identity and to reinstate the tradition of a high regard for nature, history and myth. It was above all Jospeh Beuys who sought to undermine art's traditional claim to stimulate human consciousness through creativity and positive action. In accordance with Beuys' theory of the 'enlarged concept of art', his work had a direct impact on the body, the thoughts and the feelings of the spectator, and this impact was extended to society as a whole in the form of 'social sculpture'. Materials such as fat, felt or rubber were seen by Beuys not as formal elements, but as bearers of particular qualities and energies such as warmth, cold and expansion. Art and life, politics and science were assumed to be united.

Land Art and performance art countered the conventional concept of sculpture through the notion of 'Art in Time'. New perspectives were also offered by the resort to New Media. The work of Nam June Paik and John Cage led the way for the 'video spaces' created by Bill Viola and Bruce Naumann or the electronic text-strips of Jenny Holzer, but also for a wide variety of interactive installations. Sculptors such as Baselitz and Penck, Balkenhol and Disler, however, took a stand against this mechanization of art, turning to the representation of the human figure. It is clear that this, the original territory of sculpture in the Western tradition, has lost nothing of its power and emotion.

GL

I Expressionist Sculpture

The two great ideals of Expressionism were the unity of art and life and the harmony between the liberated individual and nature.

According to the German editor and gallery owner Herwarth Walden, writing in 1918, 'Expressionist sculpture too strives no longer to imitate natural forms but to create absolute images'. In striving for a new and more direct formal language the Expressionist movement in sculpture was also an act of rebellion against the idealized sculptural forms that received official favour in Germany in the Wilhelmine Era (1888–1918).

Expressionist sculpture is distinguished by its exponents' preference for simple, true-to-life situations, often captured in an emphatic, but fleeting, display of emotion. From this creative spontaneity, which is to be found at its most exemplary in the simplified, expressive formal language of Ernst Barlach and Käthe Kollwitz, there arises a direct, emotional relationship with the spectator.

In general one can also note a preference for socially critical themes, universal human situations and politically informed subjects. On this account, the influential poet Theodor Däubler spoke of the 'revolution' of Expressionist art.

Artists such as Franz Marc and Ewald Mataré sought refuge in the world of animals, in which they found a truer sense of the religious, of the cosmic and of fate. Like other exponents of Primitivism, Expressionist artists sought out the original and the untouched.

HS

Ernst Barlach (1870–1938)
The Tippler, 1909
Italian walnut, 56 x 37.3 x 47.5 cm

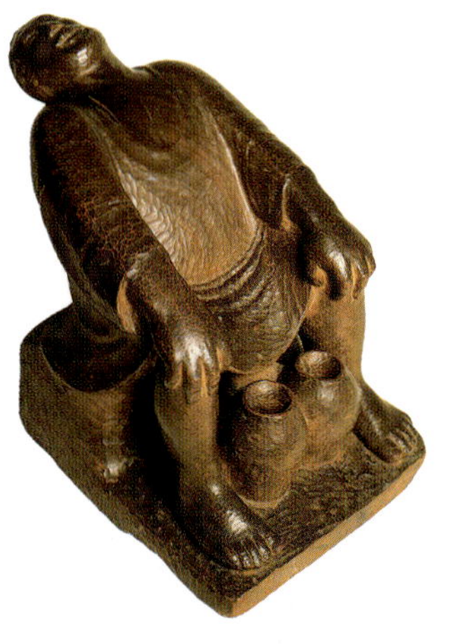

In 1909 Barlach embarked on a trip to Italy and took a studio in the German artists' Villa Romana in Florence. Here he got to know the poet Theodor Däubler (1876–1934). As a result of this meeting Barlach created *The Tippler*, sculpted out of a 'solid block' of Italian walnut. In this figure he combined the much-loved poet's physical appearance with the poetic motif of the *Astrologer*, another work created in Florence at this time. While the figure as a whole is compact and emphatically bound to the earth, the man's gaze is directed, dreamily and absorbed, towards the sky.

GL

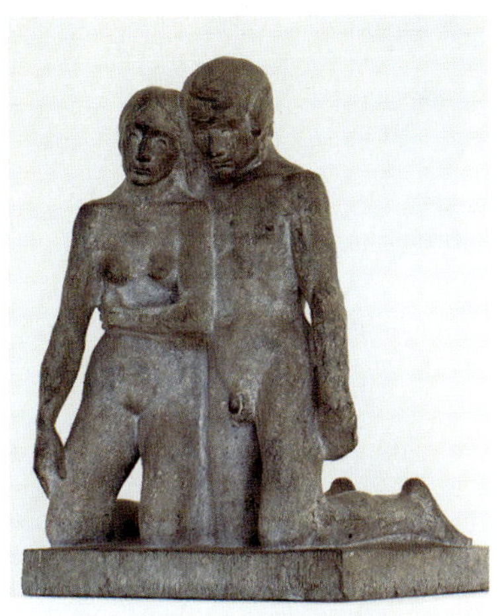

George Minne (1866–1941)
Kneeling Couple, 1889
Granite, 44 x 29 x 34 cm

In completing his *Mother Lamenting Her Dead Child* in 1886, Minne, like Wilhelm Lehmbruck several decades later, had evolved one of the central themes of his work as a sculptor – the humility embodied in the kneeling figure. While Minne's well-known design for a fountain incorporates a circle of five kneeling youths, and the figure of the *Kneeling Youth* is shown with a meekly sunken head, the frontally aligned and closely entwined *Kneeling Couple* appears to embody a collective gesture of regret for sin, guilt and poverty.

GL

Käthe Kollwitz (1867–1945)
Mother with Two Children, 1923/1937
Bronze, 77 x 79 x 84 cm

The artist's preoccupation with this sculptural group (of which the original plaster model is in the Neue Nationalgalerie in Berlin) reached its crucial phase in 1923 when her twin grandchildren, Jördis and Jutta, were born. The powerful naked figure of the mother squats low on the ground seizing and embracing the two huddled children, in an almost animal grasp. Through its unambiguously frontal alignment and its closed outline, the group has the effect of an immovable monolith, in as far as the three closely packed heads are integrated within the outline of the block and appear to have shut themselves away in a cave-like place of protection. Mother and children merge into an inner-directed unity, towards which Kollwitz was clearly working both in her numerous drawings and through the long process of execution, completed only in 1937.

GL

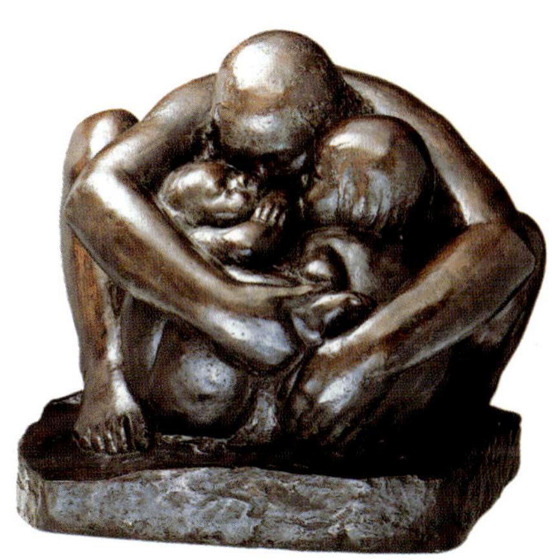

Johannes Molzahn
(1892–1965)
Summ-Summ Buddha, c 1920
Wood, 29.5 x 8.5 x 10.5 cm

Sharply angular and diagonally crossed legs signal the typical squatting pose of a seated Buddha viewed from the side. Especially characteristic is the bald and rounded head while the facial features are marked by one vertical and several horizontal lines. Information on the dating and significance of this work are to be found in a letter written by Molzahn in 1920 to his friend, the writer Hugo Hertwig. Here the artist announced, as a gift to Hertwig, a 'carved creature [...] a sort of Buddha, but more a Summ-Summ Buddha.' GL

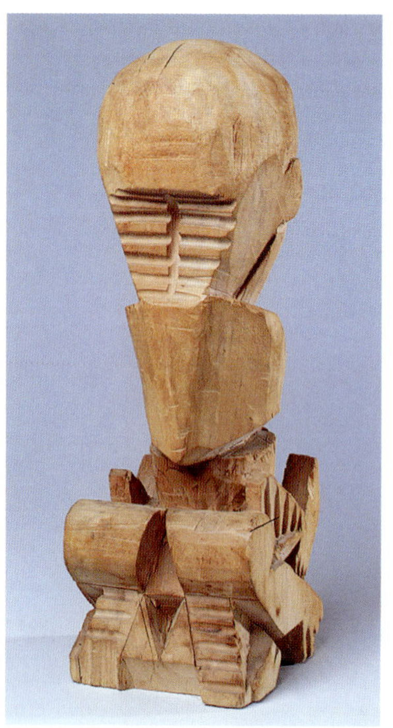

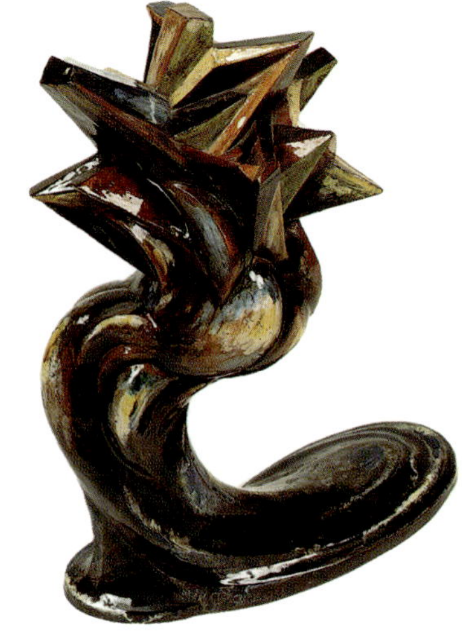

Oswald Herzog
(1881–?)
Expressionistic Sculpture, c 1920
Stoneware with coloured glaze, 46.5 x 36 x 19.5 cm

Although it has so far proved impossible to trace the later history of this artist from the early avant-garde circle of the Berlin journal and gallery 'Der Sturm', Herzog has nontheless been recognized as one of the pioneers of abstract sculpture in Germany. This expressive piece in ceramic could be termed a 'cosmic blossom' in as far as Molzahn has created an image intended to unite nature and the cosmos. The sculpture rises, as an amorphous mass, out of an undulating base, seems to lose its momentum briefly and ends in a partially visible sphere, out of which blossom-like and prismatic forms thrust in every direction. This piece, which could be termed futuristic, thus appears as a mythical and crystalline symbol for material set into motion. ChB

Franz Marc (1880–1916)
Female Torso, 1910/11
Bronze on a marble base,
third cast of six, 31.5 x 16 x 14.8 cm

When Marc wrote to the Munich publisher Reinhold Piper in May 1910, he spoke of still being at work on the wax model for this piece (now in the collection of the Lenbachhaus). According to Helmuth Macke, 'Marc was as often working on his sculptures. At that time [1911] a large female figure in wax was still to be seen on the modelling block in the corner of his studio, as yet unfinished and undergoing the wildest metamorphoses'.

The upper part of the torso is frontally aligned, yet there is a distinct turn to the right in its lower part. This contradictory treatment of movement is underlined through the positioning of the arms, with the left one (not visible from the front) held behind the body and both hands merging as they rest on the hips. It is possible that the movements thus emphasized were intended to suggest those of a dancer exercising. GL

Franz Marc (1880–1916)
The Panther, 1908
Bronze,
9.8 x 12.5 x 10.2 cm

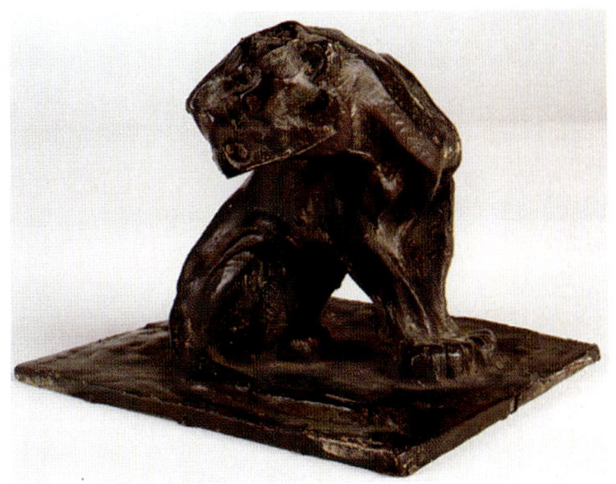

The unchased example of a total of five surviving bronze casts comes from the collection of Dr Paul Marc. Probably inspired by the work of August Gaul in Berlin, Marc first started to model figures of animals in order to give form also in this genre to the elemental expression he found in such subjects. The bulky body with its overly large head abruptly thrown back head signifies the savagery and energy of those beasts of prey to which Marc was to give definitive form in March 1912 in *The Tiger*. The title of this piece derives from Maria Marc, although the anatomy of this particular animal resembles more closely that of a tiger. GL

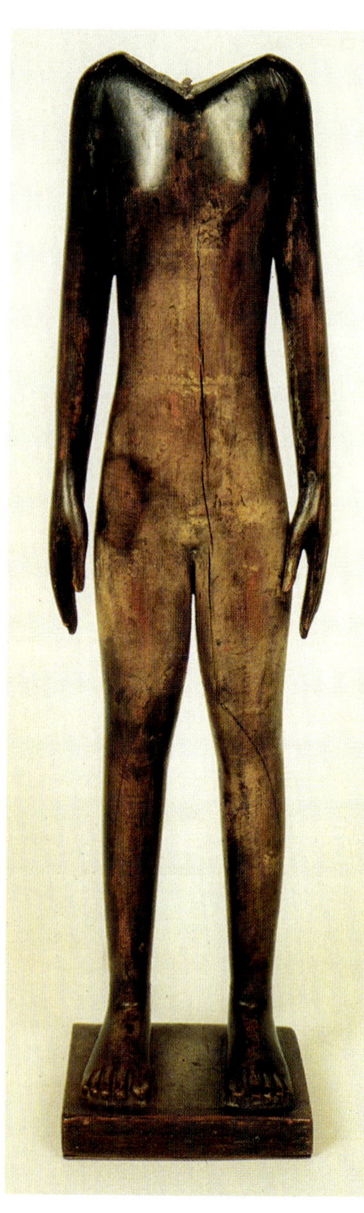

Ewald Mataré (1887–1965)
Female Torso, 1924/25
Walnut, originally gilt,
55 x 14.5 x 11.5 cm

The slender torso of a female figure stands, in emphatic frontality, on a shallow base. This piece is a pendant to the figure *Walking Man (Torso)* of 1922/23 (now in Kleve). Both arms hang straight down in the manner of the sacred sculptures of Ancient Egypt; the feet are positioned stiffly, slightly apart, and parallel to the lateral sides of the base; in place of a head, a notch is cut deep into the upper torso. This also serves to mark the central axis, dividing the body into two almost equal halves.

Out of this very clear and 'purged' form, according to Mataré, 'there arises an entirely new figure, whereas in nature the individual parts are assembled in order to serve a particular purpose.' In his diary Mataré describes in detail his work on the wood for this piece, which involved gilding the surface in order to achieve greater unity (only part of this gilding has survived). This gleaming patina underlines the archaic character of the form, which recalls the 'severe' style of Antiquity. According to an entry in the sculptor's diary for 1924, this headless torso may be seen as a 'portrait' of Hanna, his wife. GL

II Cubism and Constructivism

The fact that Cubism essentially evolved out of a six-year dialogue between two artists, Braque and Picasso, makes it a phenomenon without equal in the history of modern art. More than ever before in the arts, a comprehensive intensification of form was underway.

Soon, however, building on this simplification of elements, against the background of a reduction of the forms of nature to cubes, spheres, cones and circles, an even sharper form of reduction – that of Constructivism – was to follow. This further simplification demanded a clear distance between art and nature in a world in the grip of technology. HS

André Derain (1880–1954)
Man and Woman/Twins, 1907
Sandstone, 39 x 24 x 24 cm

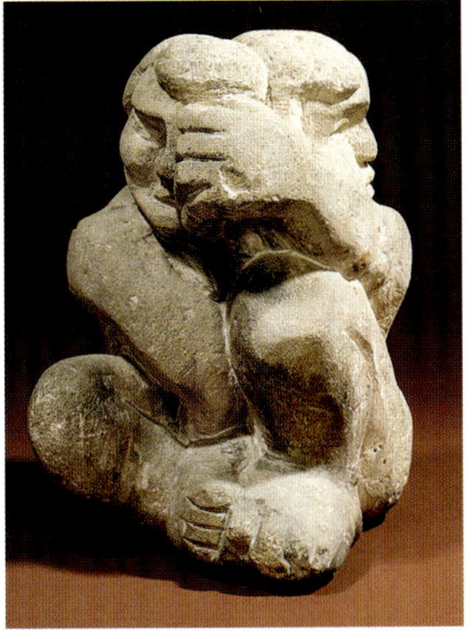

This work, along with Derain's *Crouching Figure* (now in Vienna) is one of the most important stone sculptures to be produced in Paris in the style of *art nègre*. The discovery of African and Oceanic tribal art by Matisse, Vlaminck, Picasso and, indeed, Derain (in 1906–07) heralded a new beginning in the sculpture of the early 20th century. This received its formal 'inauguration' in the Paul Gauguin retrospective presented as part of the Paris *Salon d'Automne* of 1906. Included in this exhibition was the wood sculpture of a couple, *Hina Te Fatou*, made in 1892. This would have provided Derain with a model for his own *Twins*.

This carved sandstone piece is an early 20th-century Parisian attempt to work in a primitive style. It offers clear evidence of an attempt to heighten a sense of plasticity by carving two magically and ritually interlocked nudes out of the misshapen stone block. The particular expressivity of *l'art nègre*, which Dérain found 'bewildering and unsettling', is detectable in the raw and exotic facial features, the heavy hands and the roughly hewn and almost fused bodies, which appear fated to union. GL

Alexander Archipenko
(1887–1964)
Femme drapée/Seated Woman, 1911
Bronze, second of six casts,
59.5 x 29.5 x 29.6 cm

This figure squatting on a doubly stepped base, was cast in bronze in 1911, after an original in painted terracotta. In contrast to Archipenko's powerfully painted reliefs, his so-called *sculpto-peintures* – works which are close to the Cubist collages of Braque and Gris – we have here an individual sculptural piece that can be viewed from all sides and is constructed in extremely lively outlines. While angular, crystalline, geometrically broken segments dominate within the figure, rounded outlines link the elaborately interlocking body forms and draperies. GL

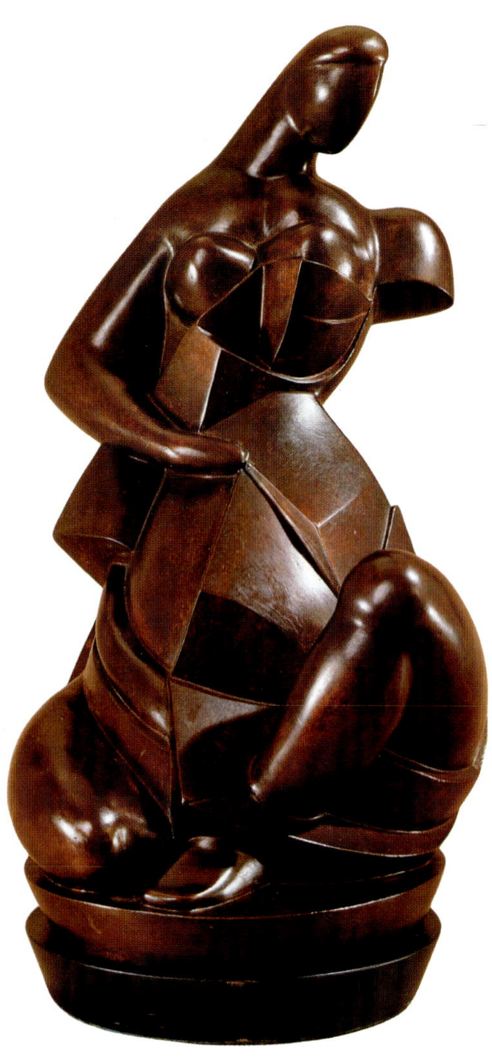

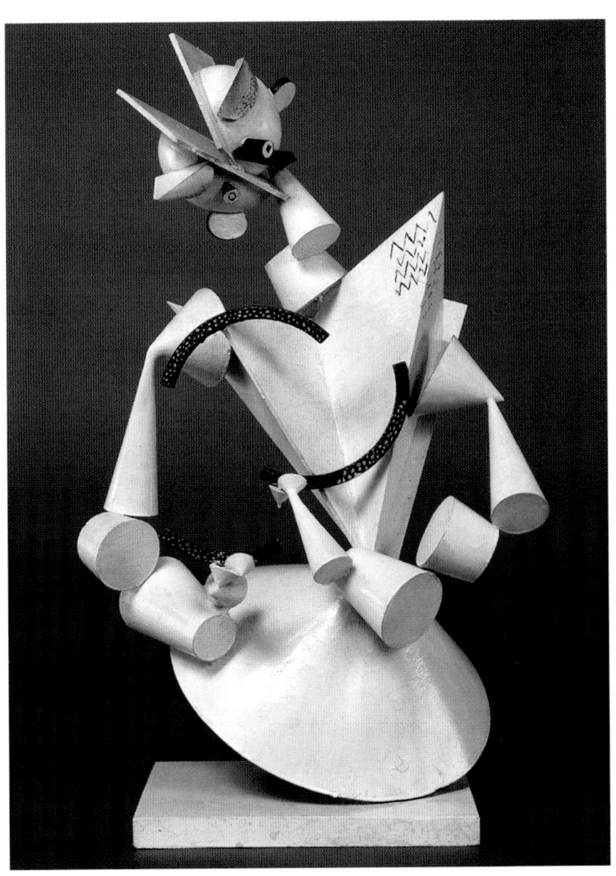

Henri Laurens (1885–1954)
The Clown, 1915
Painted wood, 51.5 x 29.5 x 22.5 cm

The Clown is one of the most important Cubist sculptures by Henri Laurens. This half-figure of what appears to be a juggler is made up of geometric, basic forms: spheres, cones, cylinders. And the balancing act consists here in the throwing and balancing of the hoop, which is shown in a number of different movements. Yet, in as far as colour also plays an important role here, it is the tubular and sculpturally rendered body shapes in the paintings of Fernand Léger, rather than the planar collages of Braque and Picasso that supply the most appropriate comparison. The bright painting unifies the surface of the various wooden sections, while graphic patterns appear as if randomly scattered on the fragments of the hoop, parts of the costume, in the eyes and on the pointed hat. Laurens claimed: 'In painting [such a figure] I'm concerned that the sculpture should have a light of its own'. It was probably for this reason that he made two further coloured versions of *The Clown*, now in the Moderna Museet, Stockholm and in the Tel Aviv Museum. GL

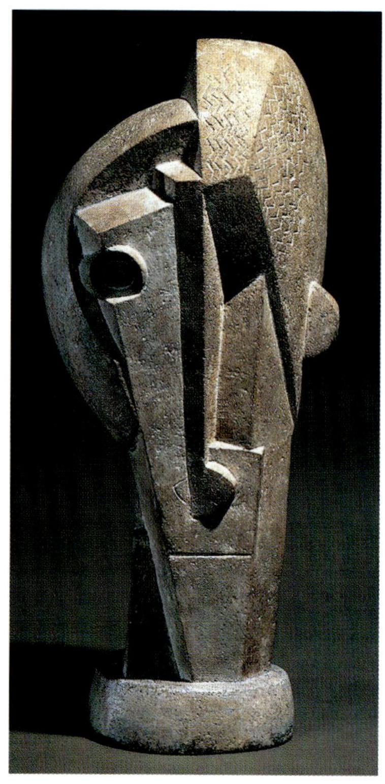

and shadow that preserves the symmetry of the human head and (originally underscored through the effect of coloured planes) nonetheless offsets the sense of stasis associated with a single viewpoint. GL

Jacques Lipchitz (1891–1973)
The Guitarist, 1918
Bronze, 71 x 39.5 x 34.5 cm

Like the Cubist painters, the sculptor Lipchitz treated one of this movement's favoured subjects – the guitarist. Conceived unambiguously with an eye to its impact as viewed from the front, Lipchitz's musician appears as a construction of concave and convex elements that are combined like building blocks in the spirit of Synthetic Cubism. The angularity of the figure is resolved into curves, the shapes are broken up into

Henri Laurens (1885–1954)
Head, 1920
Stone, originally painted
43 x 17.5 x 20 cm

Like *The Clown*, this work in stone comes from Laurens's Cubist phase. Viewed from the front, the roughly conical head on a small circular base is clearly constructed as a relief form and is made up of angular, flat and rounded units. Shapes reduced to circles, straight lines and segments of circles indicate eyes, ears, mouth and nose. Undulating lines scratched in the surface suggest hair. The various levels of the head are displaced in relation to each other, in accordance with the principles of Cubism, and relate to different levels of space. In this way there emerges a play of light

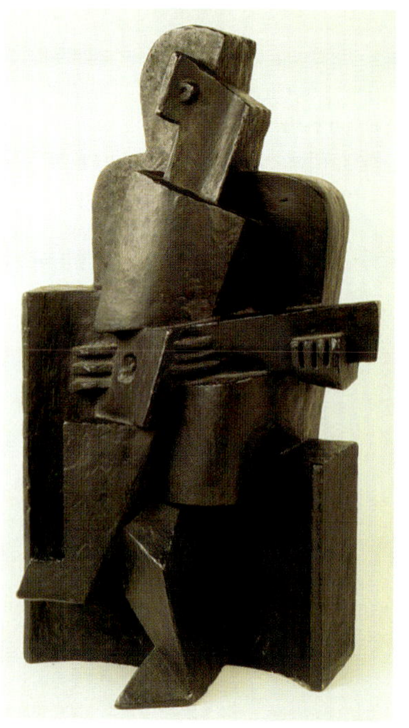

several layers and separated from each other and simultaneously set into a rhythm through sharp contours. The figure, the bench and the parts of the instrument (strings, sound box) achieve a fluent interplay of forms. The body and the instrument merge to establish a compact unity reduced to the character of a still life. In contrast to the procedure followed by other Cubist sculptors such as Archipenko or Laurens, Lipchitz respects the volumes and the solidity of his motif, neither imbuing them with new values through the addition of colour nor dynamizing them through the creation of openings and hollow spaces. GL

Fritz Wotruba (1906–1975)
Reclining Figure, 1962/63
Marble, 77 x 161 x 53 cm

Blocks hewn out with rough blows of the chisel and pushed together as if into a chain of mountains with a bizarre outline, loom up in horizontal layers from a roughly carved base. The lumps of stone are set in relation to each other like series of terraces and yet, viewed as a whole, they yield the angular forms of a reclining figure that had been turned to stone. Particularly striking is the valley-shaped declivity between the two extremes representing the head and the legs that gives the figure a new impulse of energy and tension. In contrast to Arp or Moore, with their swelling figural forms, Wotruba fully accommodates the hardness and the impenetrability of the stone block. He was, nonetheless, concerned 'with the figure, with the statuesque, with mass, balance and unity'. In all the versions of his *Reclining Woman* Wotruba emphasised pure form and frugality and dispensed with any playful accessories. As a result, according to Wotruba, these figures are 'as clear as the calm surface of a lake at the heart of a structurally complex landscape'. GL

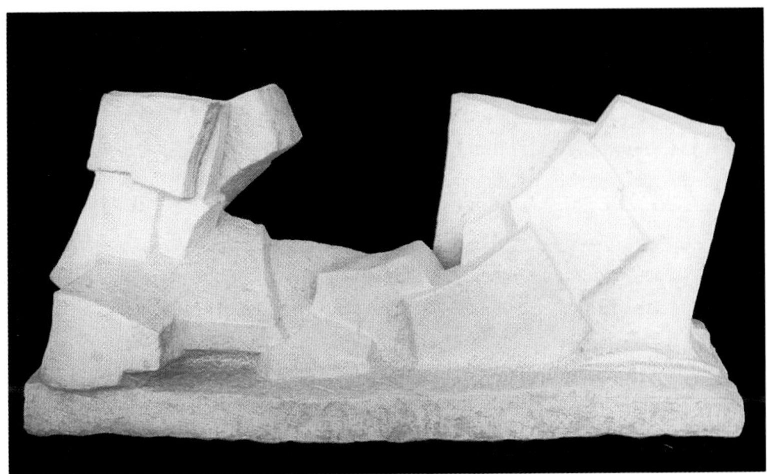

Rudolf Belling (1886–1972)
Triad, 1919/24; second version produced in 1958/59
Elmwood, 91 x 73 x 8 cm

Belling's *Triad*, made in Berlin and originally intended as a model for a sculpture in plastered brick six metres in height – to be unveiled to mark the first performance of a piece of contemporary music – is one of the earliest examples of architectonic sculpture. The piece unites the strongly abstracted figures of three dancers who symbolize the synthesis and the spatial interpenetration of the arts (painting, sculpture and architecture) and embrace both creature and vegetable elements. In this same spirit of universality, the journal of the *Novembergruppe* [November Group], of which Belling became a founder-member in 1918, was intended to have 'Triad – Painting, Sculpture, Architecture' as its title. The first version of this key work of the German avant-garde is in the collection of the Neue Nationalgalerie in Berlin. This second version was made only in 1958/59. GL

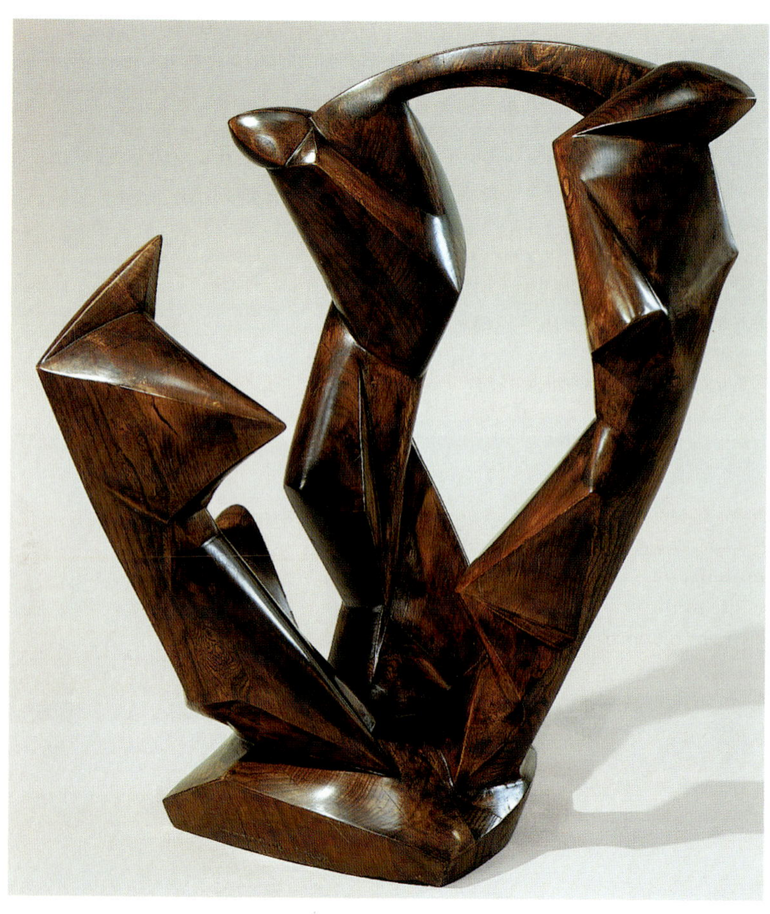

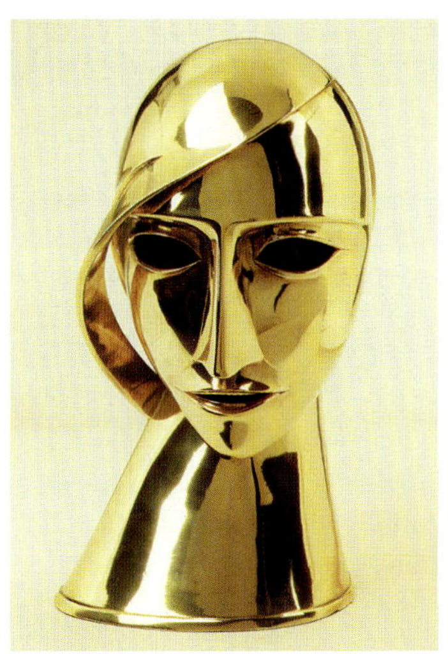

Rudolf Belling (1886–1972)
Brass Head, 1925
Brass, 38.5 x 22.8 x 21.5 cm

This female head, its elegant and decorative character deriving from the metallically gleaming 'technological' basic forms of cone and oval, is effectively a portrait of Toni Freeden, an exponent of Expressionist Dance, whom Belling had married in 1923. The vigorous diagonal of the softly curling hair adds a contrasting element to the rather severely incised eyes and mouth of the mask-like face. A sense of severity and precision, but also of modish self-confidence, pervades the generalized physiognomy of a head that expresses life in the era of technology. The element of 'portrayal' in the conventional sense disappears as the work approaches the ambivalent image of humanity associated with Dadaism, in which natural diversity was repeatedly reduced to mechanical and robotic uniformity. GL

Erich Buchholz (1891–1972)
Rising Circle, 1922
Painted wood, 71 x 52 x 4.5 cm

From the time of his meeting with El Lissitzky in Berlin in 1922, Bucholz was among the leading 'dynamic' Constructivists in Germany. Particularly in early painted wood reliefs such as *Rising Circle*, the picture-object already has something of the character of an icon (an effect intensified through the use of wood and gold colouring), a 'purity' removed from the sphere of the material, as required of art by Malevich in outlining his concept of Suprematism. The upright white plane serves as the support for an irregular vermillion relief, with a small black board as its support. This last serves as the base and 'launching pad' for a centrally inset disc in 'blood red', the colour of revolution, with its gold tinted rim surrounded by a circle of shadow. GL

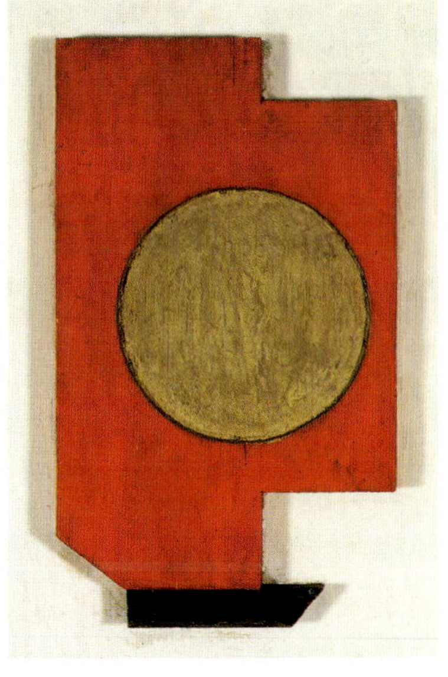

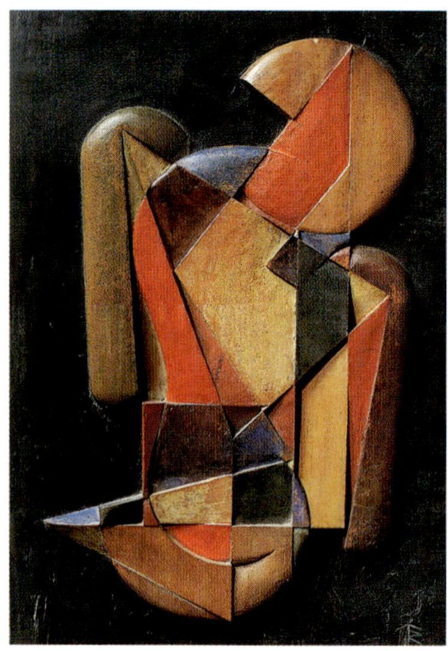

Thomas Ring (1892–1983)
Relief I, 1922
Pearwood, with colour wash,
37 x 24.5 x 3 cm

Based on a drawing dated 1922 and now in the collection of the Wilhelm Lehmbruck Museum, this shallow relief by Thomas Ring consists of interlocking geometrical planes on a black background. Rounded outer forms enclose busily subdivided inner segments, which are in turn enlivened and 'choreographed' through added colour. This structure clearly recalls Ring's non-naturalistically coloured gouaches and drawings of the years 1916 to 1921 executed in a Cubo-Futurist style. Lines are both incisive and curved, straight and rounded, and establish a unique, continuous overall structure. The constructive-linear system employed here is united, as in a relief, with the crystalline form of Cubist faceting.

GL

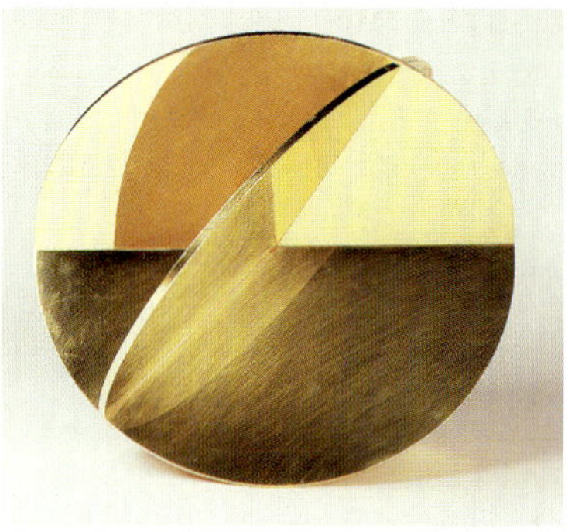

Max Bill (1908–1994)
Construction with Three Circular Discs, 1945/50
Gilt brass, dia. 49.8 cm

Max Bill presents the 'concrete' system based on size and principle in an exemplary fashion in this work made out of brass discs that combine to create a spherical sculptural form. The gilding emphasises the alternation of painting and sculpture and, at the same time, the refinement and transparency of the object that results from light-intensive reflection.

The three discs, equal in diameter and overlapping at their centres, approach each other to form separate, yet clearly demarcated, planar segments. As a result of the reflection of the outer layer, the core zone and the disc forms are repeatedly broken and subdivided into new zones of light and shadow, with the result being that the planar segments seem perpetually to change and move. Space opens up in all directions and, though perceived primarily in relation to the object, it remains open, clear and bright on every side on account of smooth surfaces and reflections. This precise cconstruction is not an end in itself but the application of a logical thought process. GL

Otto Freundlich (1878–1943)
Architectonic Sculpture, 1934–35, 1985
Bronze, first cast of six,
128 x 69 x 43 cm

Since the highly evolved civilization of Ancient Egypt the obelisk has been understood as an emblem of the cosmically far-reaching cult of the sun. Freundlich's sculpture, however, is not only the symbol of a prince's throne but rather of the seat of wisdom (*sedes sapientiae*) that, in connection with the obelisk, showed humanity the way out of darkness into light and from the oppressively brooding material realm into that of the spirit. GL

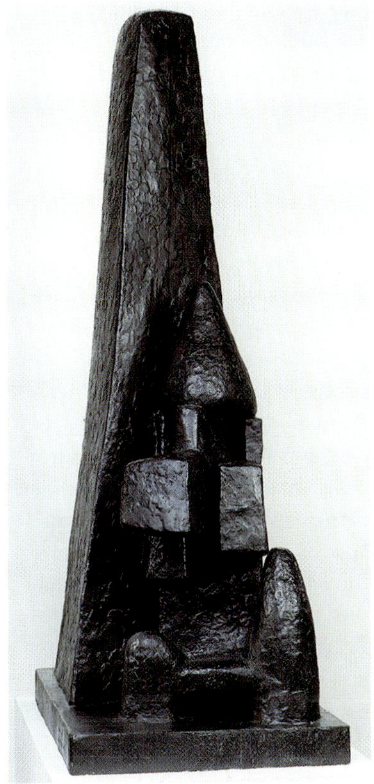

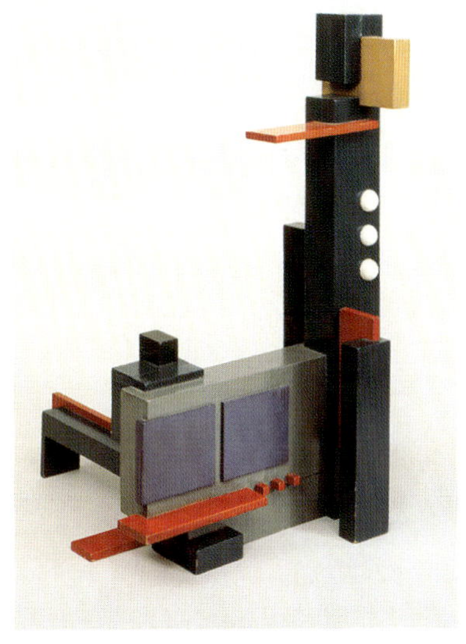

Victor Servranckx (1897–1965)
Opus I, 1925
Painted wood, 65.2 x 47.9 x 45.5 cm

In the 1920s this Belgian artist was an early member of the Bauhaus in Germany and the Dutch Constructivist movement *De Stijl*. Vertical and horizontal forms and primary colours dominate in his work. Art was no longer – as had still been the case with Cubism – perceived as capable of aesthetically enriching reality, but was supposed to fundamentally alter it. A Utopian approach of this sort also informs the sculpture *Opus I*. Made (out) of geometrical, painted and interlocking wooden building blocks, this rather resembles an architectual model. The 'building' as a whole, which has no doors or windows, is in effect a coloured design for an architectonic construction, yet not one intended to be realized architecturally. Rather, it illustrates a sculptural and rational principle. GL

III The Avant-garde in Eastern Europe

Among other portents of the approaching Russian Revolution of 1917, there evolved in Eastern Europe a number of artistic movements whose leaders clamoured for a radical break with the traditional understanding of art and the image. As a whole, these movements constituted the most significant complement to the developments in the art of Western Europe initiated by the Dutch circle of architects and artists, *De Stijl.*

Influenced by the demand for non-objectivity posited by Malevich's Suprematism, and by the broader trend towards a liberation from the object, Puni developed his constructions, Tatlin and Rodchenko their works with an emphasis on material qualities, and the brothers Pevsner and Gabo their Cubo-Constructivist forms.

The common characteristic of these achievements was their dependence on a Purist, de-individualized creative process that sought to exclude all evidence of a personal style or an expressive manner and method. Nonetheless, the work of Rodchenko, Lebedev and Tatlin, in particular, cannot be understood outside the political and social context of Russia both immediately before and after the Revolution. It was precisely their renunciation of the concepts of 'art' and 'composition' in favour of a creative, Purist simplicity that found its complement in the Soviet Russian ideal of the 'new man'.

Other artists, such as Gabo, Pevsner and Kandinsky, were able to find little to their liking in the politically motivated art that was to prove a herald of Socialist Realism, and they soon emigrated. HS

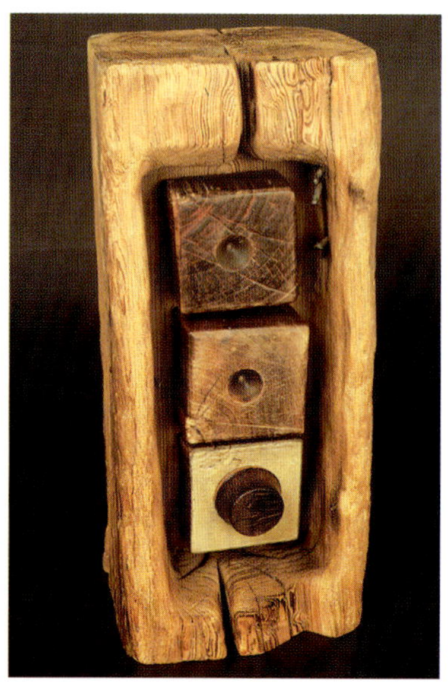

Alexander Rodchenko
(1891–1959)
Spatial Construction, 1919/20
Wood, iron nails,
47.3 x 19.5 x 17.5 cm

From 1918, the year in which Rodchenko painted his picture *Black on Black* (as a response to Malevich's *White Square),* he engaged increasingly with three-dimensional objects. The geometrical forms and the simple, 'poor' materials combine to evince an unambiguous rejection of style and manner, and to testify to the derivation of such work from the techniques employed in icon painting. This construction may be perceived as a crib-like shrine uniting carefully carved pegs and polished nails in the manner of a reliquary. Wood and nails attached to a tree trunk are also symbols of the Passion (*arma Christi*) and allude to the Crucifixion. In this context the 'nakedness' and 'poverty' of the material find their inner identity in a 'victory over painting' and the triumph of 'pure' representation. HS

Vladimir E. Tatlin (1885–1953)
Corner Relief (reconstruction), 1915/1995
Iron, wood, steel cable, third of a series of three, 250 x 101.5 x 182 cm

In 1914 Tatlin travelled, via Berlin, to Paris where he came into contact with the Cubism of Picasso and Braque. Before the end of the year, after his return to Russia, he produced his first 'syntheso-static compositions', later known as 'counter-reliefs'. The anti-static spatial structure of the counter-relief and the montage of material explicitly raised to the rank of art not only broke with sculptural tradition but also, and above all, called into question the notions of technical mastery and intended meaning in the arts.

Through rhythm and composition, Tatlin imbued with aesthetic qualities the industrial materials he employed. Here the cylindrical figure oscillates as if playing on the strings of an instrument. At the heart of this work was Tatlin's artistic utopia: a symbiosis of nature, man and technology. HS

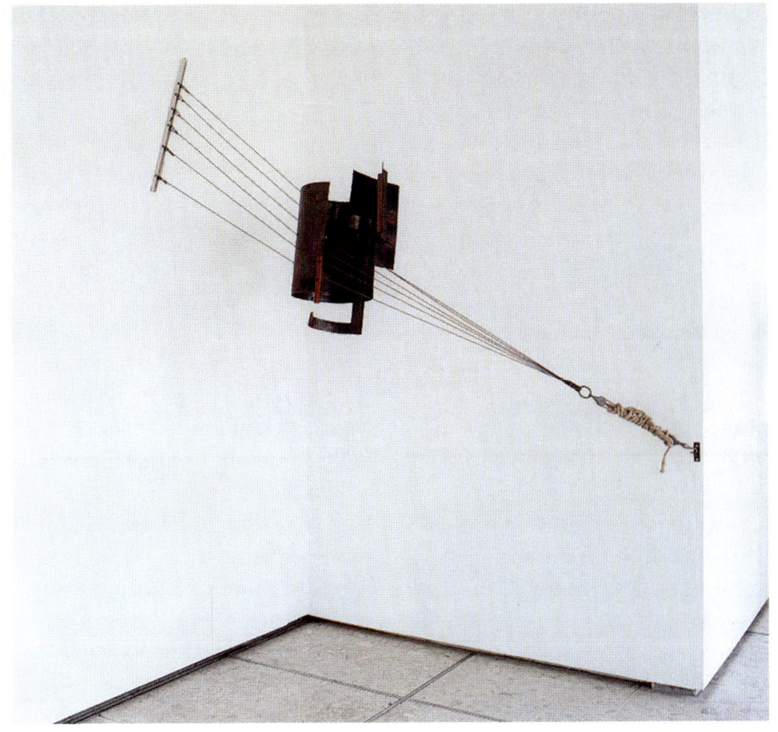

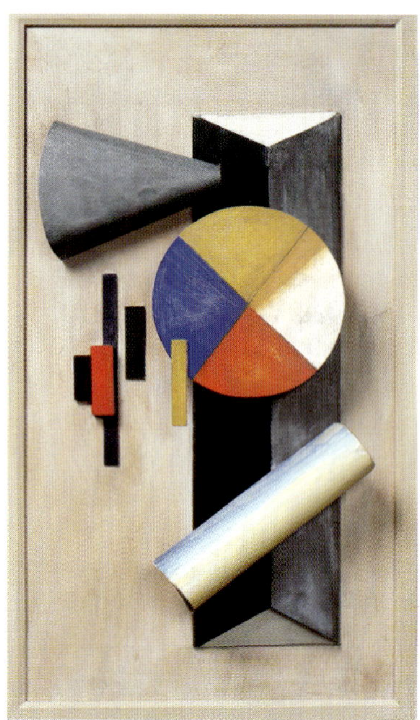

Ivan A. Puni (1894–1956)
Suprematist Construction, 1915
Painted wood, cardboard, metal,
76.5 x 44 x 11.5 cm

In 1915, together with Malevich, Puni signed the Suprematist Manifesto. The essential aims of Suprematism were 'total liberation from the object' and an art of 'pure cognition'. Arrangements of non-objective geometric and stereometric forms, dependent only on coincidence, were undertaken in the hope of achieving a break with the 'shallow striving for utility' within a world already stamped by the age of industrialization. For the Suprematist, the work of art was henceforth to assume a state of supension freed from the resonance of cause and effect in the real world. HS

Vladimir Lebedev (1891–1967)
Relief, 1920/21
48.4 x 32 x 4.5 cm

Like the Russian Constructivists, Lebedev championed the 'liberation' of the object, and he aimed at an autonomous art without a personal 'handwriting'.

For Lebedev, the simplicity of this montage clearly demonstrates the progressive shaping of a work of art. The preference for 'poor', worn materials and clear design recall Rodchenko's principles of simplification, which, particularly in the context of the Russian Revolution, were intended to shape the 'new man' through his interaction with the 'new art'. In the case of Lebedev, too, the rejection of the conventional form of the work of art, as a purely sensual indulgence – a stance derived from the Constructivists – constituted an artistic programme. HS

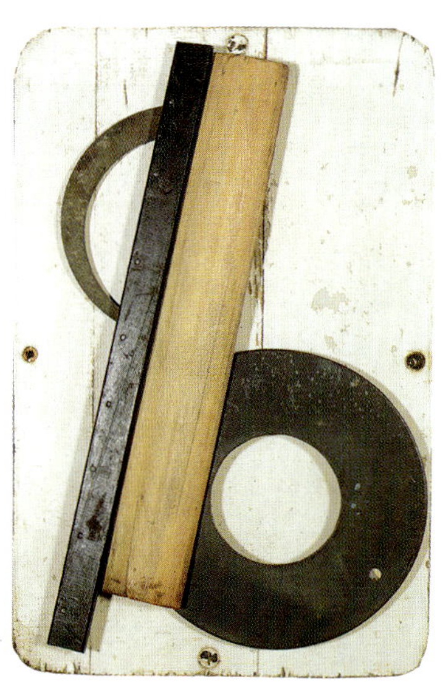

Naum Gabo (1890–1977)
Linear Construction in Space, No. 2, 1959/60
Perspex with nylon thread, 79.5 x 59 x 59 cm

From the time of the Second World War, Gabo produced 'spherical' sculptures in which a single nylon thread was tautly wound around an irregularly shaped perspex framework. In these works, the thread alone took the lead in the linear construction of space. By such means it was possible to experience, yet again, the immateriality that had been demanded by Gabo and his brother Antoine Pevsner in their Realist Manifesto of 1920 – in this case through a transparent crystalline system that was dependent as much on the play of light as on the movement and eyelevel of the spectator. The fragile construction resembles a textile woven out of 'strings' that crystallizes into a spherical form. The threads become denser as a result of their intersections towards the centre, and this makes possible a fuller reflection of light and a stronger sense of plasticity than is to be found at the edges, where the system of lines appears to dissolve.

The Rayonism that Mikhail Larionov evolved in 1910 is here linked with the Purist concept of space applied by the Russian Constructivists. The true goal is, in essence, not the sculpture itself but its character as a monument and its connection with architecture. Ultimately, the significance of this Constructivist form lies in the combination of its kinetic effect, its seeming weightlessness and the element of light. GL

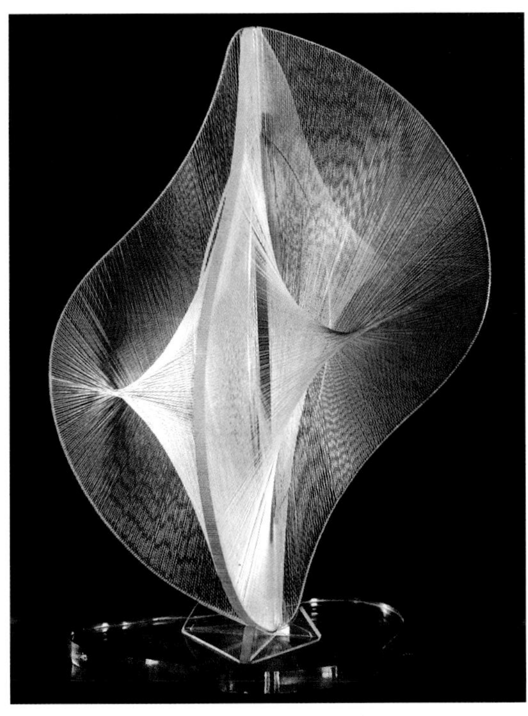

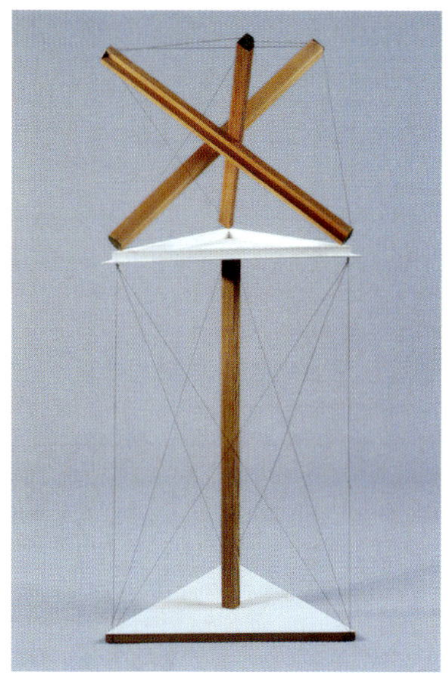

Karl Ioganson (1890–1929)
Spatial Construction, 1921/1993 (reconstruction)
Wood, wire, steel tube,
63 x 88 x 79 cm; overall h 169.5 cm

Referring to his spatial constructions, Ioganson used to speak of a 'cold structure', pointing thereby to the anti-Expressionist stance of the Russian avant-garde, which could be associated with the qualities of calculation, simple geometry and stereometry. By 'cold', he ultimately intended to convey his conviction that a work of art, like the marble sculptures of Ancient Greece, had to be free from traces of the process used to create it. HS

Antoine Pevsner (1886–1962)
Space Construction in the Third and Fourth Dimension, 1961
Bronze, in two parts; third cast of three, 99.5 x 60 x 54 cm

In 1920, together with his brother, Naum Gabo, Antoine Pevsner published the Realist Manifesto. Inspired by the complex iron construction of the Eiffel Tower, Pevsner produced abstract, stereometric formal structures through which he sought to establish a contemporary yet absolute harmony out of an aesthetic experience of the technological world. Pevsner dissolved the volumes of sculpture and, by means of sharp-edged, concave and concentrically aligned planes, achieved an effect of dynamism and dematerialization (Dynamic Constructivism). HS

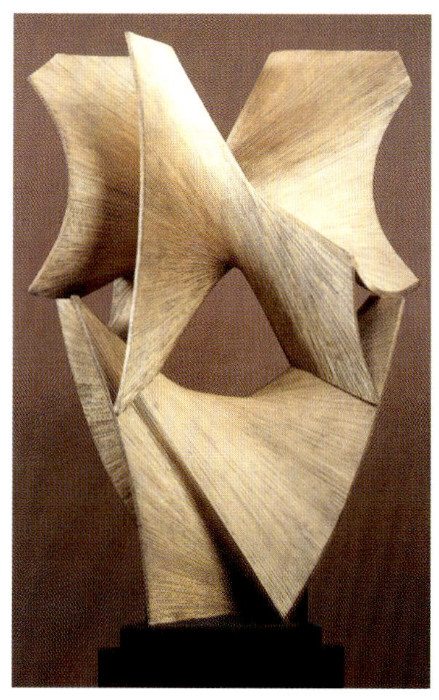

László Moholy-Nagy
(1895–1946)
Space Modulator, 1939
Plexiglass on steel plate in a wooden frame, 78.4 x 50.5 x 8.7 cm

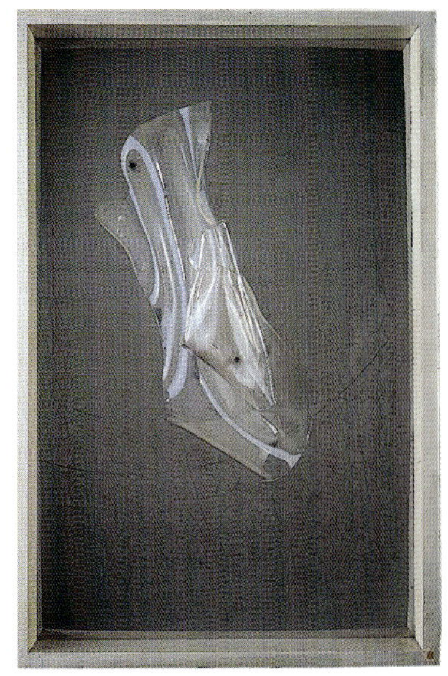

From around 1938/39 Moholy-Nagy devoted his attention to the theme of space modulation. This transparent plexiglass object, seen against the background of the reflecting steel plate, gives the illusion of being in motion, appearing to shed its own materiality and float. Through variations in the illumination and in reflected light, ever new forms emerge then again vanish, in an unbounded, and yet pictorially conceived, space. However, this space is imbued with a sense of movement. By this means there comes into being a dynamic and simultaneously floating structure characterized, in Moholy-Nagy's words, by 'the greatest poetic intensity'. HS

László Péri (1899–1967)
Spatial Arrangement in Three Parts, 1923/24
Black and reddish-brown coloured concrete, 98 x 239 x 2 cm (in total)

Péri's first non-objective Constructivist reliefs were made in 1921. The long untraced wall piece shown here was first exhibited in Berlin in 1923 and has been recognized as one of the most important examples of Constructivist art ever produced. A colour lithograph made in the 1960s indicates its original form and dimensions. With this three-part work Péri committed himself to the mission of architecture. Using the means available to Dynamic Constructivism, this architectonic function made it possible for him to develop asymmetric spatial concepts. These opened up the conventional pictorial rectangle and led towards an experimentation with alternative solutions. GL

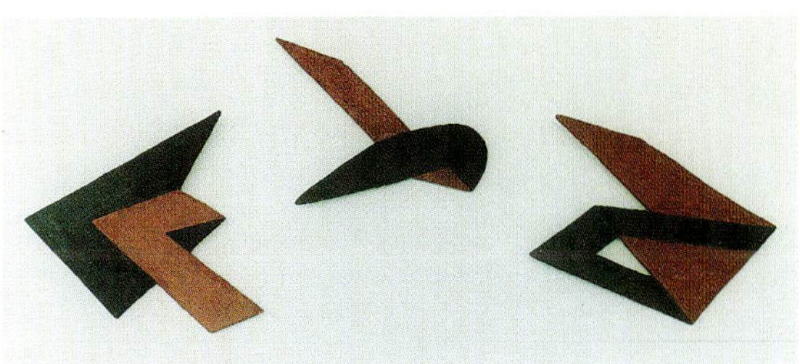

IV The Great Synthesis: Sculpture from Arp to Zadkine

There can be no doubt that it was during the extremely creative phase before the outbreak of The First World War, as also in the years following the end of the war, that the foundations were laid for what were the great stylistic blueprints of modern art. It is in this period that we can best appreciate the contribution of those painters and sculptors who have come to be recognized as the founding fathers and the pioneers of Modernism: Picasso, Matisse, Derain, Marcel Duchamp, Arp, Laurens, Tatlin, Boccioni, Gabo and Lipchitz. These and other artists created those works to which we still turn today, be it on account of their symbolism, their subject matter or the techniques employed. At the beginning of this development we find Cubist and Futurist sculpture, which was soon followed by varieties of Primitivism and Expressionism, before the 'readymades' of Duchamp (from 1913/14) introduced an entirely new concept of art and the art object. Duchamp marks the beginning of Conceptual Art, in which the idea is valued above its execution. GL

Pablo Picasso (1881–1973)
The Cock, 1933
Plaster, wood, newspaper, iron,
35 x 30 x 38 cm

This cock was made in 1933 in Boisgeloup, during one of the most important working periods of Picasso's career. Picasso had acquired this large property, near Gisors, in 1930. Long resentful at accommodating himself to the confines of his Paris studio, he appreciated having sufficient space to devote himself to sculptural work. At this time Picasso was deeply engaged with the theme of metamorphosis and, in the case of sculpture, with the evocation of texture. It is above all due to this aspect of his work that Picasso has earned a place in the history of sculpture. The cock has an internal iron framework but is otherwise constructed out of numerous, small and swiftly modelled plaster segments; in form it is simultaneously majestic and dishevelled. The feathers are partially rendered with incised leaf forms – very much in the spirit of metamorphosis, with a preoccupation for texture. The head combines elements of the human and the bestial. Life and death, animal and man, are shown to be undergoing a process of transformation – one of Picasso's most persistent themes. ChB

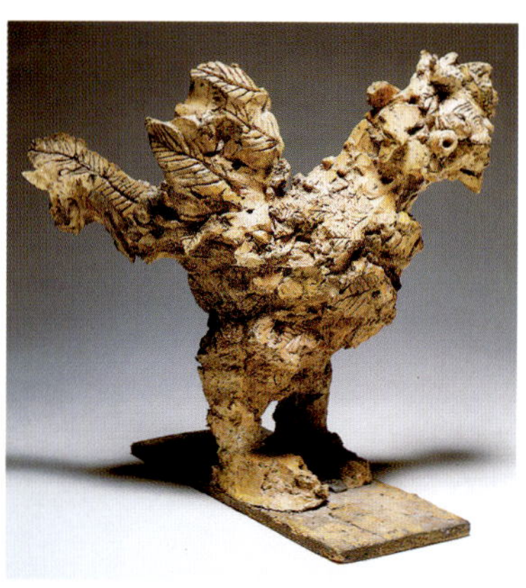

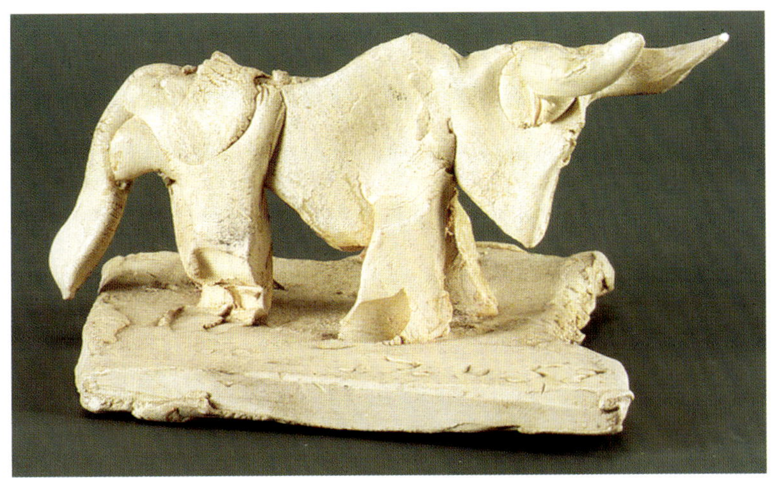

Pablo Picasso (1881–1973)
The Bull, 1957
White terracotta,
6.5 x 12.5 x 11.5 cm

This small bull, modelled in clay, of which there are also two bronze casts, is part of a group of animal sculptures made at around the same time. About 130 animal subjects have survived. Like most of Picasso's work in ceramics, these were made in the studio of Georges Ramié in Vallauris. In spite of being worked so sketchily and swiftly, the bull exhibits the characteristic features of this beast: the swelling neck, the curved horns and the powerful rib cage. At the same time this piece seems less close to Picasso's contemporary work on the theme of the Minotaur and the bull fight as it conveys the character of a piece made for a particular occasion, a 'finger exercise' for the intended subsequent production of a child's toy. Using a tool, Picasso has clearly inscribed the date 7.4.1957 on the base. ChB

Hans (Jean) Arp (1886–1966)
Arrangement of White Shapes on a Grey Ground, 1929 or later
Painted wood, 72 x 87 x 3.5 cm

The title *Arrangement* alerts us to the variable formal organization and the endless alternative possiblities implicit within this piece. In this relief there occurs an imaginary 'dance' of primitive, amorphous, amoeboid particles that, despite actually remaining within the imposed frame, arouse the impression of being in a process of mobile transformation, continuously shifting apart and then regrouping. HS

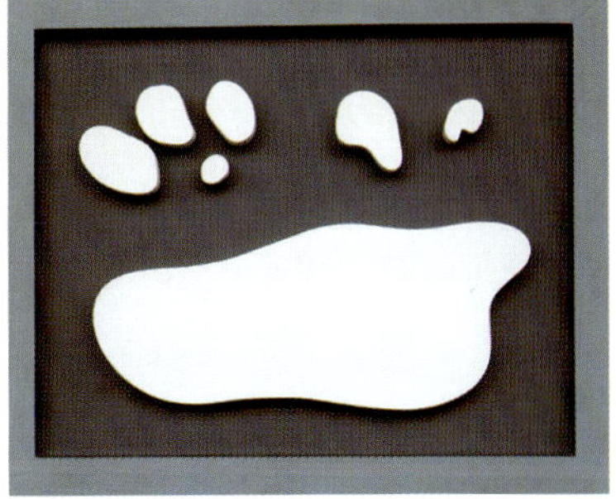

Hans (Jean) Arp (1886–1966)
Concrétion Humaine/Human Intensification, 1935/48
Bronze, in two parts,
second of three casts,
62 x 76 x 56 cm

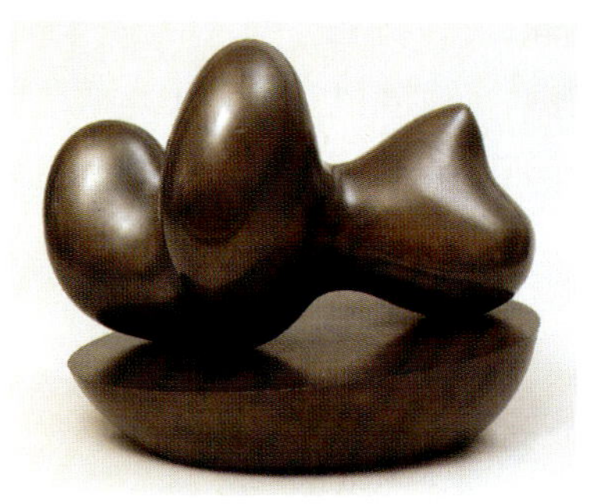

This sculpture rests on an inclined oval base yet projects beyond its edge. In size, however, it is attuned to the scale of this base, with the result that the two parts establish a harmonic unity. The transitions between the individual forms are soft and flowing. The swelling curves and the hollows belong inextricably together. Of great importance for Arp was the freedom with which he gradually established the form each of his sculptures was to assume. In poetically titling this work *Concrétion Humaine*, Arp sought to indicate both an object resulting from conscious formal creation and the necessary assimilation within the arts of the laws of nature. HS

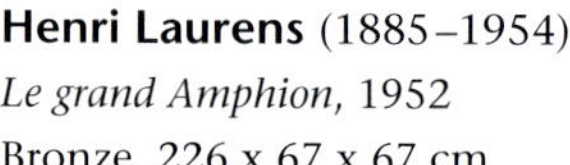

Henri Laurens (1885–1954)
Le grand Amphion, 1952
Bronze, 226 x 67 x 67 cm

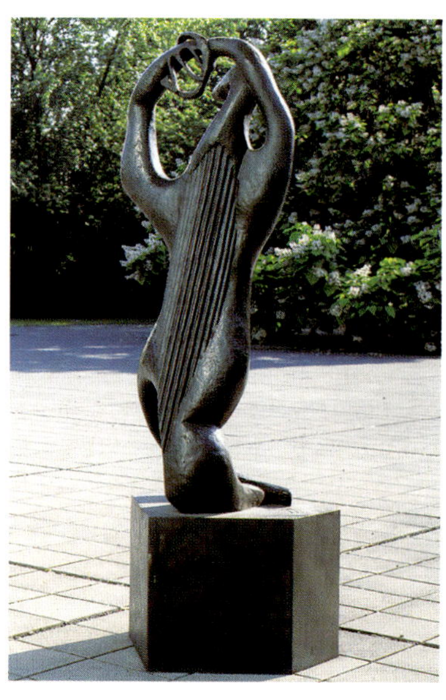

The organic and fluent figure of Amphion stands on a hexagonal base. The body, shown in a rising movement, finds its completion in the clasping gesture of the raised arms. The spread hands form a network that we may simultaneously interpret as a lyre and as the fingers playing over it. The motif of the musical instrument also recurs in the body itself, where we find unifying vertical striations that recall the strings of a harp or perhaps the fluting of a column. The architectonic character suggested by this feature is strengthened through the symmetrically inward curving sides of the body.

In Classical Mythology Amphion was the inventor of music. This son of Antiope and Zeus had a twin brother, Zethos. While the latter used his great physical vigour to erect walls, Amphion played on his lyre, causing the stones to form into architectural structures of their own accord. HS

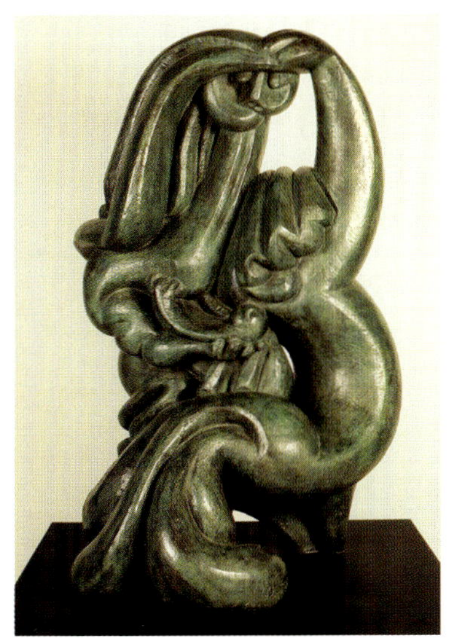

Jacques Lipchitz (1891–1973)
Mother and Child, 1940
Bronze with green patina,
120 x 73 x 72 cm

Lipchitz treated the subject of mother and child throughout his career, and he had already begun to address this motif in 1913–14. This late bronze mother and child group with green patina was made at a time when Lipchitz was forced to flee the advance of German troops and leave Paris for Toulouse. The outer contour of the group as a whole is formed by expansively rhythmic lines (inspired by the work of Picasso) that continue through the legs and the arms to the hair and the head of the mother, integrating into an organic whole. The left arm carries the infant, who constitutes the real centre of the composition, although formally part of the figure of the mother. In this way mother and child are fused into an inseparable, natural unit that, in a time of war, served as a heartening symbol of life. HS

Ossip Zadkine (1890–1967)
Orpheus, 1948
Bronze, first cast of five,
203.5 x 75 x 60 cm

A scrap of wood that Zadkine had found gave him the idea for an X-shaped figure with an emphasis on the legs and the upper torso, which literally split and merge with the form of a lyre (here resembling a tuning fork).

Orpheus, the greatest rhapsode of Greek mythology, here endeavours to win back his beloved, Euridice, with the power of his music. This piece symbolizes the sorrows of mortal humanity and the horrors of war. HS

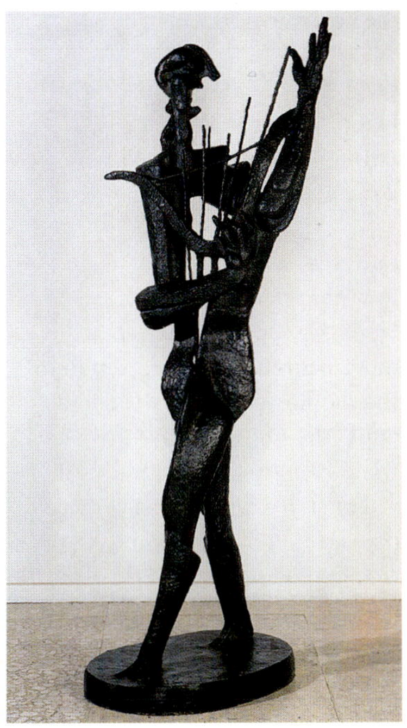

Marino Marini (1901–1980)
Dancer
Polychrome bronze, third cast of three, 173 x 58 x 39.5 cm

Marini derived his style as a sculptor from the work of the Etruscans, the former inhabitants of his native Tuscany. Marini saw himself as a 'man of the Mediterranean'. Through extreme reduction in their outlines, his figures assume a quality that is symbolic and thus also monumental. This dancer exudes an aura of timelessness. HS

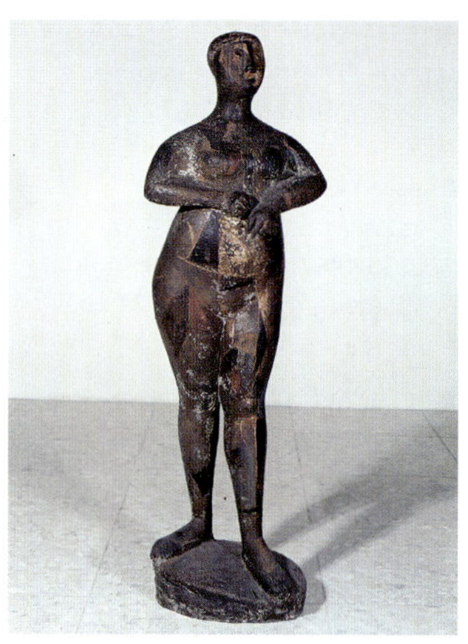

Henry Moore (1898–1986)
Reclining Figure (in two parts), 1959
Bronze on a base faced in copper, second of six casts,
143 x 215 x 138 cm

In this work Moore was able to link the 'Stone Age Archaic' of his middle period with 'Michalangelesque Classicism' and a forceful contemporary language of form. The reclining figure is a mythical one that has penetrated, like an alien creature from the primeval past, into our contemporary world. HS

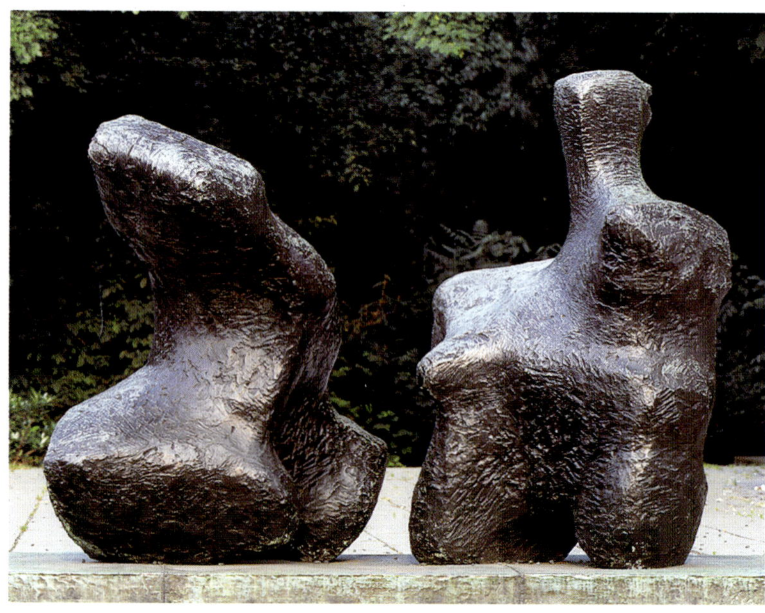

Barbara Hepworth (1903–1975)
Caryatid, individual form, 1961
Teak with thread, 202 x 25 x 15 cm

This wooden *stele* was made several years after the visit that Hepworth made in 1954 to Greece, where she was particularly impressed by the landscape and by the monuments on the islands of the Aegean and on the Cyclades.

As in other works executed after this stay, she chose here to work in hard African teak from Nigeria and adopt a 'pierced form' with hollows and openings. The slender wooden body on its base swells towards the centre like the pillar shafts of Greek Antiquity, then abruptly breaks off at its crown as if encountering a horizontal beam. The interior is hollowed out almost to the sides, as if forming a trough, and is pierced in its upper section with two upright oval openings. Threads are stretched across these in a fan form reminiscent of that of an African stringed instrument. HS

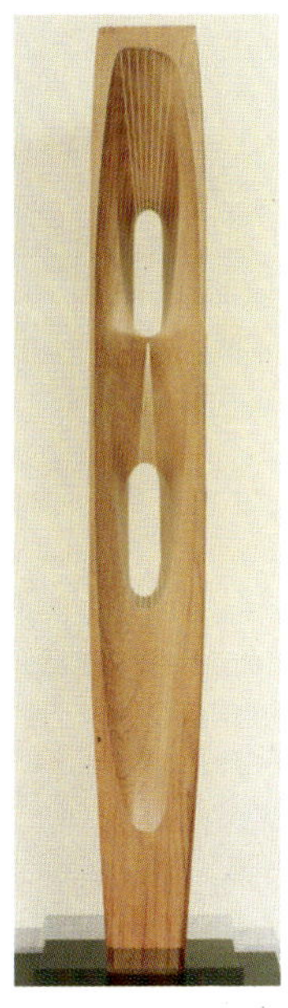

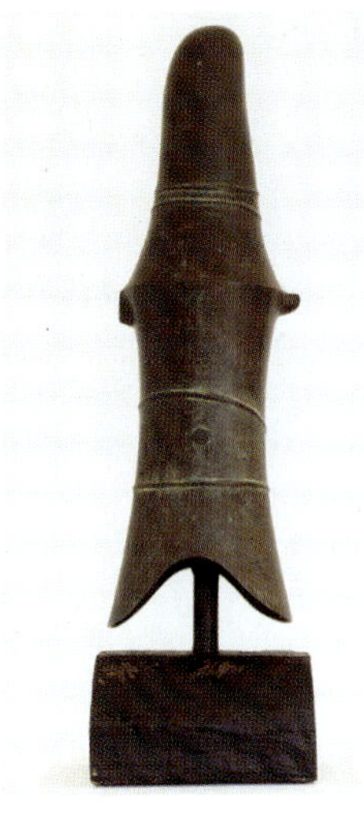

Isamu Noguchi (1904–1988)
Bell Image, 1959
Bronze on a wooden base,
98 x 25.7 x 27.2 cm

This piece is effectively a two-part work consisting of a squared-off but otherwise wooden base pierced centrally by an iron rod, on which the hollow form of the bronze 'bell' with undulating edges is mounted. The double ring winding around the smooth walls has the effect of two cords separated by a space marked with a button-like notch in the lower area, but almost touching in the narrowing upper region. Along the seam between the belly and the throat of the 'bell' there are lateral handle forms.

Noguchi was, however, not concerned to produce a functional object, but rather to give form to one that would evoke the ancient iron and bronze vessels found in China and Japan. GL

V Heads and Masks

An emphatic departure from the traditional canonization of the head is already to be observed in the work of Auguste Rodin. The traces of sculptural Impressionism, already very evident here, find their culmination in the sculpture of Medardo Rosso.

Until the mid-19th century the concept of *mimesis* [imitation], derived from the art and aesthetics of Classical Antiquity, was still valid in the fine arts. It was only with the advent of Primitivism that the situation altered. Around 1910 a new enthusiasm for Romanesque and non-European sculpture took hold. Artists such as González and Picasso saw fetishistic and transcendental qualities in these sculptures and artefacts and groped their way, experimentally, towards the essence of this art. Particular fascination was derived from the animal faces of the masks of Oceania and Africa, in which European artists recognized a unique and alien beauty and the simultaneous capacity for expressing magical powers.

The artists found a quality that had been lacking in European art on account of centuries of dogmatic canonization. Masks and fetishes thus established new points of reference because they went beyond the boundaries of the world that could ordinarily be perceived through the senses and the intellect, thus securing a new access to the primeval. HS

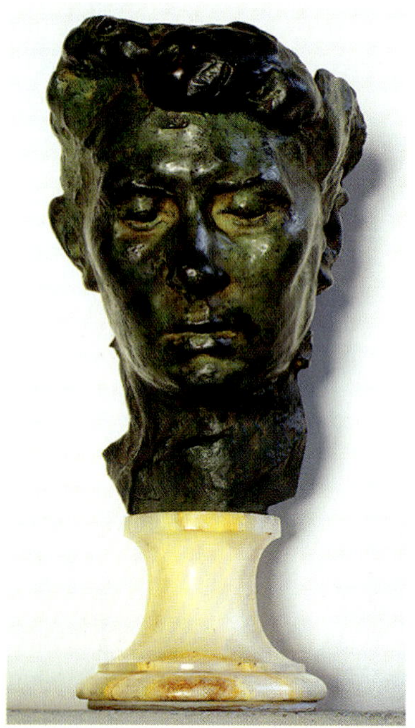

Auguste Rodin (1840–1917)
Rose Beuret, 1888–1890
Bronze, 26.5 x 16 x 15.5 cm
(without base)

This portrait mask, with its characteristic green patina, which comes from the Deneke Collection, shows Rose Beuret (1844–1917) at the age of around 45. Rodin's companion, who came from a peasant family, was a seamstress. She had met Rodin when she was twenty, but it was only on 29 January 1917 that she married him, just two weeks before her death and less than a year before his own (in November 1917). The face is rendered in softly modelled features, the slight sideways incline of the head with downturned eyes underlining the effect of modesty. KL

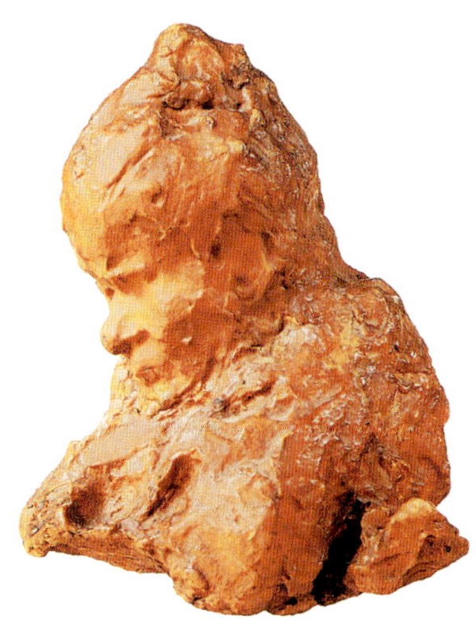

Medardo Rosso (1858–1928)
La Portinaia/ The Concierge, 1883–1884
Tinted wax on plaster,
37 x 32.5 x 19 cm
Wedding present from the artist to his son, Francesco

Rosso, who moved from Milan to Paris in 1889, was one of the pioneers of what has been termed Impressionist sculpture. Exploiting the softness and malleability of plaster and wax, he produced images of the human figure that would be transformed in the play of light into specific but dreamily entranced individuals. The reduction of the depicted parts of the figure and the seemingly floating, hazy overall effect combine in Rosso's work with a socially critical approach to contemporary problems (housing the destitute, solitude, prostitution). The deeply withdrawn and contemplative head of *The Concierge* of which there are several versions, conveys the sorrow and loneliness of a 'marked woman. GL

Constantin Brancusi (1876–1957)
La Négresse Blonde, 1928
Polished bronze, stone base,
8 x 28.2 x 27.8 cm

While the surface of Brancusi's polished bronze reflects every earthly and cosmic phenomenon, in the two-part cruciform stone base we find the axial pattern of earthly stability and fixity. The upright, oval, egg-like form is humanized through the negro lips, the jagged chignon and the head decoration. At the same time Brancusi seeks even here for the archaic and purified primal form as an expression of vitality and originality.

As Brancusi wrote in 1917 to Tristan Tzara, wood and stone signified the truth: 'In humanity I see the moon, plants, the negro, metal, stars and fish.' GL

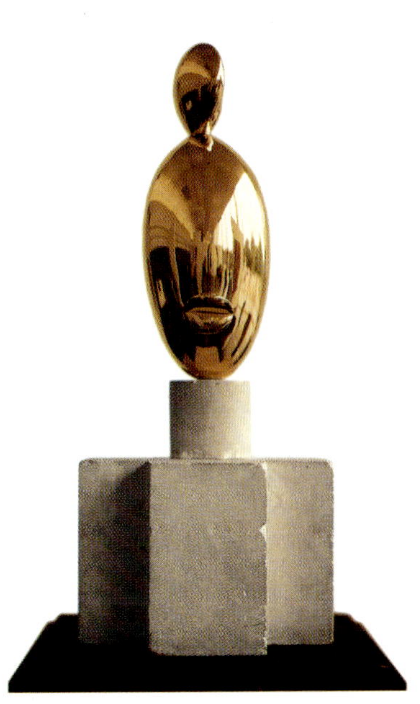

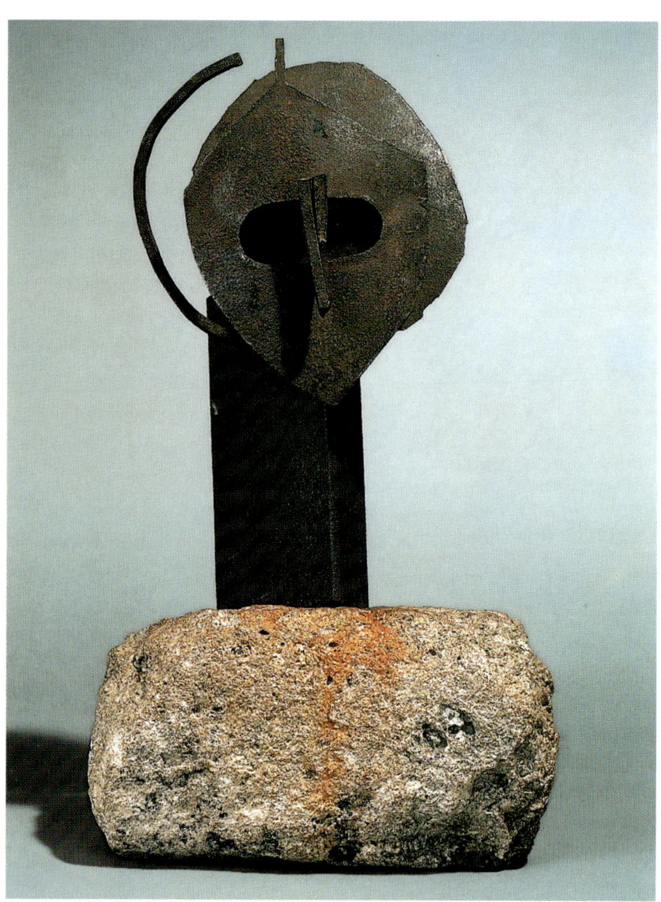

Julio González (1876–1942)
Head with Large Eyes, c 1930
Iron, shell limestone base,
44 x 25 x 21.5 cm

In collaboration with Picasso, making heads, masks, figures and still lifes, González succeeded in ennobling a new material that had long been used in art only for work of lesser aesthetic significance: iron. In *Head with Large Eyes* the sculptor effectively opposes Brancusi's harmonic geometry to a roughly worked iron plate which is mounted on the sloping surface of a rectangular base made of shell limestone. Out of this base there emerges a longish neck, V-shaped in outline, with its opening towards the rear. The head itself – which is simultaneously a mask – is welded on to the upper edge of the neck. Through the deft treatment of the head as an iron sculpture and its combination with the rough and irregularly shaped stone base, this image assumes a character that draws on both the archaic and the fetishistic.

ChB

Victor Brauner (1903–1966)
Fantastical Head, 1934/1940
Painted field stone,
22.5 x 11.6 x 2 cm

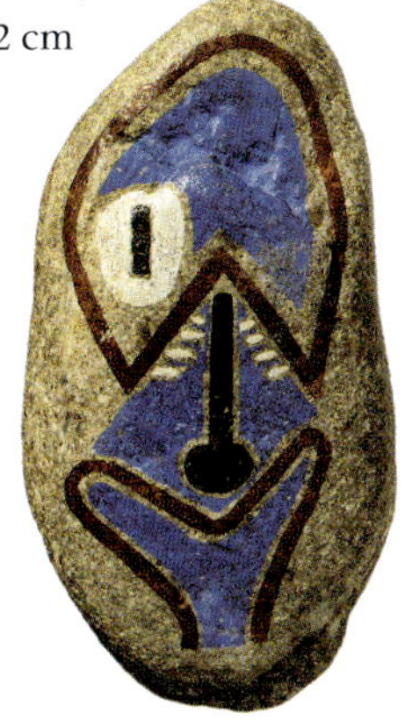

Brauner treated this 'head' as a Surrealist *objet trouvé,* intensifying its magical effect through painted markings. He thereby drew on a tradition that goes back to the rock paintings in the South of France and in Spain, to the rarely occurring natural rocks with the appearance of relief carving and to the sacred objects of pre- and early history, a tradition that was taken up in the mid-1930s by the Surrealists (Alberto Giacometti, Max Ernst and others).

This object can be interpreted in a number of ways, not least because it can be approached as both an upright and a horizontal form. While in the upright reading, it is possible to make out a one-eyed face; when the stone is placed horizontally we find a frieze-like ordering of events: the frontal view of a human face is complemented by the tail of a fish, a phallus and an aggressive monster with open jaws. During the course of a fight in 1938 Brauner lost his left eye, and one might see in his *Fantastical Head* a form of self-portraiture.

GL

Max Ernst (1891–1976)
Un ami empressé/An Indefatigable Friend, 1944
Bronze, 66.8 x 38.4 x 40 cm

This work was made in the summer of 1944 (though not cast until 1957), when Max Ernst stayed with Dorothea Tanning at Great River on Long Island. Viewed from the front, the flattened torso takes on the character of an animal on account of its spinal column and mask-like face. The back view, on the contrary, shows an apparently female creature with arms hanging at her sides, neck craned forwards and legs that appear with their natural direction reversed so that they reach up over her head. This grotesque form of corporeality, corresponding to the style of Ernst's American years, alludes to the hermaphrodites in the paintings of Hieronymus Bosch. In its Surrealist versatility, the 'indefatigable friend' demonstrates the reversal of male and female, of inner and outer life. GL

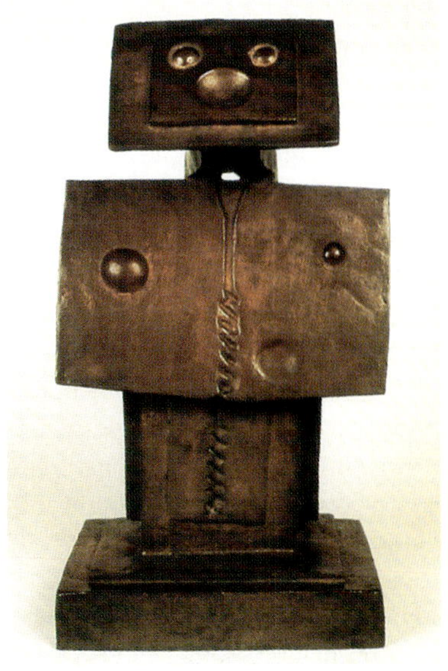

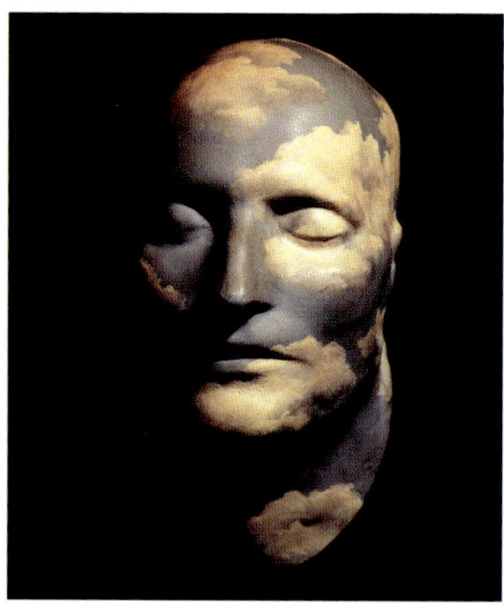

René Magritte (1898–1967)
L'avenir des statues/The Future of Statues, 1932
Painted plaster, 35.5 x 16.5 x 19 cm

Between 1931 and 1937 Magritte made several slightly varying versions of this visionary work (others are also to be found in London, Stockholm and elsewhere). He discovered the plaster cast with the death mask of Napoleon in an antique dealer's. In its Surrealist adaptation, this object embodies the theme of the reciprocity of influence between dreams and reality, here in parallel with that of the interpenetration of the genres of painting and sculpture.

The face and the throat are painted blue with white clouds, evoking the illusion of an open sky. This travesty of Napoleon's death mask and the undermining of any element of 'reality' signals the contradictory nature of this work. Ultimately, Magritte is here asking: 'Does the "future of monuments" live in the clouds?' This is a question that has not yet lost any of its relevance. GL

Salvador Dalí (1904–1989)
Head of Dante, 1964
Bronze with green patina, spoons in silver gilt, marble base, fourth version of six,
27.2 x 20.1 x x 20.7 cm

This deeply lined face depicts the greatest Italian poet, Dante Alighieri (1265–1321), as an aged poet-prince. The markedly lively surface of the emaciated visage assumes a certain independence, with ridged, curvilinear folds of skin that curl in the chin into a spiral, twist above the right eye into an extension of the eyebrow and traverse the right cheek like furrows. Dalí has here 'crowned' the poet with a wreath of gilt silver spoons of an Art Deco style, their surface assuming an organic character through the addition of veining and ribs. GL

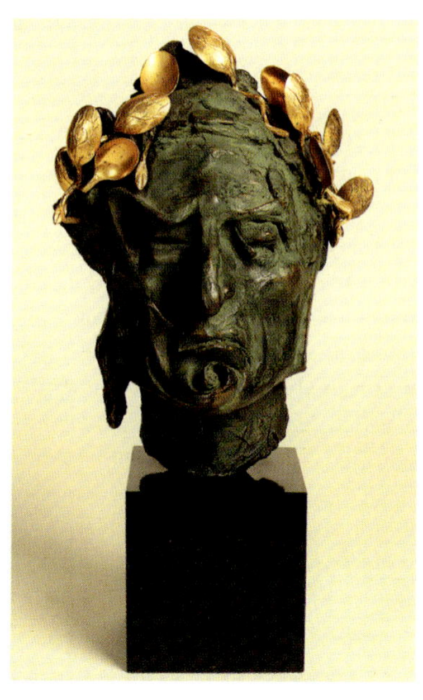

VI The Wit and Magic of Objects

Dadism and Surrealism were the creation of a group of like-minded friends who countered the perceived oppression of bourgeois society through total shamelessness and irony.

These artists felt distrustful of a society governed by reason because it was precisely such a society that appeared to be responsible for war and tyranny.

The dream, the hypnotic trance and the hallucination were credited with more significance than rationally determined experience of the world. Pairings originally seen as opposites, such as reality/dream or objective/subjective were henceforth intentionally combined, with artistically fruitful results.

The alienation of objects of everyday life bestowed on them both magical and playfully witty qualities. In as far as these objects were removed from their original context and thus further alienated, they acquired something of the aura of a mystery.

In the works of Max Ernst and Man Ray we can observe a process of 'enchantment' taking place. These artists were so able to free things from their original context, both spatial and temporal, that they appeared cosmically transfigured. HS

Man Ray 1890–1976
Cadeau/The Gift, 1921/1974
Multiple, made in Milan,
131st of 1300
Bronze, 16.5 x 9 x 10.5 cm
(in a cardboard drum)

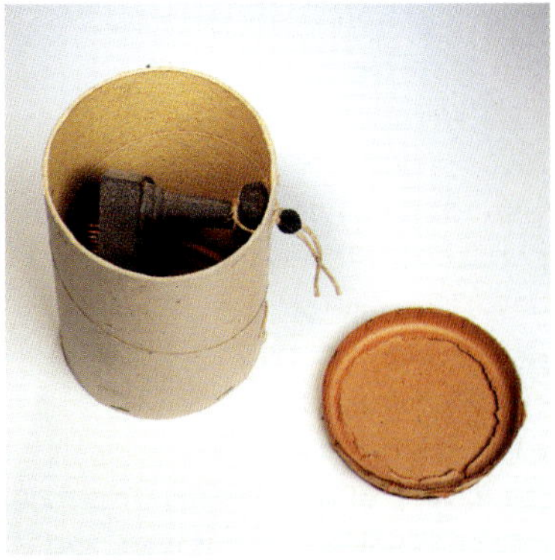

One day, when he was with the composer Eric Satie, Man Ray went into a hardware store. 'I picked out an iron, one of the sort that you have to heat up on the hot plate of an oven, and asked Satie to come into the shop with me. There, with his help, I got a box of nails and a tube of glue. Once back in the gallery, I stuck a row of nails on to the flat side of the iron, gave it the title Cadeau and added it to the exhibition. This was my first French Dada object.' As the original of 1921 was lost, three replicas were made in 1963, and, in 1974, 300 were produced in bronze. This 'gift for a guest' surely counts as one of the most striking and well-known examples of Object Art. GL

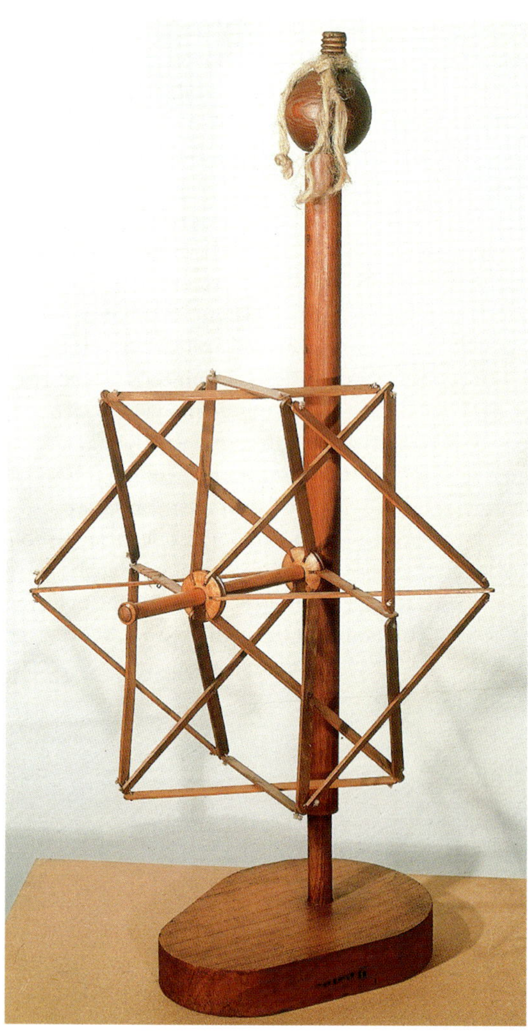

Max Ernst (1891–1976)
Objet mobile recommandé aux familles, 1936
Original version in wood and hemp, 98.5 x 57.5 x 46 cm

This object montage consists of several parts: an ovoid base holds a vertical rounded pole, its diameter narrower at its foot and its upper end crossed by a 'head' formed out of a knob wound about with strands of hemp. Into an opening in this pole there is inserted the central rod of a yarn reeling frame, which is made out of thin mobile slats. The two wooden rings on this central rod can be moved horizontally back and forth so that the criss-crossing slats are alternately distended and collapsed. It is also possible to set the entire frame into radial rotation. When this movement is made to take place energetically, a distinctly erotic element enters into play – such as André Breton expressly sought to achieve in the Surrealist object as he understood it. This sexual aspect is emphatically underlined by the decoration of the knob with hemp, suggestive of curly female hair. The traditional operation of spindle and distaff by women is here interpreted by Max Ernst with a melancholic irony as a sexual act between man and woman that establishes an instinctive bond between the couple that is reflected throughout the entire family. GL

Christo (b. 1935)
Three oil barrels, one wrapped, 1958
Oil barrels, textile, wire,
enamel paint,
h 122 cm, dia (each barrel)
37 to 38.5 cm

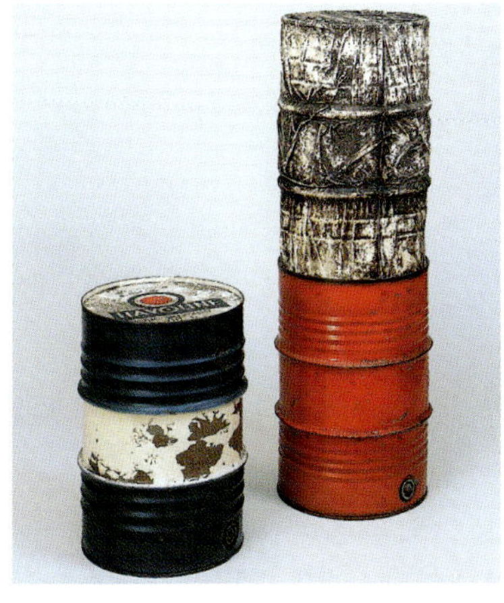

This group of oil barrels is among the earliest examples of Christo's 'wrappings' from a time when the artist embarked on systematically assembling various containers, intending to create 'temporary monuments' with them. The barrel painted red, and that in blue and white – the colours of the French national flag – were cleaned, while the third was wrapped in canvas, soaked in size (the conventional material of the painter) and tied with a fine wire. This distinct treatment of each group of objects is of particular significance for Christo, for it was by this means that he sought to sharpen the spectator's awareness of the difference between disguise and core, facade and content, everyday reality and aesthetic quality. Christo hides objects and thereby arouses in the spectator a curiosity that is not provoked by them in everyday life. GL

Jean Tinguely (1925–1991)
Baluba XIII, 1961/62
Iron, electric installation, rubber,
bird feathers, plastic,
218 x 46.5 x 46.5 cm

This piece is one of a series of 'movement machines' constructed spontaneously out of found objects and made to generate vibrations with what Tinguely called 'pantomimic associations' – by means of a motor and a timing mechanism hidden within the container. The name *Baluba* – that of one of the tribes of the Bantu people in Central Africa – is intended to introduce a suggestion of ritual dance, as if we were here confronted with a medicine man hung about with fetishes, souvenirs and magical instruments. GL

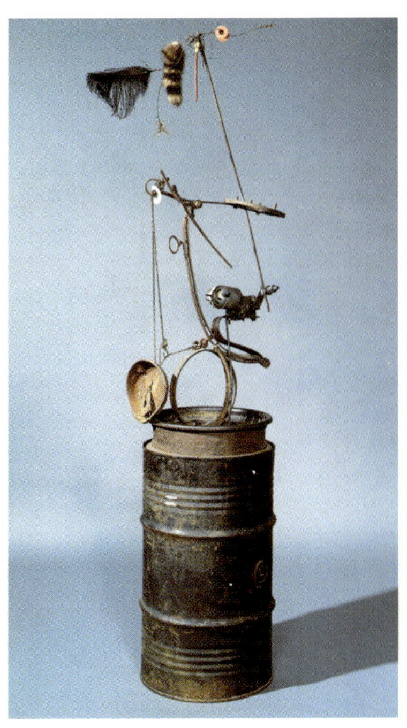

Antoni Tàpies (b. 1923)
Cadira coberta/Covered Chair, 1970
Wood, canvas, plastic,
77.5 x 69.5 x 56.5 cm

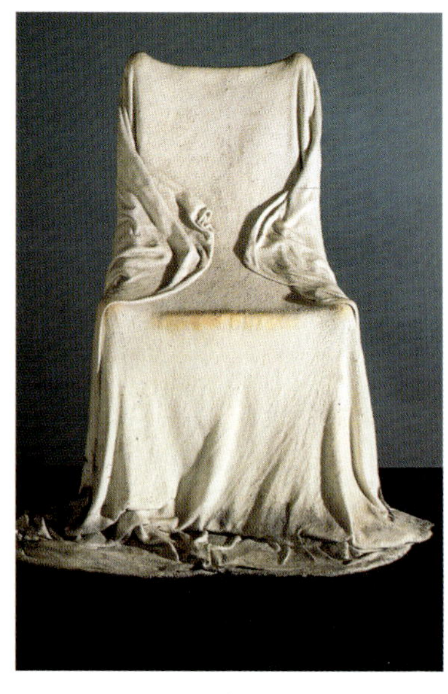

Carefully, like the robe of a monk or a saint, the white canvas covers the chair and then settles into taut columns and intricately gathered folds to establish a sculptural immobility. Out of the firm outline of this veil the edge of the seat and the protruberance of the chair back stand out very clearly. In the œuvre of Tapiès, chairs are invariably empty and also removed into a state of magic and mystery. Here, the emphatic veiling of size-soaked and stiffened canvas as well as the small scale (this appears to be a dwarf's chair) effectively prevent the spectator's approach. GL

Jean Tinguely (1925–1991)
Fairy Tale Relief, 1978
Wood, iron, rubber, toy, garden gnome, electric motors,
280 x 620 x 150 cm

The mechanization of every element in this piece can be experienced as if in a game. In its clamorous and simultaneous *mise-en-scène*, this object appears well suited to telling 'fairy tales'. It was this aspect of the machine that allowed Tinguely 'to achieve, above all, poetry'. *The Fairy Tale Relief* was intended to fulfill this function and to be used like a mobile 'travelling circus'. GL

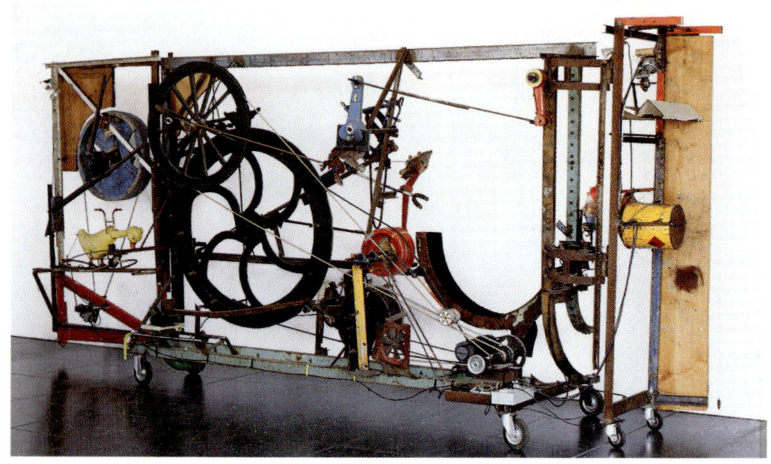

Andy Warhol (1927–1987)
Brillo Box, 1964
Painted wood, 43 x 43 x 37.5 cm

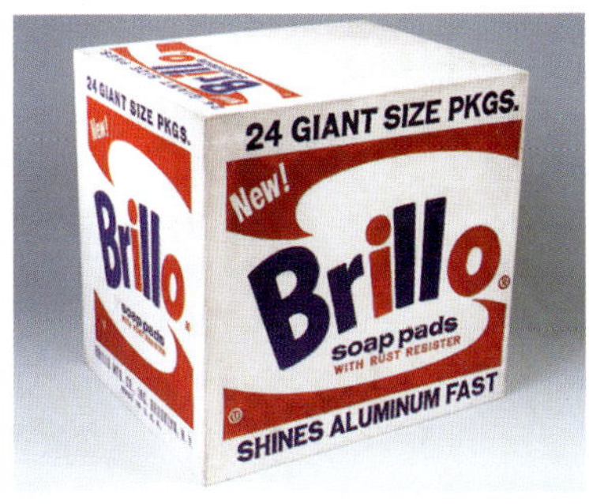

This object was originally exhibited at the first large 'Box Show' that Warhol organized at the Stable Gallery in New York in 1964. Stacks of boxes of products and foodstuffs produced by Brillo, Del Monte, Heinz and Campbell's filled out the gallery as if it were a supermarket. This Brillo Box was printed by hand and is signed on the blank underside. The object derives its particularity from the playful implication of serial production and simultaneous isolation from the world of the consumer. In Warhol's own words: 'At the time when I was painting old tin cans on canvas, I also took a box and painted it on all sides. It looked really extraordinary and yet seemed quite unreal. That's how I got the idea that it would be great to make boxes of this sort. The Brillo company liked my paintings but Campbell's Soup was quite horrified.' As an aspect of Pop Art, Object Art was at once readily accepted by both public and critics. According to Barbara Rose, the general public was 'pleased to see objects that it recognized instead of having to struggle to understand Abstract Expressionism.' GL

Louise Nevelson (1899–1988)
Black Chord I, 1964
Black-painted wood,
101.5 x 62.9 x 8 cm

The paint applied to all the wooden parts before they were mounted on the board neutralizes superficial differences between them and evokes a dark resonance, the 'black chord' of the title. Here and there the glinting light reflected by the gold underpainting breaks through the 'dust-covered' upper layer. We do not register the wooden objects as waste products but, rather, see them in their individuality as precious things. As a result of the effect of a unified

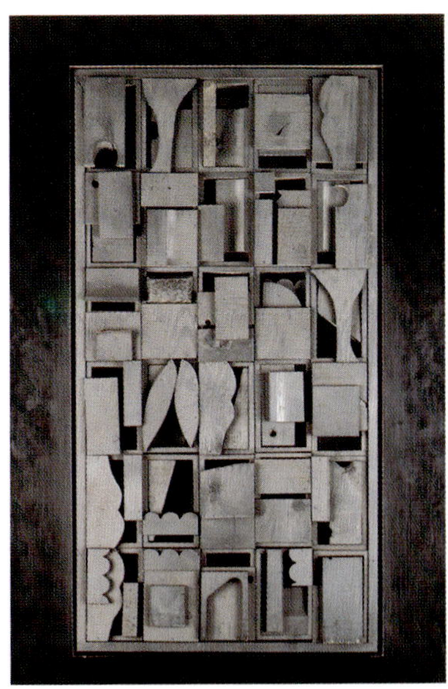

facade, the layers of relief embraced within the reflecting frames assume a sense of the sacred, of dignity akin to that associated with a shrine or an icon. This work is one of a series of five versions. GL

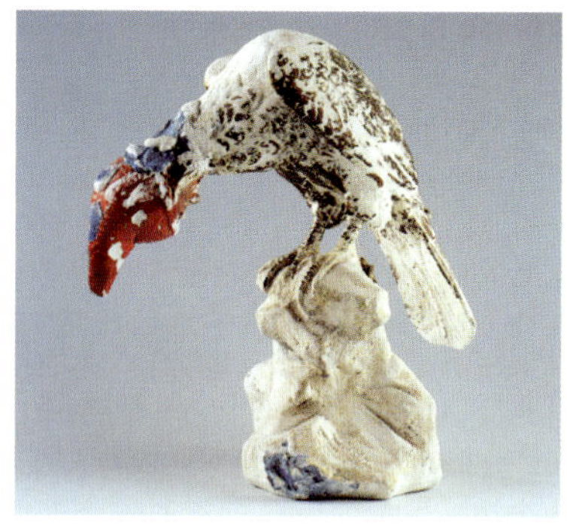

Paul Thek (1933–1988)
Garden Gnome Bird, 1971
Ceramic, wood, plaster, paint,
41.6 x 19 x 37.5 cm

Thek was one of the first artists to work with perpetually altering spaces in which furniture and plants, both stuffed and living animals, newspapers and other everyday objects were amassed and piled up to create a 'Pyramid of Death and Rebirth'. One object to be found in these walk-in chambers that rather resembled a nomad's tent was this garden gnome bird, who might have served as a sort of fetish and a guardian of these unreal cave-like formations. GL

Allan Kaprow (b. 1927)
Basic Thermal Units, 1973
Zinc bath tub, thermometer, photograph, plastic dice,
41 x 86.7 x 63.4 cm

In 1973 Kaprow staged a 'Four-City Happenning' in Essen, Duisburg, Bochum and Remscheid. The work now in the Wilhelm Lehmbruck Museum is a relic of the Duisburg event and combines a zinc bathtub, a thermometer and a photograph of the seated artist. According to the motto, 'if you heat the room you cool the body', the temperature of a room was raised so that after three hours the difference could be registered on a thermometer. Then, by means of the application of ice cubes and the gradual removal of clothing, the artist's body temperature was lowered – until the surrounding space became too hot or the body too cold'. By this very obvious means, Kaprow treated 'the fundamental insight presented in the work', as a form of anti-art that can only be experienced through participation and imitation. GL

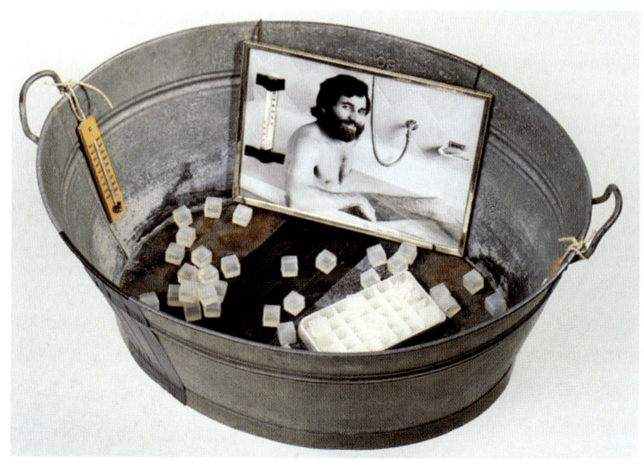

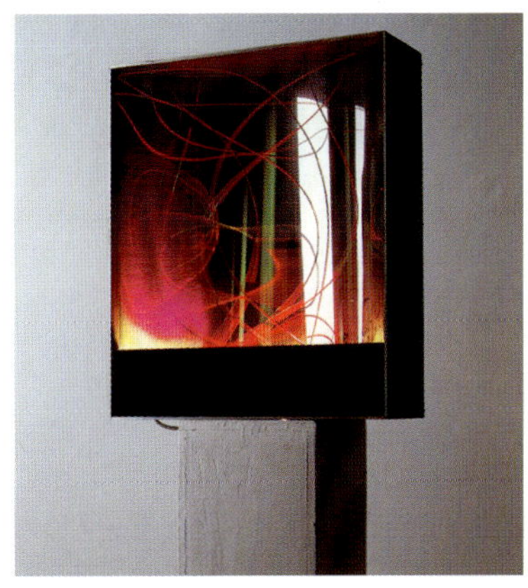

Aleksandar Srnec (b. 1924)
Object 200173, 1973
Aluminium, painted wire, motor, ultra-violet lightbulb,
61 x 50.7 x 17.2

Alekandar Srnec, a Croatian sculptor, was one of the founders of the Zagreb artists' group EXAT 51, the first such association in former Yugoslavia to openly take a stand against Socialist Realism and to proclaim itself in favour of Abstraction. From 1953 Srnec, like Picelj and Richter, was in close contact with the *Nove Tendencije* [New Trends] movement, one of the leading avant-garde groups in Europe. Srnec made objects out of coloured wires and highly polished mirrors that were powered by electronic motors to make 'coloured movements'. The markedly playful and painterly aspect of these light boxes shows Srnec to be one of the most experimental artists of the post-war generation to work with light. The exhibitions of the *Nove Tendencije*, held every second year until 1973, with a section devoted to international contemporary music, determined the cosmopolitan character of this Croatian movement. GL

Reiner Ruthenbeck (b. 1937)
Metal plate with viewing slit, 1971
Black-painted metal,
200 x 100 x 0.3 cm

The monochrome painted panel obstructs a part of the wall against which it leans. Wall and panel, stable architecture and unstable object, are here presented as interrelated elements. Although the viewing slit, placed at the spectator's approximate eye-height, offers the possibility of a glimpse through the panel, it nonetheless offers no new knowledge. The gaze thus limited swiftly turns away from the inaccessible portion of wall and comes again to rest on the black surface of the panel. The mute object character of the latter now arouses subtle associations with opening and closing, with internal and external space. Fixed habits of seeing are thus circumvented and collective fundamental experiences may be extracted from these 'contradictory states'. GL

Klaus Rinke (b. 1939)
12 Barrels Full of Water Drawn from the Rhine, 1969
Installation with galvanized 60-litre barrels, black-and-white photographs, poster, scoop, 175 x 860 x 75 cm

In June 1969 Klaus Rinke was invited to take part in the exhibition '14 x 14' held in Baden-Baden. Armed with a long-handled scoop and galvanized 60-litre barrels, he set off to walk upstream along the Rhine for two days, stopping at twelve towns en route. In each one, he staged a happening that consisted of filling a barrel with water from the river, which at that time had been poisoned by an environmental catastrophe. As shown by the photographs above each of the barrels, and as a poster at the entrance to the installation explains, Rinke drew water from the river, sealed each barrel and provided it with a label recording the place and precise time of the event. According to Rinke, his intention was to 'make the Rhine exhibitable.' ChB

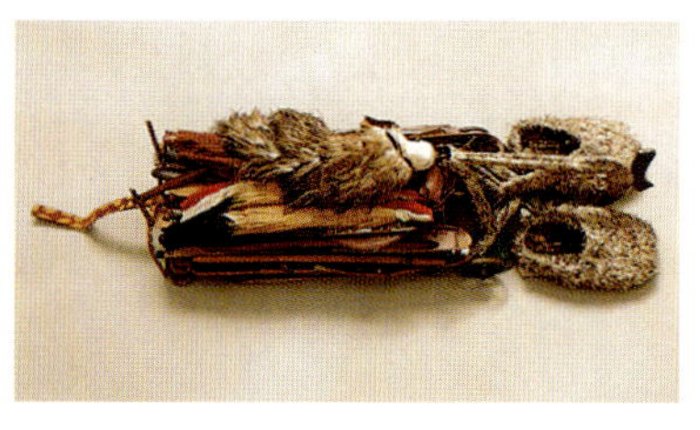

Nikolaus Lang (b. 1941)
A Heap of Culture, 1986–191
Historical and contemporary objects representing the material culture of the Aborigines of Australia, 98 x 424 x 105 cm

In the 'preservation of evidence' movement that, from 1974, defined its joint goals as 'Archeology and Memory', pictures, photographs and objects relating to a particular region were collected in a manner resembling systematic field work and arranged as documentation. This is the approach adopted by Lang for his 'field research' in Australia. In this work he documents the cultural heritage of the people in the south. A homemade coat of horsehair and emu feathers and over-sized, trouser-like shoes are among the heaped-up products. GL

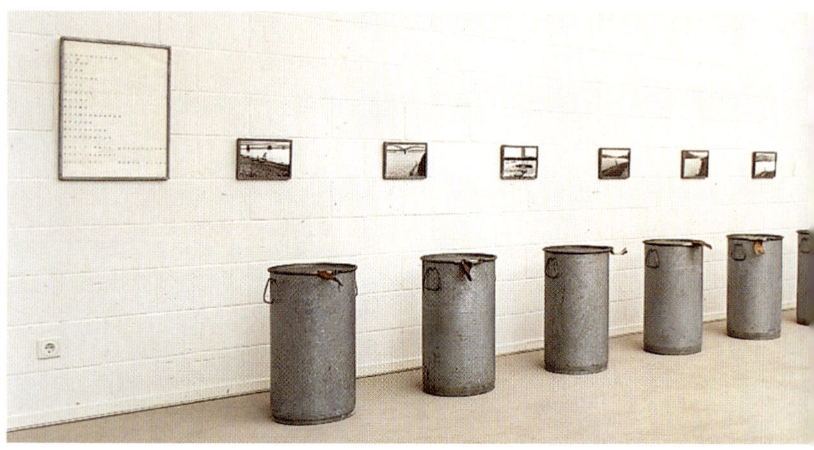

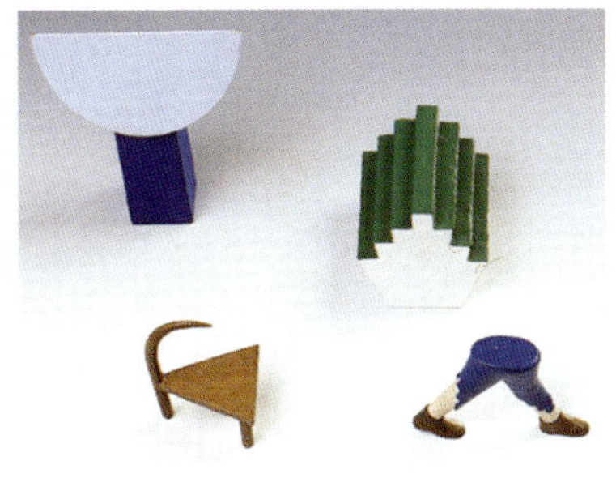

selection of 'pots', 'birds' heads' and 'blonde hair'. These so far exist in very small editions of only two. GL

Fritz Schwegler (b. 1935)
Group of Small Sculptures, 1963–1968 (devised), 1991–94 (executed)
Bronze or wood, partially painted
H (each item) 7 to 31.7 cm

The multi-talented Fritz Schwegler – draughtsman, creator of artist's books, writer, painter and exponent of Object Art – has preserved his roguish and absurd ideas in what he terms *Urnotizen* [primal notations]. Through series of independent preliminary stages, numerous designs issue, usually several years later, in wood and bronze sculptures, their compact size characterisizng them as small-scale sculptures. Out of a total of around 500 objects the Wilhelm Lehmbruck Museum possesses a

Adolfo Riestra (1944–1989)
Anthropomorphic Vessel, 1988
Terracotta, 65 x 48 x 39 cm
Long-term loan

This Mexican artist worked exclusively in terracotta, producing figures that were sometimes lifesize, and was regarded as one of the most important of his country's sculptors. Although the vessel-like figures are rough, unpolished and ascetic in appearance, their austere gestures, slit eyes, open mouths and protruding ears convey that magical, anthropomorphic expression that distinguishes traditional ceramic products. According to the critic and art historian Erica Billeter, Riestra 'frees clay from its functional connections and returns to it the dignity that it had enjoyed in the old cultures as a material out of which images of the gods were made.' GL

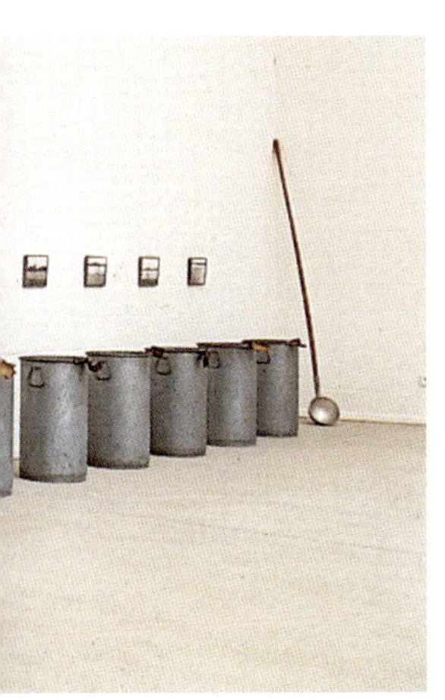

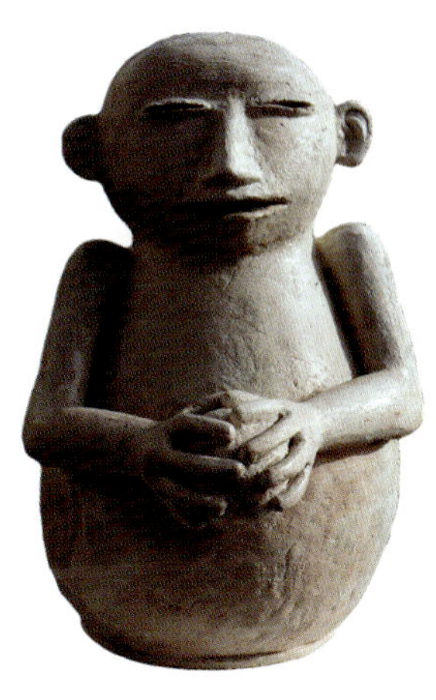

VII Sculpture in Iron and Steel

The dominant presence of iron in the era of industrialization led to a rediscovery of this material in modern art. Sculptors effectively became artisans once again in as far as they would work the material themselves. Through acquiring expertise in welding and forging techniques, they were now able to assume overall responsibility for their work, from the original idea to the final stages of its execution. The return to manual activity of this sort increased the amount of physical control over the desired formal progress. Starting with the work of the Cubists and Constructivists (Picasso and Tatlin), sculpture in iron increasingly came to resemble the products of engineers or architects.

While Pablo Gargallo and Julio González (see p. 74) are regarded as the first to have used metal in this 'modern' way, both the kinetic rhythms achieved by Alexander Calder and the constructions of Richard Smith were created with the aim of removing a sense of mass. This is also true of the work of Chillida, in his case through the use of space as a counter to the weight and density of the metal. It would appear that Minimalism has spelt the end of the 'Iron Age' in sculpture, just as the post-industrial era has transformed the economy.

HS

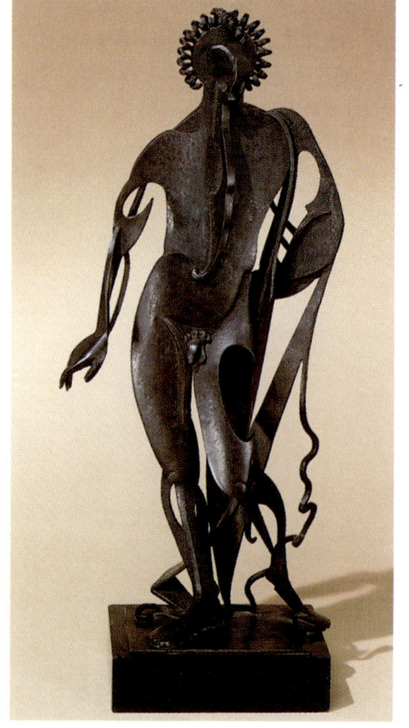

Pablo Gargallo (1881–1934)
Antinous, 1932
Iron on a black marble base,
84 x 33 x 19.5 cm

Partially perforated planes cut out like silhouettes with curvilinear outlines create the framework for this naked standing figure. The central panel of the torso functions as a stabilizing shaft, on to which the delicately boned and buoyantly long and curling crosspieces are added. The figure is intended to be viewed frontally. Emphatically corporeal and abstract segments interpenetrate and set up exciting contrasts, overlapping each other in ways that vary with each change of viewing position. Closed and open, concave and convex forms seem to illustrate the Classical canon of a sculptural work from

Antiquity. Gargallo's model was the life-size marble statue of the so-called Belvedere Antinous in the Vatican. His own *Antinous* was intended as an imitation of, and homage to, the image of man evolved in Ancient Greece and Rome. In parallel with the Neo-Classical tendencies of the early 1930s, it was also a means of bestowing a new dignity and validity on the normative character of the art of Antiquity. GL

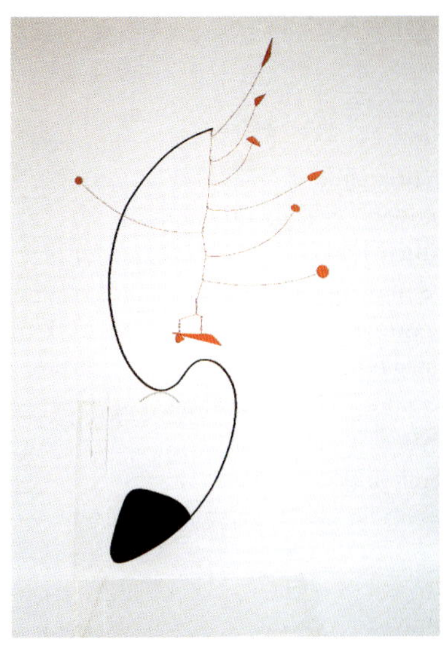

Alexander Calder (1898–1976)
Untitled, Mobile with S, c 1940
Black-and-orange-painted table mobile in steel with iron wire, h 243 cm

Calder's mobile sits on the edge of a table. The slightest movement in the air sets its lateral arms and their leaf and disc finials into motion. Calder opened up a new dimension for sculpture with his mobiles: variability. These creations were, in effect, a new and unique type of 'living thing' made of wire, sheet metal and steel, gently gliding, rising and falling at various speeds in directions not always controllable, moving around an imaginary axis, evolving a variety of rhythms and offering true enchantment in a problematic era. They seemed to free themsleves gracefully from the order imposed by weight and to evade the imperative of gravity and stability.

This mobile, intended to spur 'work done at the table', takes up position on its edge, its oscilating motions set off by the gentlest movement of the air against its arms attached by fine wires. Towards the base of this freely devised form – in analogy with the weighting of the S-shape – abstract and biomorphic forms effectively maintain a balance.

Art and technology, ingenous reasoning and poetic perception, stability and movement, weight and lightness, earnestness and gaiety, design and nature are rarely to be found poised in such a compelling interrelationships. ChB

David Smith (1906–1965)
Blackburn, Song of an Irish Blacksmith, 1949/50
Iron, bronze, marble base,
117 x 103.5 x 58 cm

Until 1940 Smith was employed as an industrial labourer at the Terminal Iron Works in Brooklyn. The sculpture *Blackburn* was made ten years later 'in memory' of that very place, where there had been two workmen called Blackburn and Buckhorn. *Blackburn* is, then, dedicated to one of these two men; its planned counterpart, dedicated to Buckhorn, was never executed.

From the formal point of view, this work may be seen as one of the 'Landscapes' that Smith started making in 1946. As a 'drawing in iron', it unfurls like a tree, with the marble base serving as both root and trunk and the curving strips elastically branching to meet again at the head of the central vertical.

When viewed from the front the abstracted forms sprouting from the branches and suggestive of leaves, circles and rings, combine to arouse the suggestion of natural growth; the view from the side reveals a bewildering wealth of much smaller self-contained shapes. The central axis of this construction is crowned with a formation resembling the burst husk or pod of a fruit, an image that adds greatly to its playfully buoyant character. Smith's sculpture is effectively the 'song' of the artist identifying his own calling with that of the blacksmith. GL

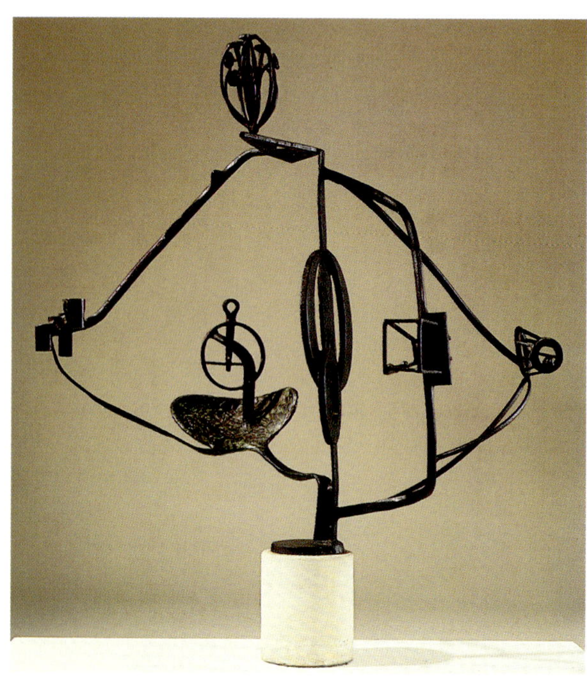

Norbert Kricke (1922–1984)
White Spatial Sculpture: The Temple, 1952
White painted steel, black wood base, 203 x 67 x 46 cm

The spatial sculpture 'Temple' stands out, not least in terms of its shape, among the group of six sculptural pieces by Kricke to be found in the collection, all made between 1949 and 1976. This item is a key instance of the application of a principle first adopted by Kricke in 1952: that of the autonomously developing line, its rising and falling rhythm the product of a continuous, unbroken movement. 'The problem that I address is not that of [sculptural] mass, nor that of the figure, but that of space and movement – space and time'. The line embraces the entire shape of the movement and the emptiness oscillating in space, these condensing into a sort of architectonic whole. The directedness of the movement and the transparency of the space generate that 'poetic energy' that has always been a characteristic of the image of the cathedral. GL

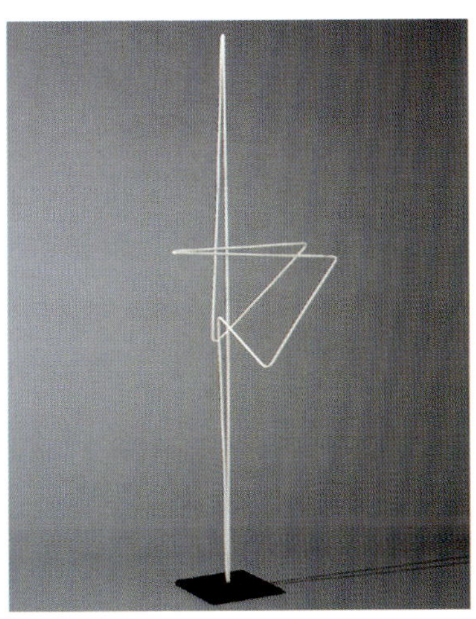

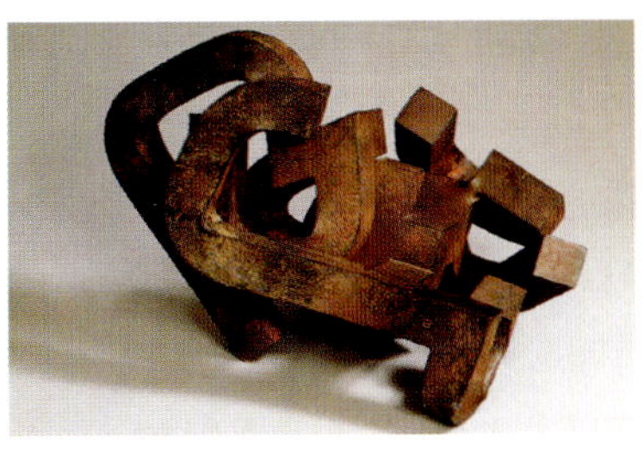

Eduardo Chillida (b. 1924)
Modulation d'espace II, 1963
Forged iron, 57 x 78 x 61.5 cm

Since 1959 Chillida has forged dynamic, entangled, space-enclosing constructions out of compact iron girders. He is particularly interested in the creation of space by means of angular iron beams that outline it as a gesture of modulation. As a result of the way they cling to and penetrate each other, the metal forms generate a sense of volume and assume the role – in analogy with a human fist or a bird's claw – of a container for this volume. In addition, the angular bars embody the dynamic flow of energy that seeks to evade any gravitational pull even while it participates in the dramatic play of light and shadow.

With his concept of a space-creating sculpture – compared by Chillida himself with the process of breathing in and out – the artist assumes a decisive position in opposition to both Object Art and Minimal Art. In 1966 Chillida was the first artist to win the Wilhelm Lehmbruck Prize in Duisburg. GL

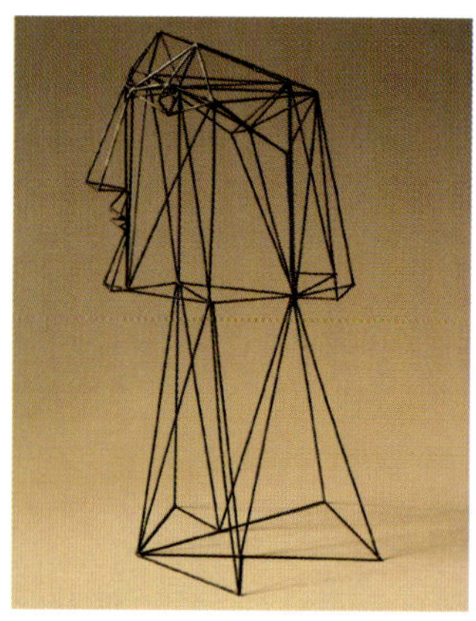

Hans Uhlmann (1900–1975)
Head, 1937
Steel wire, 55 x 20 x 25 cm

The Berlin artist Hans Uhlmann, with his 'open, transparent sculptures', is one of the pioneers among Germans working with iron and wire. An outstanding example of his work is to be found in *Head*, the basic structure of which was outlined in the drawings of the portfolio 'Heads, Plaits, Curls and Brushes in Wire' published in 1934/35. Working 'outwards from within' and engaging directly with the thin, soldered wires, Uhlmann created from the varied play of intersections a frontally aligned sculptural head without a base. GL

Donald Judd (1928–1994)
Five-unit Wall Sculpture, 1992
Corten steel and coloured Plexiglas, each unit 50 x 100 x 50 cm

Judd's 'wall sculpture' consists of five open, wall-mounted bodies in steel, grouped at the same height and with the same distance between them. The box or hollow space that provides the basis for many of Judd's geometrical series as an embodiment of regularity is here 'individualized': each unit is divided into two by a central iron bar and thereby conceptually 'enlarged', while the backgrounds are filled with monochrome, coloured Plexiglas. Each central bar ends at a visible distance from each background. In no way, therefore, does it interrupt the coloured surface as at first appears to be the case. Around the yellow tone gleaming from the centre of the series are purple and black panels (on the left) and green and white panels (on the right). The firmly interlocking bodies and their serial arrangement become part of a symbolic coloured 'orchestration' that transforms the sobriety of the form into shimmering Colourism. GL

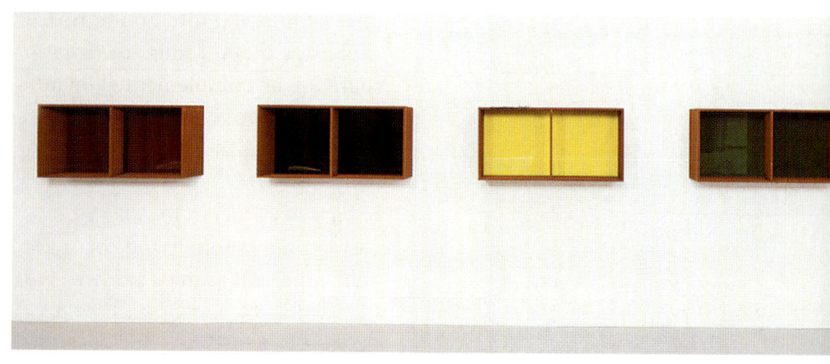

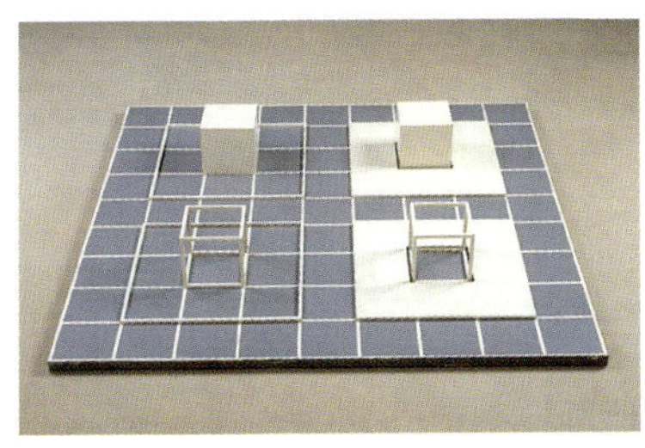

Sol LeWitt (b. 1928)
Four-part Piece 'ABCD 2', 1968
White-painted steel, 145 x 145 cm
(overall base); 17 x 17 x 17 cm
(each individual cube)

The American representatives of Minimalism, such as Sol LeWitt, countered Pop Art and its cult of consumer society with a Purist system of serial and anonymous industrial products. This multi-part floor-work made in 1968 is to be understood as the blueprint for a structural analysis of bodies, volumes and space. As in a game of chess, the grid system becomes a module for each of the individual 'figures' that are arranged in accordance with an intensive process of comparative perception. These are not to be interpreted through any iconographic content, but purely through the process of observation and sympathetic contemplation. GL

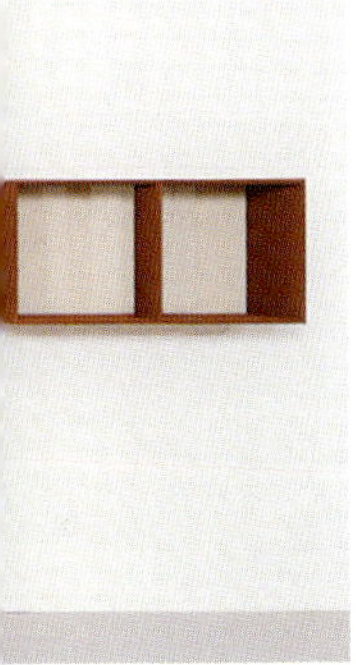

David Rabinowitsch (b. 1943)
Metrical (Romanesque) Construction in 5 Masses and 2 Scales, 1973/1991
Steel, in several parts,
250 x 290 x 6 cm
Long-term loan

Floor-sculpture, a genre favoured also by Rabinowitsch, proved an especially appropriate form for exponents of Minimalism. This extremely heavy work in steel consists of five parts, each irregular in outline. Their positioning and grouping define the outline of the sculptural equivalent of a 'shaped canvas' and at the same time determine the internal structure, which is characterized by a few drilled holes and a network of orthogonally and diagonally drawn lines. The construction thus formed consists, in terms of its layout, of two units

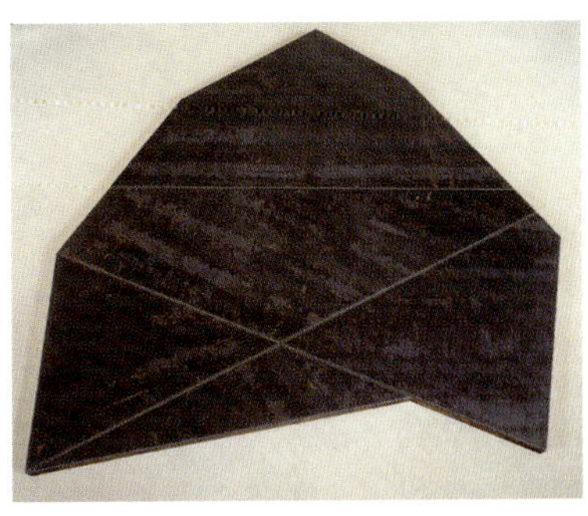

distinct in scale, with an undivided, expansive shape dominated by a sharp angle, complemented by multiple and angular smaller spatial units. Rabinowitsch's encounter in 1971 with the Romanesque architecture of churches in Cologne clearly had a profound effect on his own approach to mass and weight, line and surface – not least in this floor piece of 1973. GL

Wolfgang Nestler (b. 1943)
Alterable Square, 1983
Feather steel and steel, dimensions variable (L of each rod 200 cm)

Nestler, who had been a pupil of Erwin Heerich in Düsseldorf, first forged iron rods and sheet iron into simple shapes. He started out with geometrical forms such as the circle, the triangle and the square, forms that in fact still characterize his work to this day. His aim, however, is not (as exemplified in *Alterable Square*) Minimalism – that is to say the emphatic confinement to the floor of a specific closed form – but rather the achievement of a work in a state of transformation and alteration. In moving towards this goal Nestler presents elements that can be separated and perpetually rearranged within a given space. Almost all his works are variable in as far as one can alter the positioning and the 'basic plan' of the indiviudal parts in relation to each other simply by moving the pieces. While the iron rods are linked together at their ends by means of forged rings, they can nonetheless, and without the exertion of any great physical effort, be moved into a formation that evokes a cube or a square, in each case with the corresponding emphases. Out of the manipulable quality of the square, and as a form of Concrete Art (in the tradition of Erwin Heerich or Josef Albers), there come about the dramatic shifts and openings of perspective that, in a positively playful manner, bestow lightness and grace on the sculpture. According to the critic Paul Wember, writing in 1985, 'personal engagement with the object results only from a true and inner connection between work of art and spectator'. GL

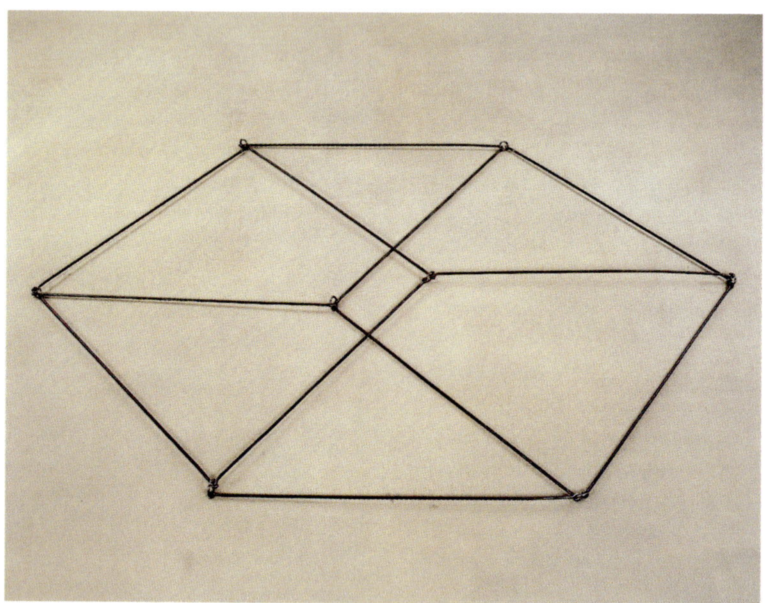

VIII Against War

The traumas of war, which – directly or indirectly – marked the entire 20th century made it imperative to find new forms of representation in the fine arts. Wilhelm Lehmbruck, who experienced the First World War directly, if briefly, as a medical orderly, rendered his own sense of despair in his sculpture *Seated Youth.* Gerhard Marcks's *Prometheus Bound,* a work formally indebted to that of Lehmbruck, encompasses the Second World War through reference to the devastation visited upon the city of Cologne. These are sculptures entirely imbued with resignation and sorrow. Already, in a work of 1915, Baranov-Rossiné used a wooden crutch as an *object trouvé* to allude to the wounded, whose fate was very much a part of the war in the East. The verisimilitude and classically posed figural groups made by the American Duane Hanson capture the fatalism and the awareness of the ever-present threat of death associated with the war in Vietnam.

All of these sculptures show the senselessness and the powerlessness of humanity in the face of the incomprehensible nature of war. HS

Wilhelm Lehmbruck
(1881–1919)
Seated Youth, 1916/17
Bronze, h 114.8 cm

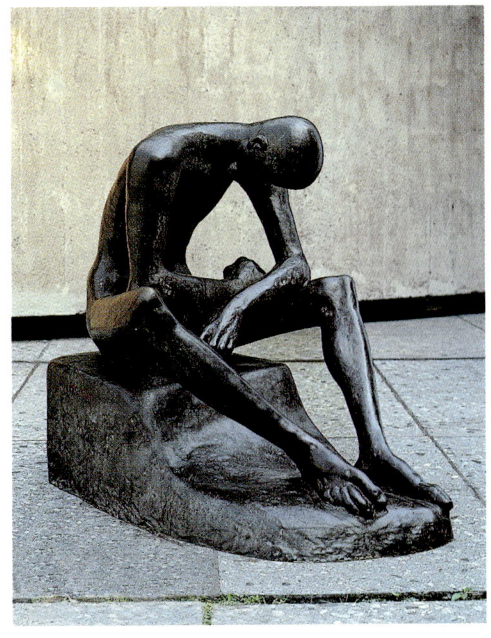

Combining the figural types and poses associated with the Wretched Christ and the seated Thinker, Lehmbruck here created a symbol of defeat and meditation. According to Kurt Badt, writing in 1920, this work was 'a child of the war, of the powerless breakdown of the [significance of the] individual under the imperative of the plurality' (see text on pp. 13–20). GL

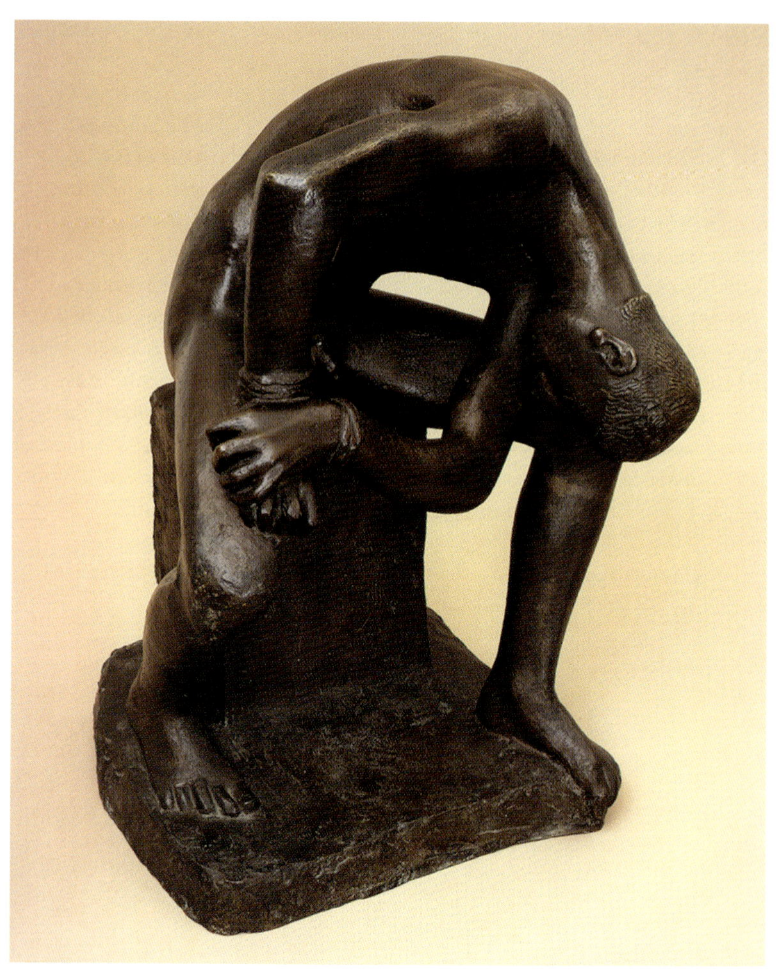

Gerhard Marcks (1889–1981)
Prometheus Bound II, 1948
Bronze, fourth cast,
78 x 53 x 46.5 cm

By 1916/17, in his *Seated Youth* (illustrated on p. 93), Wilhelm Lehmbruck had already found a valid formula for rendering the fate of man crushed by war and misery. Marcks gave the traditional form of the Wretched Christ a newly mythical and timeless dimension in his own sculpture. He shows the chained hero in the mute and bowed pose of lamentation and anguish. Already during the war (1943) Marcks produced the first version of his seated *Prometheus*, based on numerous sketches and in connection with a series of four further seated figures. This, however, was destroyed in Marcks's Berlin studio during an air raid. He again began work on this piece and produced his *Prometheus Bound* in 1944; illustrated here is the subsequent version of 1948. HS

Vladimir D. Baranov-Rossiné
(1888–1944)
Counter Relief, c 1913–15
Assemblage mounted on wood,
140 x 85.5 x 10 cm

This so-called *Counter Relief* by the Ukrainian-Jewish sculptor, painter and inventor of multi-media is one of the great incunabula of the history of art. Baranov-Rossiné, who died in 1944 in a German concentration camp, here pushes the specifically Russian compositional and material language of Cubo-Futurism to its limits. The *Counter Relief* is also important both as a document and within the history of art: it shows an articulated mannequin with an icon-like gold head, a gas mask, crutches and a false leg. For all the ostensible 'neutrality' of these assembled elements, there is no escaping the fact that they allude to the destitution, misery and tyranny that were inseparable from much civilian experience during the First World War.

The extraordinary position of Cubo-Futurist *sculpto-peinture* and the new life it suddenly breathed into early 20th-century European sculpture is evident in this work. HS

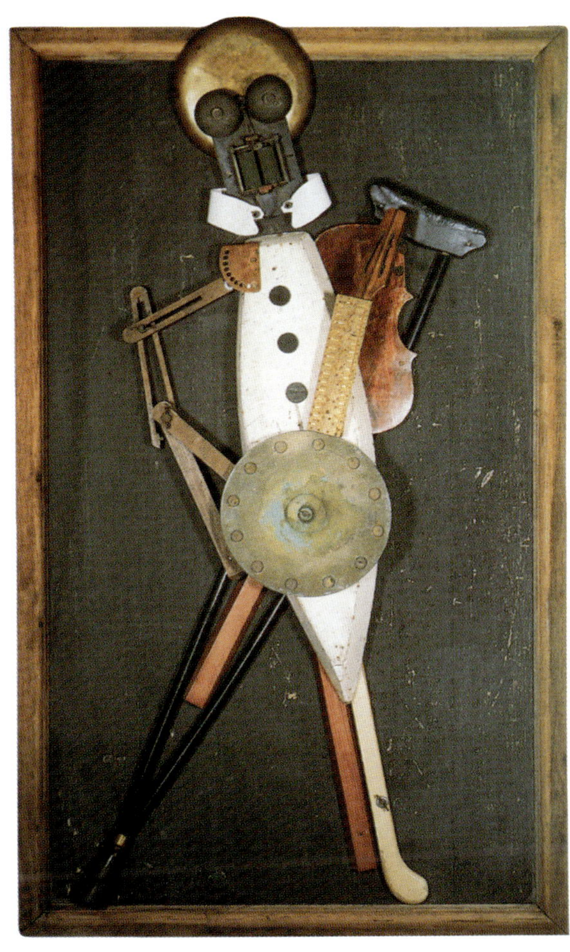

Duane Hanson (1925–1996)
War (Vietnam Piece), 1967
Fibreglass, textile, iron, earth,
77 x c 560 x c 370 cm

The essence of Duane Hanson's achievement lies in a sublime and insistent reconciliation of art and reality.

Through the troubling verisimilitude of this five-figure, life-size group of dead and severely wounded soldiers in the Vietnam War, Hanson aimed at provoking in the spectator a perplexed speechlessness. The subtle mixture of an event in the real world and classical poses from the history of art gives the work a shocking credibility. The war in Vietnam was the first to be reported day by day on television. Hanson, however, mistrusted technological devices such as film and cameras and refused to rely on them because he was aware how such machines could convey illusion and veil reality. In contrast to the deceptive TV pictures, Duane Hanson succeeds with his own art in arousing real compassion, while at the same time not losing himself in sanctimonious consternation. The emphatically earthbound quality of the individual figures of the soldiers on the sandy soil also appears to allude to a passage from the Old Testament: 'For dust thou art, and unto dust shalt thou return' (Genesis 3: 19). HS

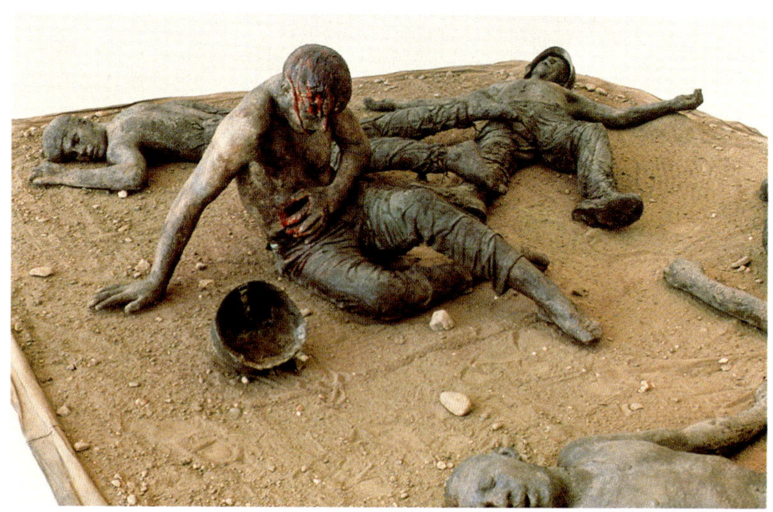

IX Sign and Material: Informal Sculpture

Informal Sculpture, about which everyone had talked since the Fautrier exhibition in Paris in 1945, did not achieve the same degree of formlessness and non-objectivity as had Informal Painting. Dependence on the materials used and the analogies with natural forms initially remaining all too significant. It was only with the 'Ideograms of Sorrow' and the 'Testament to Dread' that a more compelling sculptural informality was achieved. The creation of the work occurred in reality 'always only in response to resistance' and was linked with the search for the 'unknown element in art' as Willi Baumeister defined it in 1947 in his celebrated 'creed'. The powerful, incomprehensible cosmos made up of heaven and earth was evoked as the embodiment of an archaic myth. GL

Alberto Giacometti (1901–1966)
Femme au chariot I/Woman on a Carriage I, c 1943
Plaster, pencil, painting, wooden cart, h 164 cm

This is the only plaster sculpture by Giacometti in a German museum collection, and it illustrates far more of the artist's handwriting and working methods than does the 'distant' bronze cast. This work dates from the middle years of the Second World War when Giacometti had left Paris and was working in Geneva and Majola, where he remained until 1945. This is also Giacommetti's only large-scale work from this period (the majority being diminutive), a time in which the Surrealist element definitively retreated in favour of what Giacometti called the 'totality of form' (in which proximity and inner vision united to achieve figures of immense fragility). In 1950 Giacometti made a second version of the *Femme au chariot*, in which the figure appeared almost to float within a vehicle with outsized wheels and long spokes. In the first version, too, movement is only to be understood symbolically, for the wheels are mounted on their own base so that any real movement is prevented. Both works may be seen as illustrating one of Giacometti's principal themes: the emergence out of nothing and the subsequent disappearance of the vision of a woman. GL

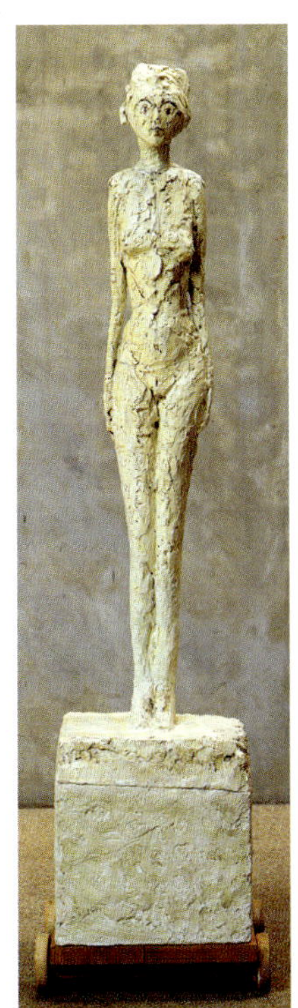

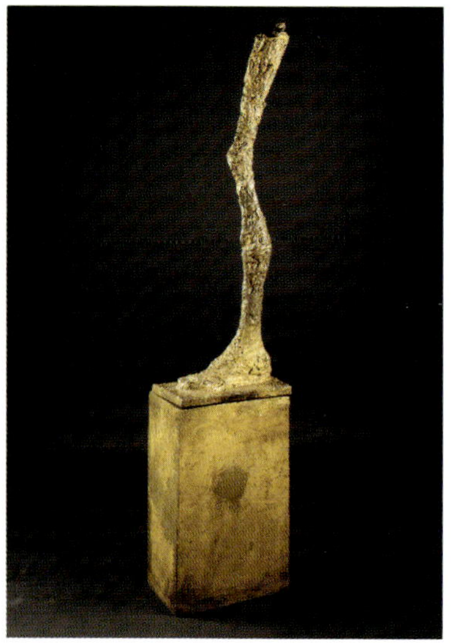

Alberto Giacometti (1901–1966)
La jambe/The Leg, 1958
Bronze (two parts) with gold patina, second of six casts,
218 x 30 x 46.5 cm

This over-life-size human leg rising from a smooth, separately cast base is the last of the works in a series of body-torsos. *Hand*, *Nose*, and *Head on a Rod* had been made in 1947. *The Leg* came about as part of Giacometti's reaction to a car accident in Paris on 10 October 1958, when he was taken to hospital with a broken right leg. As a result of this experience, and in fear of losing his foot, Giacometti made *The Leg* into an independent sculpture, alost akin to a votive object, that embraced an acknowledgement of the processes of magic-ritual healing, thoughts of death and 'secret infirmity'. GL

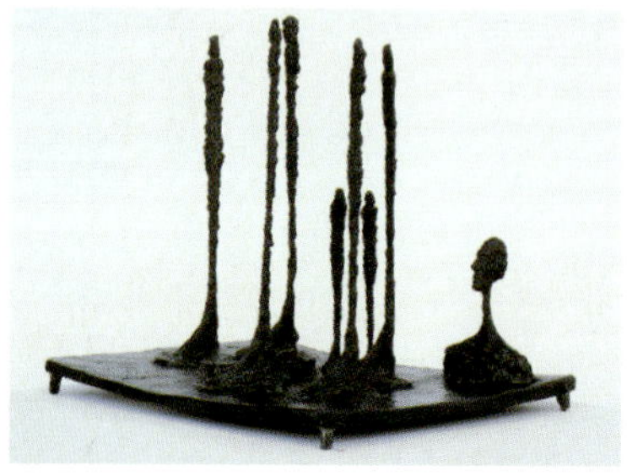

Alberto Giacometti (1901–1966)
Composition sept figures – tête (La forêt)/Composition with Seven Figures – Head (the Forest), 1950
Bronze, fifth of six casts,
55.5 x 61 x 49.5 cm

On a dipping base with peg-like corner supports we find trees that resemble the wasted bodies of seven motionless standing figures, between whom we catch a glimpse of a male bust placed directly on the ground. As usual in Giacometti's work, the skeletal figures are frontally aligned, but here they clearly maintain a formal relationship with the bust in the background, the only figure supplied with a face and eyes. Through this figural grouping, which resembles a still life, Giacometti gave form to his vision of a 'corner of the wood that I once saw years ago (in my childhood), where the trees (behind which one could see granite boulders) with their naked, slender trunks (without branches almost to their tops) always seemed to me like human figures frozen while walking along, yet continuing with their conversations.' GL

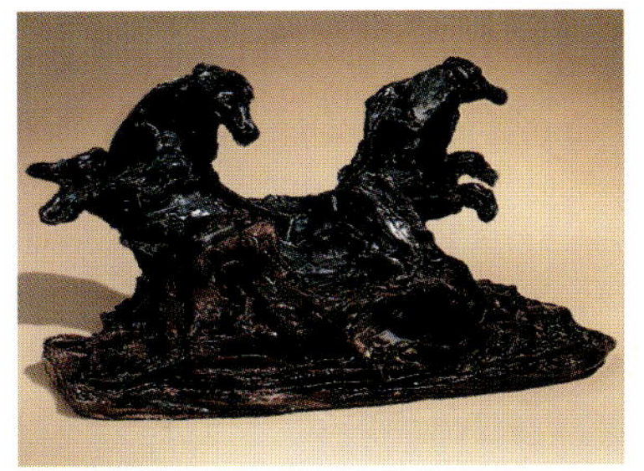

Lucio Fontana (1899–1968)
I cavalli/The Horses, 1938
Ceramic, 38 x 47 x 62 cm

In 1935/36 Fontana went to work in the studios at Albisola (known for their reverence for tradition), in order to acquire experience in working with ceramics. Years before formulating his theory of *spazialismo*, the works that were made here have an emphatically expressive character that derives, without doubt, from the example of the painterly, 'Impressionist' strain in the work of Medardo Rosso and others. The group *I cavalli*, made at this time, is designed with one, frontal viewing position in mind and shows the turbulence of gallopping horses. In the almost 'errupting' and randomly modelled material out of which the main motifs emerge, one can detect a restless imagination fascinated by inner movement and already approaching the peculiarities of Informal Sculpture. The rearing horses thus appear to be only a pretext for setting rough but dynamized material into motion in a way that pushes it to the boundaries of abstraction. Fontana's pieces in ceramic thus create a sort of provisional solution on the way towards his later goal of achieving vibrating surfaces and a pervasive vitalization of space. According to Fontana (in his so-called Manifesto written in 1946), 'existence, nature and [the sculptor's] material together create a perfect unity unfolding in time and space'. GL

Germaine Richier (1904–1959)
La toupie/The Spinning Top, 1953
Lead, with painted elements by Hans Hartung, 130 x 53.5 x 72.5 cm

This artist's œuvre is characterized by human-animal hybrids with frayed limbs and scaly, restless surfaces. The individual figure shown here, who stands in front of a protective shield, also has something of this 'diabolic' character. The emphatic backward slope of the walking woman clearly relates to her fear of the 'spinning top', while this itself resembles, rather, the rising head of an antagonized cobra – the threat it poses appearing to be the cause of the instability and mood of irritation conveyed by the figure. GL

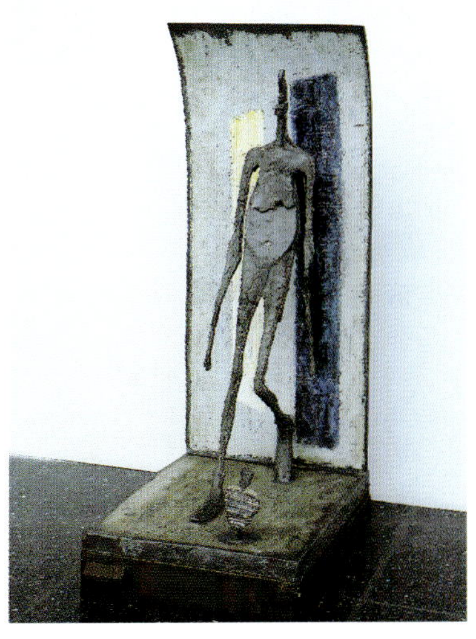

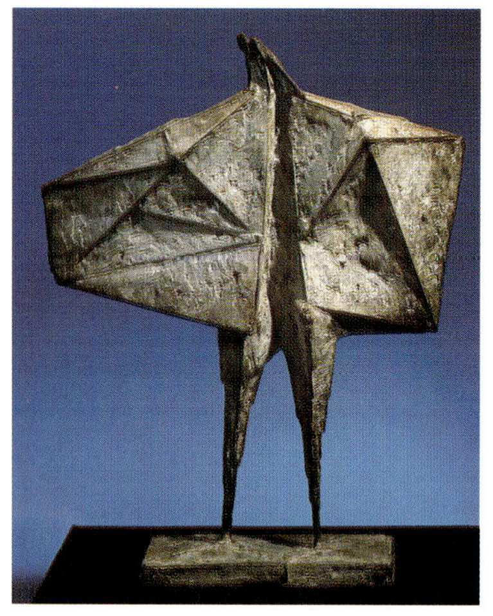

Lynn Chadwick (b. 1914)
Stranger II, 1956
Iron, cement, plaster,
109 x 87 x 30 cm

This winged, two-legged hybrid, which is to be understood as a sort of 'watchman', was made as part of a series of seven versions dating from 1956 to 1960. Half-animal, half-human, the 'alien' stands on stilts resembling the legs of a bird. From either side of its 'spine' angular wings extend, their skin pulled taut over a pattern of bones and sinews. The threatening gesture of the 'watchman' here combines with the armoured idol shape of an 'alien' being. The true significance of this figure only became apparent in 1957, when Chadwick produced *Alien III* as a design for a monument to the first flight across the Atlantic, in July 1919. GL

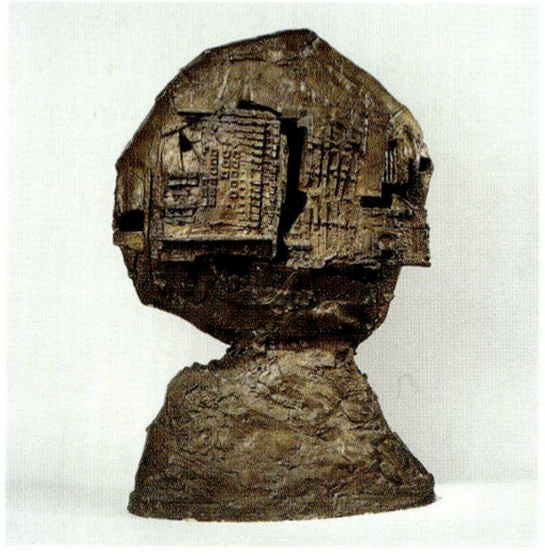

Eduardo Paolozzi (b. 1924)
Crocodile, 1956
Bronze, 93 x 63 x 25.5 cm

Impressed by the work of the *nouveau réalistes* in Paris, Eduardo Paolozzi followed them in assembling machine men and fetishistic *stele* out of pieces of scrap metal. This work, made out of *objets trouvés*, is one of a series of heads and busts made from machine parts. Paolozzi employed these now useless products 'in order', in the words of the critic R. Melville, 'to cover the nakedness of his forlorn figures, and he bestowed on these the dignity of saints [...] and Japanese gods of war'. Using the raw material of the block of wax, its surface covered with the impressions of the objects he had found, Paolozzi created something resembling a robot. The obtrusive evidence of parts from computer wiring circuits and electrical appliances allude to their origin in the world of technology. These have here been incorporated within the electrical currents of the brain. The head, accordingly, looks like a sort of 'maze' that has unhinged the rational system of technology. GL

Bernard Schultze (b. 1915)
Forest-Migof, 1956
Bronze, 65 x 58.1 x 44 cm

'I was always interested in decay in the forest, and a drawing by [Alfred] Kubin, of an overgrown train in a wood became a symbol for me of my view of life, of decay, of the victory of all-devouring nature over technology [...] While I was working on this sculpture my head was full of such thoughts, as also of memories of wartime episodes in the Russian forests'. His imagination aroused by Kubin's autobiographical novel *Die andere Seite* [The Other Side] and Max Ernst's series of pictures of 'Forests', Schultze created a series of such fantastical environments, to each of which he gave the name 'Migof', by merging Surrealist dream landscapes

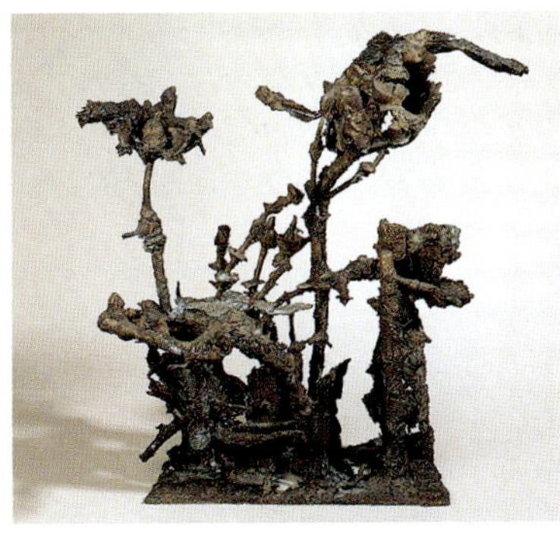

and inventions. The notion of the 'Migof' indicated images and creatures 'that stand somewhere between animals, plants and man'. This forest piece of 1965, made out of scrap and found objects, was created by a process of smelting and forging that allowed the detailed and varied structures and surfaces to be united into a bizarre whole. GL

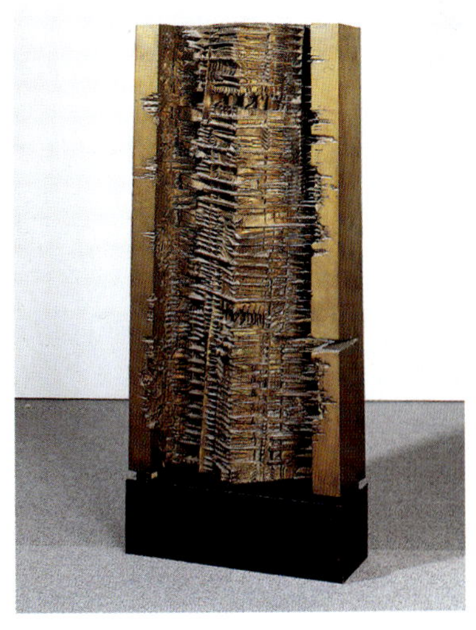

Arnaldo Pomodoro (b. 1926)
Successioni 4/Sequences 4, 1962/63
Bronze, 137 x 66.5 x 21 cm
(without base)

Along with his brother Gió, Arnaldo Pomodoro is one of the most influential sculptors to be associated with Italian Informal Art. Freed from any element of figuration, his early works, such as this *stele* with a filigree structure, evoke architectonic bodies incorporating bony and cuneiform elements. At the same time these works make clear Pomodoro's debt to his early training as a goldsmith. This graphic high relief extends over the sides and edges and submits further to a clearly emerging process of inner disintegration and decomposition. The structure in the form of a honeycomb, meanwhile, calls to mind organic living processes, while the lattice of inherent symbols is equally associated with uncontrolled states such as smouldering and solidification. GL

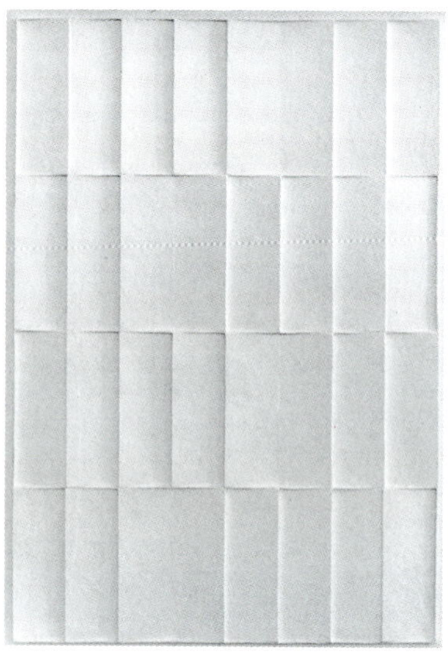

Jan Schoonhoven (1914–1994)
White Relief Rbg 25, 1969
Wood, cardboard, white paint, 123.5 x 84 x 3.8 cm

In the early 1950s Schoonhoven was still painting in the style of the COBRA group, but in 1957 he made his first structure-reliefs in *papier mâché*, a technique he was thereafter to favour. In 1960, together with Armando and Peeters, Schoonhoven founded the group *nul* [nought], which adopted a position comparable to that of the German group *ZERO* based in Düsseldorf. For Schoonhoven, the series of reliefs using white geometric basic forms established what was to become the distinctive feature of all his work. In contrast to the relief fields made up of sunken squares, in which internal shadows gather, this *White Relief* is distinguished by a subtle and sublime forward-vaulting alignment of uniform subdivisions. The arrangement with vertical gradation in four rows, one above the other, corresponds to a repeatedly doubled – and thus eight-part – horizontal internal structure. It is the light, coming from different directions, that will assume the central task of setting the surface into vibrations and enlivening it. By this means the white form is intended to activate that 'breathing' that leads to calm and to the sort of reverence one might feel before an icon.

GL

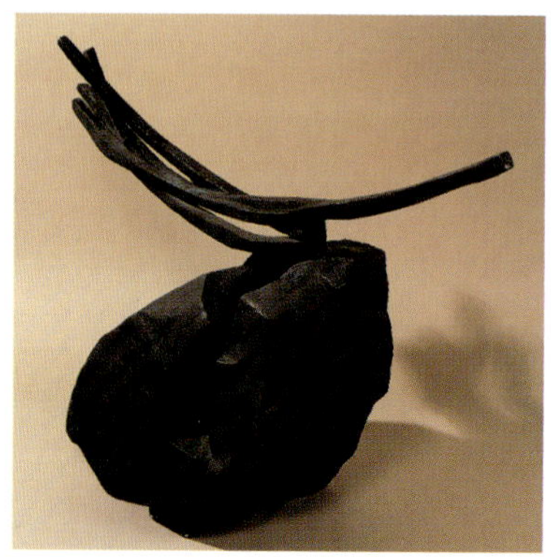

Wilhelm Loth (1920–1993)
Figure 4/59, Seated Woman, 1959/1960
Bronze, 80 x 108 x 40 cm

Loth treats this bi-partite block squatting on the ground as a collapsed spatial shell. To its broken and rising surface is attached a set of curving bars, these vigorously extending in several directions. The metal rods, positioned as a double fork, reach beyond the block, which serves as a counterweight. In this construction, which is rich in contrasts, Loth concentrates his formal elements not according to anatomy but according to types of action or behaviour such as 'breathing' and 'sitting'. GL

X Artists' Spaces

When a Berto Lardera retrospective was held at the Wilhelm Lehmbruck Museum in 1976, this artist's *Salle de récréation plastique* of 1970/71 was exhibited for the first time. Eleven movable elements, consisting of cut-out silhouettes in aluminium, copper and iron, were mounted on steel rods over a floor area of 3 by 3 metres. In their horizontal positioning, these rods give a distinct structure and density to each of the three walls of the room, which can be entered through an entrance inserted into the fourth. The possibility of moving and regrouping the wall objects draws the spectator into the room installation and encourages him or her to adopt an active and creative role, in effect to 'recreate'. The spectator thus moves 'between two worlds' (the title of one of Lardera's steel sculptures) in a space that is simultaneously static and kinetic.

An interior similarly evincing artistic intervention on three of its sides, although not permitting entry, was made by Christian Boltanski in his *List of Duisburg Children* of 1993. Boltanski selected a poorly lit corner oriel and filled its built-in floor-to-ceiling shelves with the 'favourite objects' of the city's children and young people. The individual objects, such as shoes, dolls, caps, teddy-bears, sunglasses and numerous other playthings were in each case identified with a label indicating the identity of the donor and 'co-player' with his or her signature and passport photograph. Peering through a lattice, the spectator encounters a 'list' made up of countless accumulated relics from everyday life. Like a child peeping with longing through a keyhole, the observer here assumes the role of a *voyeur* who finds himself confronted with the desires and memories of a spent youth in a now 'lost time'.

A 'list' of another sort was presented by Joseph Beuys in his *90,000 DM* Room of 1981. Originally installed in the Galerie Jöllenbeck in

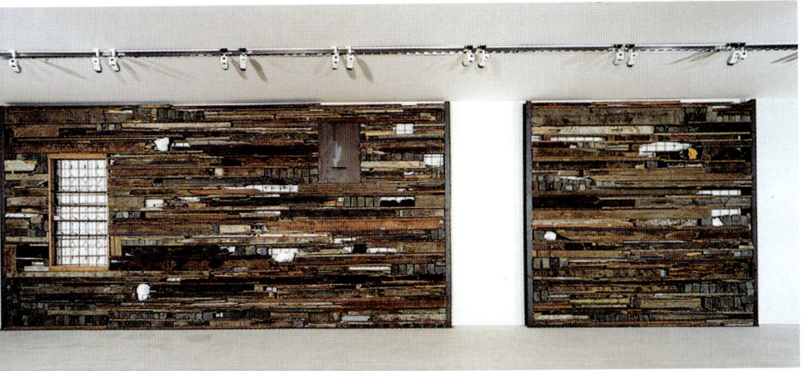

Jannis Kounellis (b. 1936), *Untitled*, 1982/1999, Two-part wall installation, 380 x 1430 x 30 cm

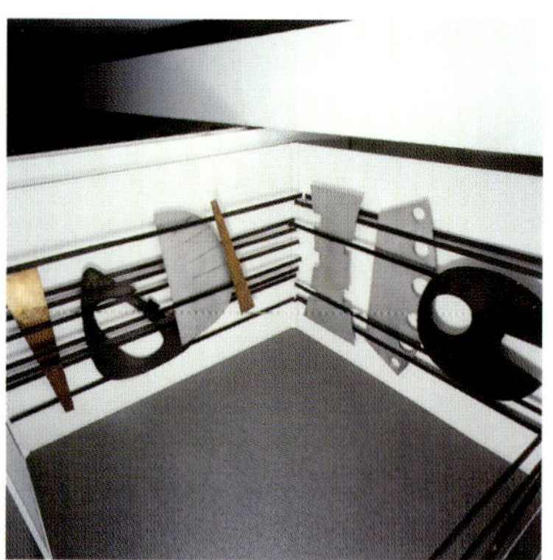

Berto Lardera (1911–1989)
Salle de récréation plastique,
1970/1971
Room installation,
353 x 231 x 332 cm

Cologne, this was intended by Beuys (as his collage between two panes of glass makes clear) as a corner space into which a bath, filled with water and covered with clay, was to be pushed. In the damp clay Beuys inscribed the figure 90,000 DM, the price at which the work was offered for sale at that time, and he named the installation after this. Around the bath are grouped several rusty vessels still bearing labels and filled with fused clumps of metal. These pieces came about in connection with the works made in Italy on the theme of the *terremoto* [Earthquake] and the *difesa della natura* [Defence of Nature]. The scoop and the now formless lumps of aluminium and rust heaped in the containers are testimony to the performance piece in which Beuys had had letters and numbers from a printer's shop smelted over an open fire. The purity and clarity of the water and the panes of glass leaning against the wall were emphatically opposed to the receptacle for poison, symbolizing the power to destroy both nature and mankind. As Christoph Brockhaus has argued, the apparent lack of specific alignment for the containers, the displacement of the glass sheet, the cracks in the clay covering and the emphasis on the monetary value of the work could not refer more clearly to the 'dislocation of values' and the caesura occurring within a materially oriented society. The human dimension disappears, only in ghostly form in the outline of a figure at the base of the bathtub.

In 1997 the museum acquired an entire room installation with several groups of works by Franz Erhard Walther – after Beuys the most important performance artist in Germany. This was a hitherto unique assembly of three sculptural works from the legendary First Work Phase of 1963–69 – 32 sheets, with drawings, on both sides and 61 photographs arranged into 7 photo-tableaux, illustrating the individual stages of the performance. The photographs of 6 tableaux were taken by Timm Rauten (in 1969) and those from Work Phase no. 33 by Jens Rathenau (in 1980). The arrangement of objects, drawings and photographs, established by the artist and presented in this way for the first time, made possible the coincidence of elements in that more complex, receptive and interactive experience at which Walther's comprehensive concept of the 'work' aims. The First Work Phase perfectly illustrates the 'thinking in terms of process' so characteristic of Walther, whose interest was not concentrated on

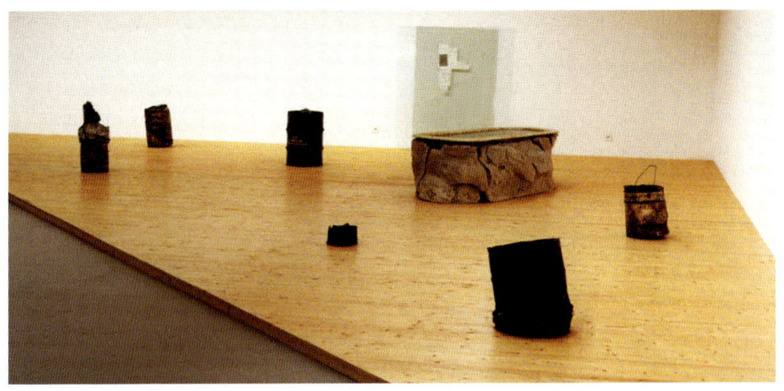

Joseph Beuys (1921–1986), *The 90,000 DM Room*, 1981, Room installation

the 'fixed form' of the individual work but on its transparency and on its openess within a space that could be entered by the spectator.

Another type of Process Art has been practised since 1966 by Richard Long, to whom the prestigious Wilhelm Lehmbruck Prize was granted by the City of Duisburg in 1996. The modest titles that Long gives his painstakingly produced and well-documented works should not blind us to their almost mythical exploration of place. In the 'Landscape Pieces' Long links the 'miracle' of nature with its emotionally and cosmically freighted history. In the complex of 'Mud Works', as in the wall piece RIVER AVON MUD CIRCLE, which Long created in 1997 along the inner wall of the museum, the corporeal is transformed into a cosmic star sign. In a natural setting the circle and the line appear to be the products of artifice, but in the space of a museum they allude to the powers of nature. Long's technical discipline and rigour is in tune with this purist view of the world in terms of simple gestures and symbols. For Long, man does not stand at the centre of what he creates. He is, rather, a 'tool'. Long has claimed: 'I like the idea that the world was made out of stones'.

With an equally purist approach, Erwin Heerich has evolved an autonomous 'universe of spatial bodies', sufficient unto itself, which enables him to produce 'concrete' art with a Minimalist rigour. However, to

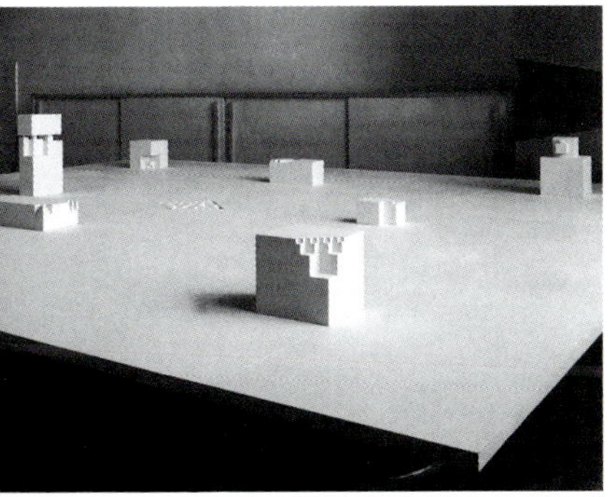

Erwin Heerich (b. 1922)
Group from the 'Architectural Landscape',
1 of a total of 12 works, 1975
White painted wood

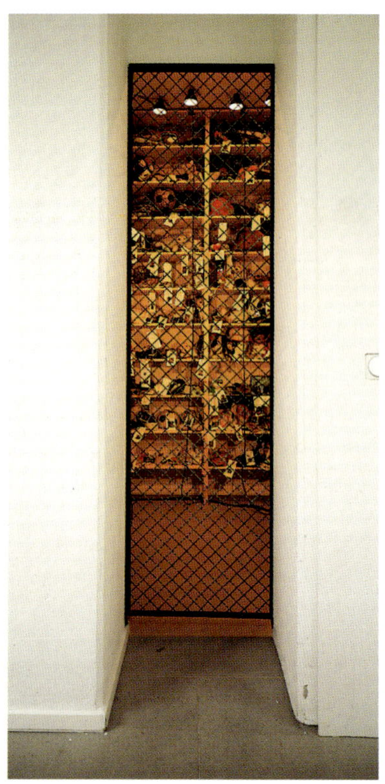

Christian Boltanski (b. 1944)
Réserve des enfants de Duisburg, 1993
Oriel

the Minimalist preoccupation with mathematical regularity and symmetry, Heerich opposes a diversity of arrangements. Especially in his isolated 'architectonic landscapes', he shows a diversity of idiosyncratic, stereometric bodies that illustrate purposeless, rationally verifiable and yet extremely complex experiences of space. The wood sculpture conceived as a model posseses all the forms and proportions of the large-scale pieces executed in stone and metal for internal and external spaces.

The museum's most recent acquisition of particular significance is the impressive wall piece by Jannis Kounellis, *Untitled*, first shown at the 'Zeitgeist' exhibition in Berlin in 1982 and most recently in Cologne in 1997. Transferred to Duisburg, the materially complex relief was substantially extended in relation to its new setting. Its most dominant characteristic is the sense of a wall enriched with squared timber, paving stones, plaster casts and 'poetic material' (oil barrels, musical instruments, wine glasses), resting on a bulky steel frame. While a window is visible on the left, a door reaching to the ceiling (an empty plane) appears to have been inserted on the right. Encountered in the context of works by Merz, Beuys and Long, this piece has to be understood as part of an expanding space, as a 'wailing wall' haunted by 'fate', as the cladding for an architectural structure that bears the scars of history and the passage of time. The wall unites the still surviving traces of that archaically rooted sense of a blueprint for life that finds its raw material in nature and a fleeting and fragmentary memory in the work of man. Materialistically-oriented, industrialized society is urged to return to its roots and reflect on its origins and history. GL

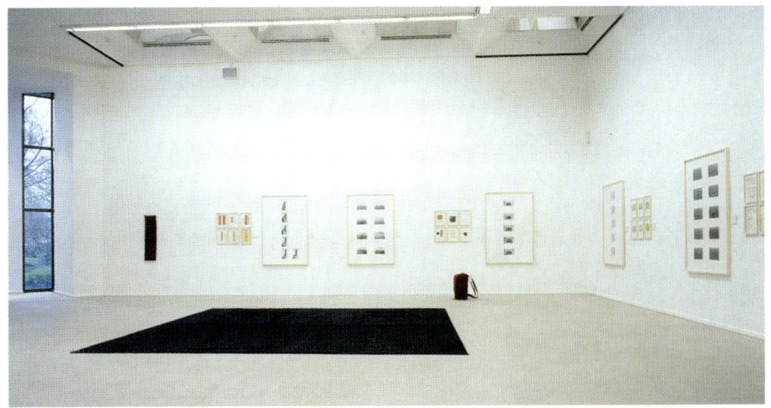

Franz Erhard Walther (b. 1939), *Objects from the First Work Phase*, with the addition of drawings and photographs, 1963–1997, Room installation

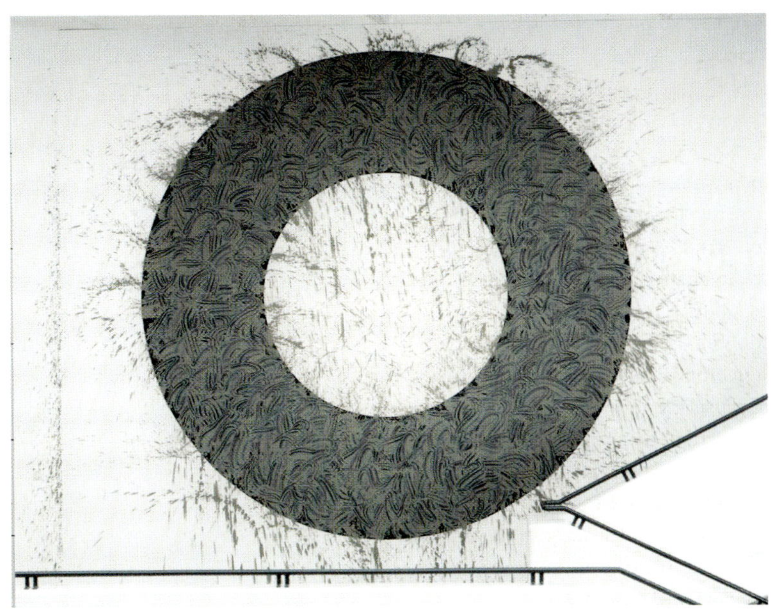

Richard Long (b. 1945), *RIVER AVON MUD CIRCLE*, 1997, Wall piece in acrylic and mud on painted plaster, dia 456 cm

XI Sculpting with Light

Dan Flavin (1933–1996)
Untitled, 1969
Yellow and red fluorescent lights, mounts, electrical installation, second version of three,
244 x 64 x 20 cm

Flavin was the first artist to make industrial fluorescent lighting (which he started using in 1963) central to his work. Using this medium, he opened up new dematerialized worlds of colour and illumination that flooded and transformed gallery spaces. According to the sculptor's very precise plan for this corner piece, the desired effect depends on the combination of one vertically and two horizontally placed light tubes. A vertical light rod is positioned in the corner, clasped both above and below by a short crossbeam so that a double T-shape results. While the red light of the crossbeam dazzles the approaching spectator, the yellow light of the vertical tube is directed into the corner: its dematerialized glow thus irradiates the surrounding space, enclosing the spectator. GL

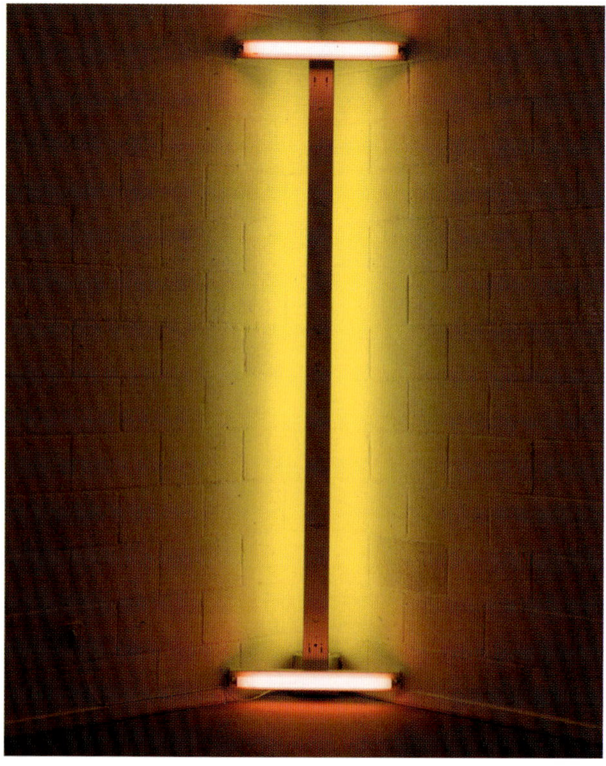

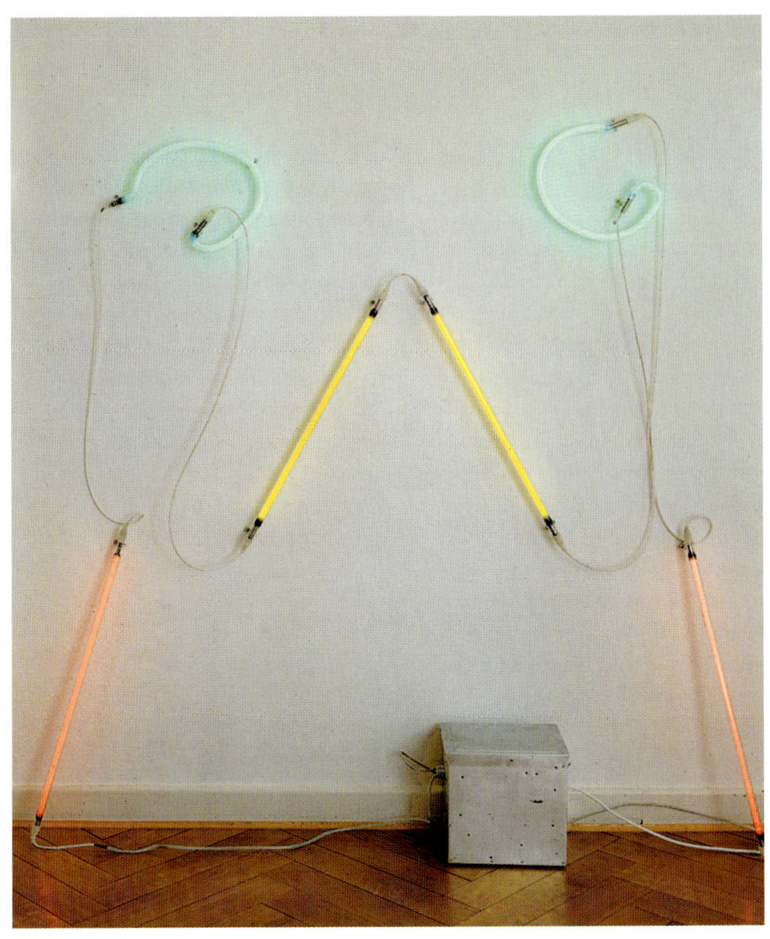

Keith Sonnier (b. 1941)
SA, 1969–1974 (BA-O-Series), 1969
Green, yellow and red neon tubes and transformer, 180 x 200 x 35 cm

This installation is arranged according to a precisely drawn plan supplied by the artist. Sonnier does not work with either fluorescent light (as Flavin did) or with neon lettering and spiral forms (as in the case of Bruce Naumann or Mario Merz); rather, he assembles ingeniously bent neon tubes with selected coloured light in correspondence with a semantic system of his own. As the majority of wall installations permit numerous variations with regard to form and colour, Sonnier produces his work in series, each of which is calligraphic and simultaneously painterly in character. According to Sonnier, the 'BA-O'-series, to which the illustrated work belongs, is titled with a Franco-Haitian term meaning a 'shower of colour and light'. Sonnier started work on this series in 1969, and it proved to be the starting point for his early videotapes and films, their pictograms 'colouring' the spectator's habitual ways of seeing. GL

Mario Merz (b. 1925)
8–5–3 m, 1985
Three-part igloo installation, structure in iron, glass, stone, brushwood and neon,
800 x 500 x 300 cm

Merz made this installation in 1985 out of what had originally been three indiviudal igloos in different materials. He titled it *8–5–3*, thereby inverting the sequence of numbers in the Fibonacci series that he has always favoured for his work (with the next figure at every step provided by the addition of the two immediately preceding figures). The centrally placed igloo, its iron ribbing covered in several layers of glass, shelters a considerably smaller igloo made of stone. The third igloo, made of layered bundles of brushwood, is pushed near to the glass structure, the two in fact being cursorily linked. In Merz's view, the mutual penetration and sense of belonging found among all 'nomadic' forms of housing embody a Utopian view of the world that is attuned to the heavens. The semi-spherical primitive stone mound stands beneath the glazed dome conveying clarity and transparency, while the bundles of brushwood recall the 'prehistoric wind from the icy mountains'. The cosmic associations implicit in the semi-spherical form are strengthened through three long neon tubes that pierce the glass skin as if they were lances of light or streams of energy that penetrate into the still dull and lifeless stone. Each individual igloo already shelters within itself the elemental powers of nature and the cosmos, but in this installation Merz intensifies the notion of modest habitation to a potentially extensive 'unreal' igloo city, a *città irreale*. GL

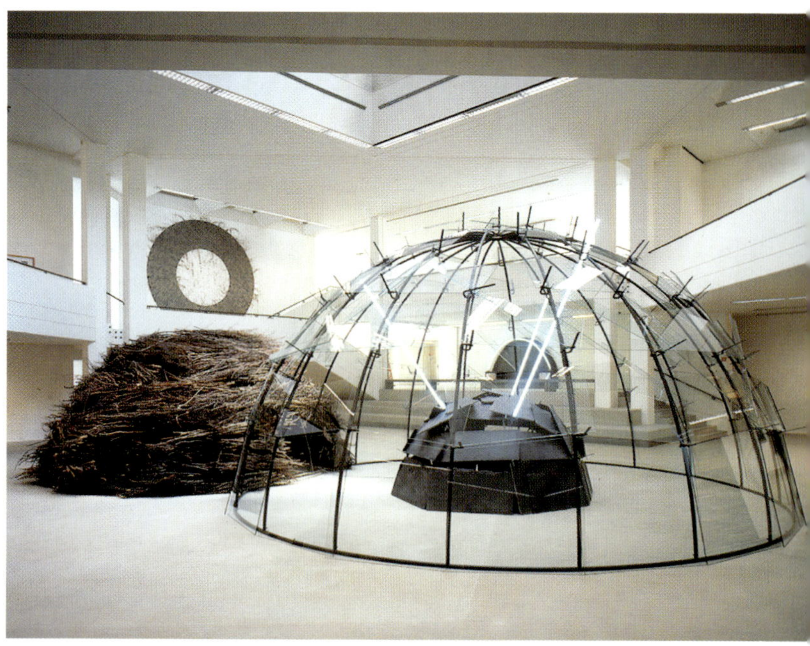

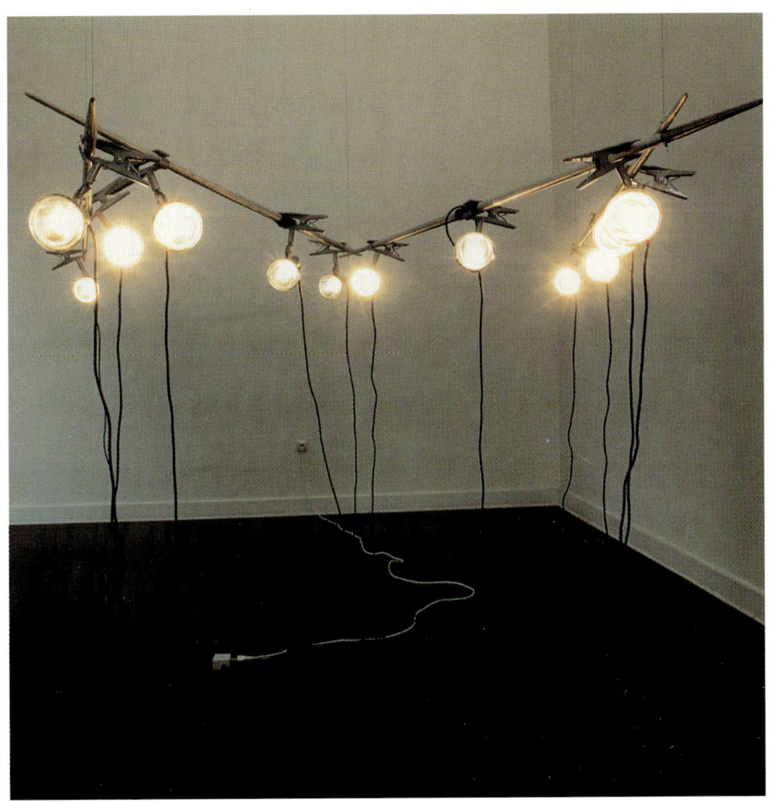

Gilberto Zorio (b. 1944)
Evviva i giavellotti e le lampade/Long live the javelins and the lamps, 1974
Javelins, lamps, electronic installation,
170 x 250 x 250 cm (as installed)

Zorio is a member of the group of Italian artists who, in the spirit of *arte povera* [Poor Art], chose to work with 'poor' materials in order to demonstrate genetic connections, to liberate energy inherent in material and, at the same time, to explore its mythical dimension. As a sculptor, Zorio desires to mobilize a society ossified in consumerism and to call upon all its members in order to draw every individual back into the cycle of cosmic energy. The four suspended javelins are decorated with lamps that dangle at about eye height. The weapons are positioned so as to form a double V-shaped victory sign. In combination with the dazzle of the lights, these polished and aggressive objects imbue the space of this installation with energy, excitement and dynamism. GL

XII Contemporary Positions

The conventional conception of sculpture as an individual work or part of an installation has survived, even if Land Art, expansive Object Art and, in particular, sculpture using the New Media have all introduced quite new perspectives. Both painters and sculptors (Penck, Jetelová, Disler, Balkenhol) have taken a definitive stand against the dominance of technology through their explicit regard for the figurative. Artists such as Schwegler, Stalder and Breloh have reintroduced an emphasis on the handmade object with wit, irony and subtle melancholy. Through the Wilhelm Lehmbruck Stipends (awarded from 1977) and the annual prize offered by the Museum Supporters' Circle (from 1983), the Wilhelm Lehmbruck Museum has been able to provide support for a younger generation of sculptors both from Germany and abroad. GL

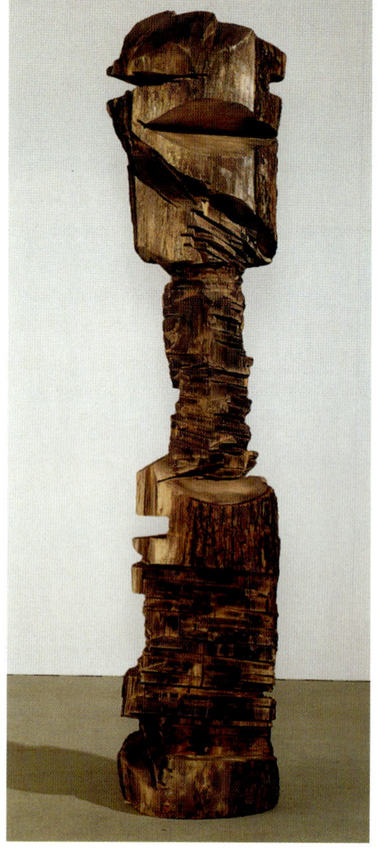

A.R. Penck (b. 1939)
The Spirit of L. II, 1982
Limewood, 268 x 70 x 55 cm

This work, acquired from the Hahn Collection in Cologne, was made after Penck had started work (in 1980) on a sculptural series of 'Idols for Germany'. In this second version the artist commemorates his stay in the village of Lindenau (the 'L' of the title), where he had a studio from 1972 to 1975. In its renunciation of colour, the work evokes archaically reduced figural forms, their cracks, splintering and deformations prompting thoughts of what Penck has called the 'primevally present'. This monumental piece, which nonetheless embraces the self-assertion of the individual, mirrors both the contemporary world and the potential future forms of society. GL

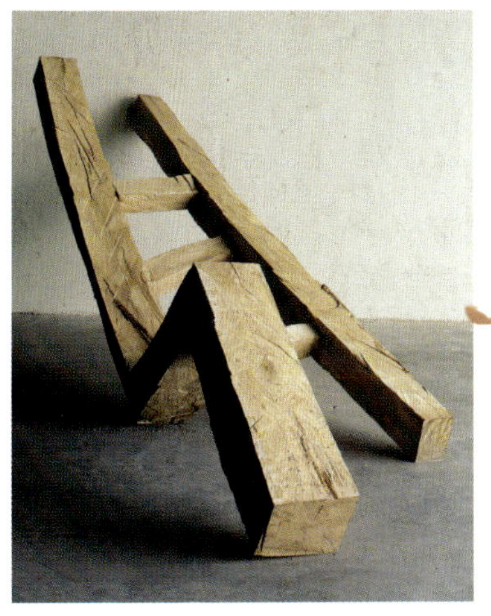

Magdalena Jetelová (b. 1946)
Reclining Female Figure, 1996
Oak, 135 x 185 x 320 cm

Jetelová has addressed the motif of corporeality in numerous works – both wood sculptures and drawings. In this case the rough, splintered wooden beams create a frame in the form of a ladder, partially broken and thus non-functional. While the basic structure endures, the whole requires the support of a wall. The ladder, traditionally a symbol of reconciliation and ascent, here responds to an image of humanity impeded in its natural mobility and so threatening to topple over. GL

Heinz Breloh (b. 1940)
Meeting of the Sculptors II, 1992
Eight pieces in terracotta,
h 30 to 53 cm

This sculptor from Cologne creates his vigorous basic figural forms out of clay that retains the traces of hand-modelling. The eccentrically and complexly deformed entities, appear, on account of their elemental character, to have derived from primitive life forms. The process of making by hand is, however, not only to be interpreted as a merely expresssive gesture; rather, it illustrates an elementary working process. Out of this 'mythical act of creation' there arises what the art critic Manfred Schneckenburger has termed a 'counter-force to the world of machines and electrical circuits', a poeticization of matter and a synthesis of all the powers of art. Terracotta is thus here transformed into an assembly of imaginary 'diagrams' of personages – Getrude Stein, Richard Wagner or the mythological figures Philemon and Baucis – who take on power and shape through a process of metamorphosis. It is also in accordance with this principle that the freely modelling sculptor, whom Breloh equates with the act of creation, shapes his own work. GL

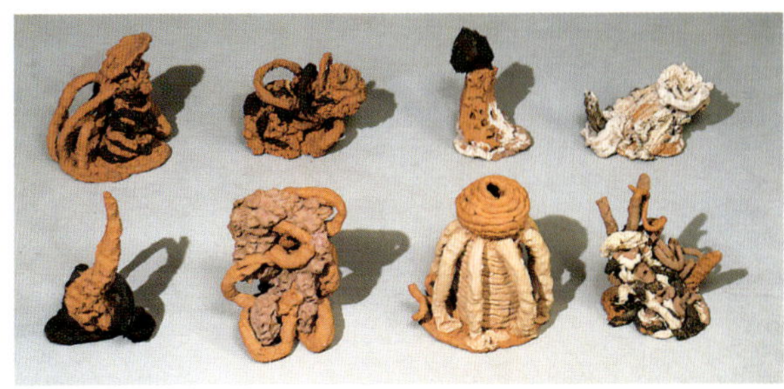

flesh' and solitude readily assciated with death. GL

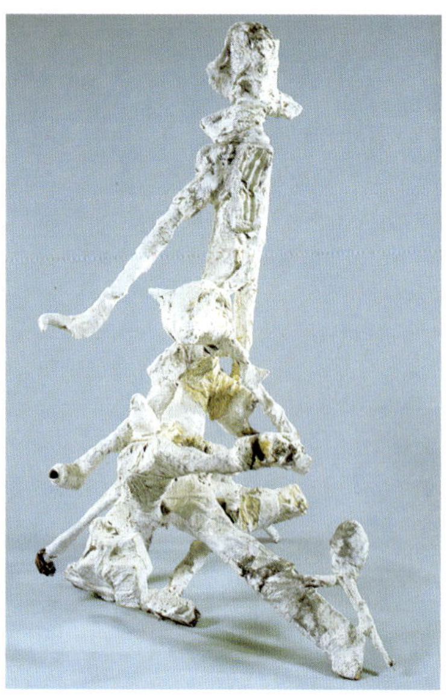

Martin Disler (1949–1996)
Odysseus, 1987
Assemblage, 202 x 152 x 142 cm

Disler's figural form is distinguished by its rendering of the human body in all the ecstasy of movement and in a state of aimless frenzy, and yet firmly attached to the unstable ground. Like Breloh and Stalder, Disler counters contemporary 'computer culture' with, as he phrases it, 'the most up-to-date cave paintings'. For Disler, the rocking ship is a metaphor of this approach. In this vessel Disler has set up home, and he offers a penetrating description of it in his essay 'Häutung und Tanz' [Moulting and Dance]. One among several mythical figures to be found on board this ship is Odysseus, who represents those heroes who were arbitrarily exposed to fate and the whims of the gods. As this sculptural work shows, the end of any odyssey may also signify decay and deformation, and that sense of 'quivering

Anselm Stalder (b. 1956)
The Excavation, 1984
Polystyrene and 'Moltofill'
75 x 50 x 50 cm

In the sculpture *The Excavation* the artist has proceeded by taking apart a head. The top of the skull has been removed and the contents clawed out by hand, leaving clearly visible traces of fingers in the rust-red coloured wall of the cavity. As the head is emptied and robbed of its functions, it also sacrifices its face. This has lost its positive sculptural form and appears as if drawn inwards by the act of excavation, being effectively eroded from within. As the emptied head nonetheless also appears as an open and potentially fillable vessel, it is clear that new content may give rise to a new face with a new sculptural identity. GL

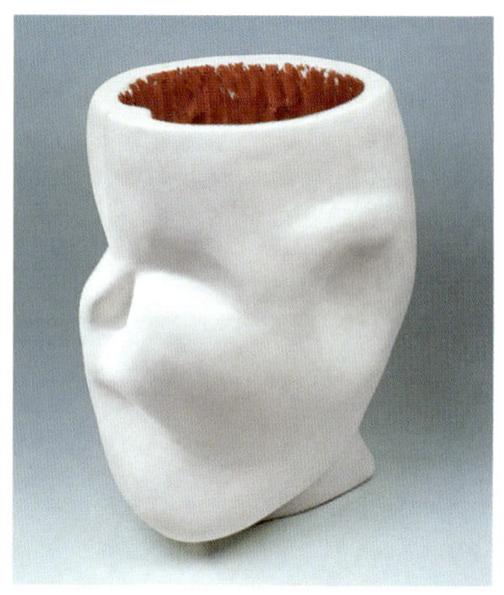

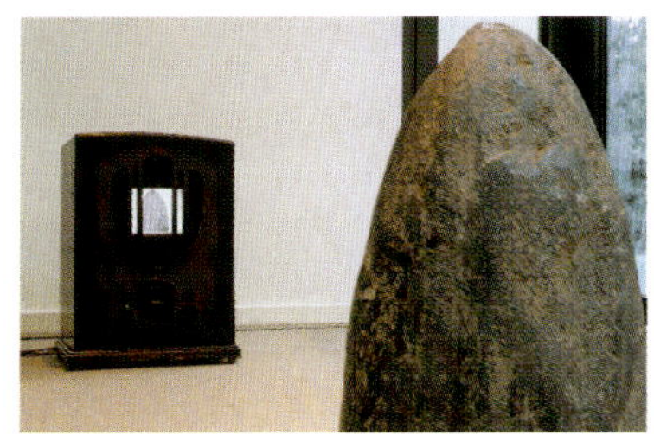

Nam June Paik (b. 1932)
TV Buddha, 1997
Buddha statue in stone, TV set in radio casing, video recorder, 36.5 x 26.5 x 10 cm (statue); 40 x 29 x 22 cm (radio casing)

It was in 1973 that Nam June Paik, the father of video art, first started making the various versions of his TV installations incorporating Buddha statues. In each case the same formal principle recurs: a Buddha statue or, as in this work, a fixed image of a group in relief, recurs on the screen of a TV set. The spectator thus becomes a witness to a confrontation that is absurd but compelling. The power of religion and that of the media are here positioned motionlessly opposite each other. ChB

Andreas M. Kaufmann (b. 1961)
'Alone with far too much', 1993/95
Room installation, dimensions variable

Andreas M. Kaufmann paints with light. In his room installation *Alone with far too much*, the film *Rashomon* (by the Japanese director Akira Kurosawa) is projected acrosss the walls and the floor of the surrounding space. The three film sequences, which are extremely slowed, create an 'enchanted' environment and a fascinating disorientation for the spectator. As a result of their spatial distortion, the projected images have the effect of a mirage, setting off ever new fleeting associations. Almost unselfconsciously, spectators move about in the vain attempt to grasp the projected image in all its detail. It is indeed the impossibility of doing so that accounts for the curious aesthetic pleasure and the excitement of Kaufmann's 'video paintings'. SD

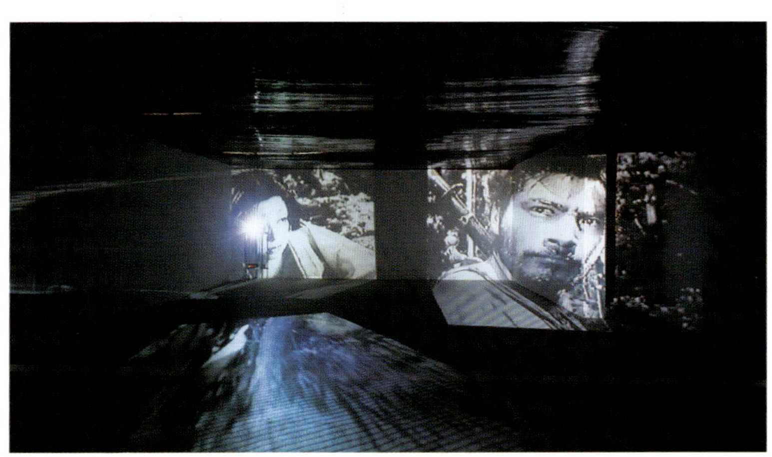

XIII Large-scale Sculpture in the Museum Park

With only a modicum of enlargement, as in the case of sculpture oriented to the scale of the human body, it is less often the private sphere than the publically accessible interior to which it is best suited, be it in terms of theme or of form. Large-scale sculpture is in every respect appropriate for public spaces. And it is also for such pieces that a museum of sculpture requires space. In 1989/90, in the course of preparations for the exhibition 'Sculpture of the Second Era of Modernism', the Wilhelm Lehmbruck Museum was able to expand its display area for large-scale sculpture to encompass the neighbouring Kant Park.

Since this time not only has the *Kneeling Woman* by Wilhelm Lehmbruck (positioned by his son, the architect Manfred Lehmbruck) served as a landmark, pointing the way to the main entrance of the museum, but other sculptures too have moved beyond the confines of the sculpture court (a space still closely related to the museum interior). Now, certain large-scale sculptures (if curatorial criteria are met) can be placed within the landscape of the park. This has been the case with pieces by Tollmann, Lechner, Hauser, Reichert and Hermanns. Even more importantly, works by Abakanowicz, Ecker, Fainaru, Karavan, Paolozzi, Sciola, Serra, Simon, Sonfist and Volten have been placed together, and/or new works created, in locations chosen by common agreement.

In the year 2000 a procedure for the redesign of the park will be introduced.

ChB

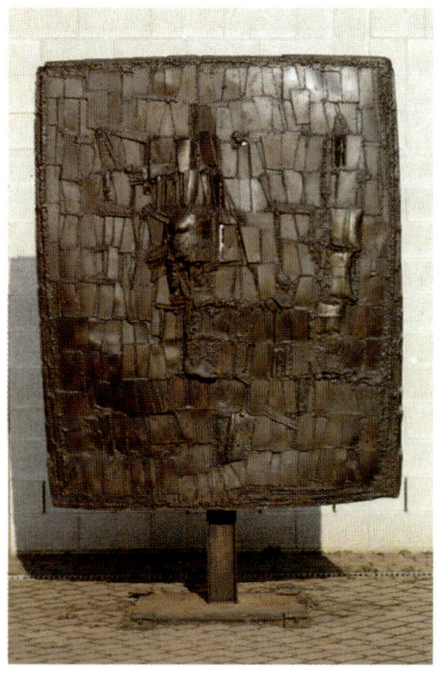

César (1921–1998)
L'Homme de Figanières/The Figanières Man, 1964
Iron, 260 x 170 x 70 cm

The inward-curving and largely scaly 'panel', as César termed his numerous early iron reliefs, is mounted on a base with both vertical and horizontal segments. The overall impression is of a form resembling a *stele* that nonetheless conceals within itself a precious 'relic'. This is especially so on account of the illusion of the fossilized image of a prehistoric human body, the result of aeons of compression.

GL

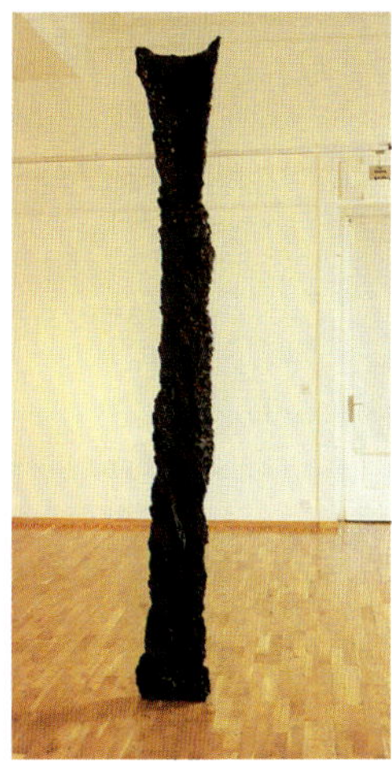

Bryan Hunt (b. 1947)
Falling Water – Bear Run II, 1977/78
Bronze, unique cast,
301 x 42.5 x 24 cm

Since 1977 this American sculptor has taken his inspiration fom waterfalls, being fascinated by their dramatic plunge from a great height. The form of floor sculpture he has always favoured is here countered by an extreme vertical element, which recalls the visual experience that a waterfall does indeed, as Hunt says, 'have a head and feet but no beginning and no end'.

The element of water, found in perpetual and vehement motion, required a corresponding surface structure, and this can be seen in the plaster model for this piece in bronze. The artists' hands and fingers left behind meandering tracks that were re-emphasized, when the plaster was dry, through vigorous blows of the chisel. The sense of movement frozen in the cast was finally and decisively imbued with rhythm through the light playing over the surface with its dark patina. GL

Dani Karavan (b. 1930)
Dialogue, 1989
White concrete, water, bush,
60 x 600 x 2400 cm

The repertoire of forms found in this sculpture has three characteristics: it is indebted to Minimalism, it is used in a site-specific fashion and it assumes a social function. With its white concrete material the sculpture is a variation on the grey concrete of the wing of the museum that houses the Wilhelm Lehmbruck collection. Positioned in relation to the large tree in the sculpture court and ending at the pond, it also serves as a 'bridge' between the museum and the park. The six cubes positioned on the platform occurring approximately half-way along this 'bridge' provide a place where people can sit and talk. Above this the sculptor has squared off the foliage of the trees and planted a bush. ChB

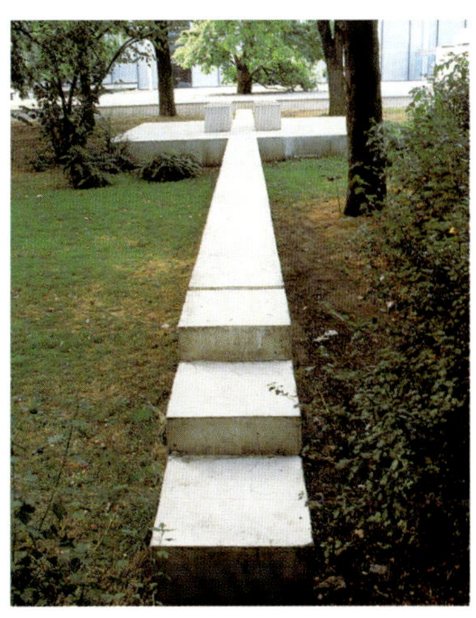

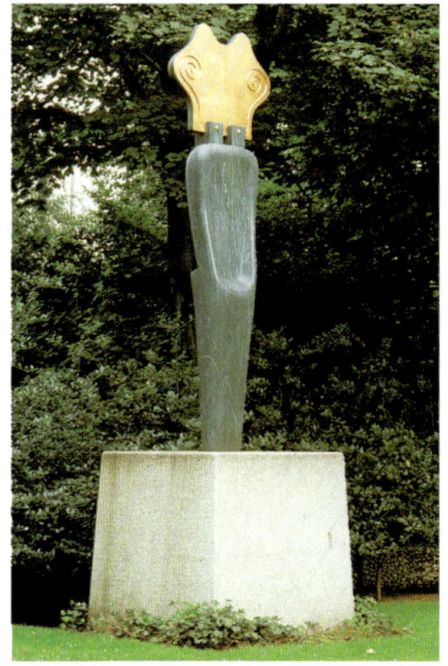

Meret Oppenheim (1913–1985)
The Green Observer, 1933/1976
Green marble, gilt copper panel,
total h 332 cm,
of which base h 142 cm

This work, which bears the subtitle 'One who watches another dying', was completed after a sketch made in 1933. In this late phase of Surrealism, Oppenheim was much preoccupied with large-scale sculpture. *The Green Observer*, with its combination of a palmette-crowned and gilt 'head', extremely slender 'limbs' and a pyramidal lower section, assumes the 'elevated' character of a monument. Through its setting in a meadow sown with ivy, this *stele* is also clearly evocative of a Cult of the Dead. GL

Richard Serra (b. 1939)
Weitmar, 1984
Rolled and curved Corten steel,
450 x 500 x 8 cm

This monolithic freestanding sculpture has been positioned so as to underline its connection with the architecture of the museum building. Serra concentrates his material (steel) by reducing it to extremely simple forms. The extreme heaviness and hardness of this material embraces the force implicit in its role as a support, as a weight or as a towering form, allowing the spectator to experience these qualities through the tracks they have left in the work. GL

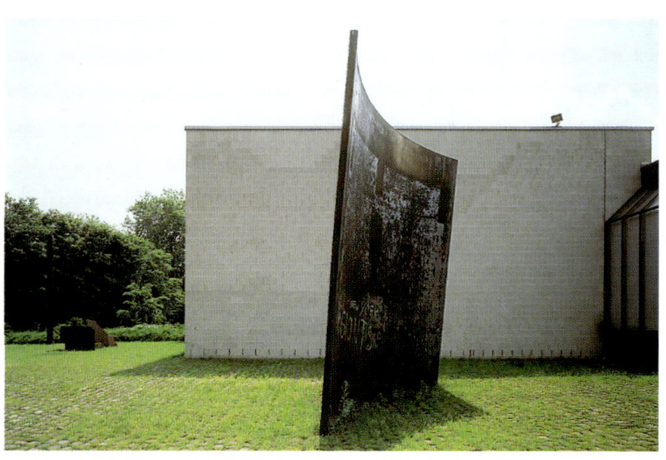

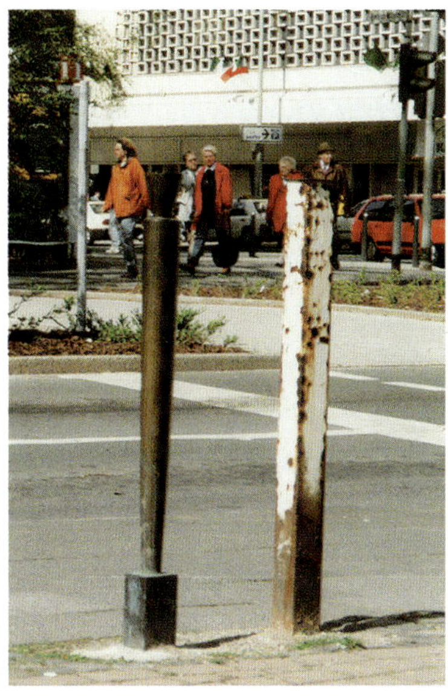

Norbert Radermacher (b. 1953)
The Posts, 1989
Polished bronze, h 118 cm

Radermacher made his bronze posts as a reaction to a pre-existing street barrier in the form of an angular iron stake of the same height. He can thus be said to be using an art object to oppose both fixity and the functional. According to the artist, writing in 1987: 'Out of the limitations of ones' own thoughts and four walls [one advances] into the open space of the street. In relation to the scale of the city the pieces are small. Like a lifebelt floating on the vastness of the ocean. In the last analysis all you can do is hold on to what you have.'

GL

Eduardo Paolozzi (b. 1924)
Egypt, 1990
Bronze, 110 x 430 x 275 cm

This bronze piece was executed after the plaster model made by the artist and installed in 1990 in Kant Park near a childrens' playground. The title is derived from the attributes of a scarab beetle and a grasshopper, while the motif of the open hand alludes to the hand of God the Creator and to Medievel reliquaries in the form of a hand. As is so often the case in Paolozzi's work, there are also elements that allude to technology (robots), here perceived together with knowledge and play (a sphere, steps and a wheeled vehicle). GL

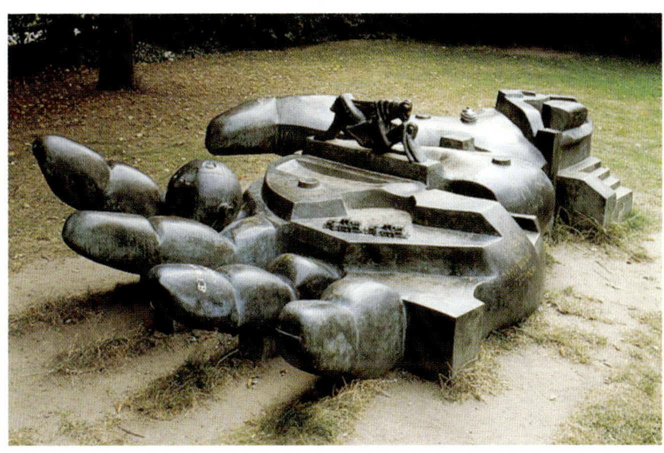

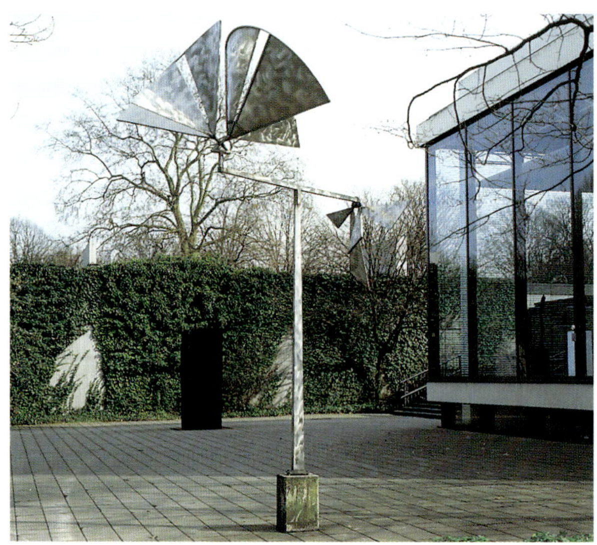

George Rickey (b. 1907)
Two Congenial Segments: Rotation IV, 1980
High-grade steel, 500 x 470 x 140 cm

While the 'lines' in Rickey's work are delicate, reminiscent of needles, the planes are made up out of triangles and 'wind wheels' on a transverse pole. Ball-and-socket joints and mobile pegs allow the movement of the blossom-like swaying segments driven by the wind, the autonomous rotation of which cuts through the air. The light as it falls on the moving surfaces enhances the dematerialized, playful quality of the structure.

According to the artist: 'The wind plays over these blossoming leaves, but it does not alter them, except in as far as it transforms them into the bearers of a lyrical message'. GL

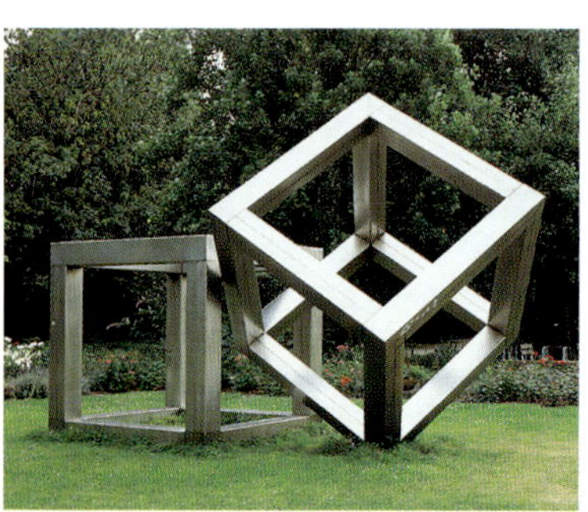

Alf Lechner (b. 1925)
Construction in Cubes, third version of seventy-three, 1973
High-grade steel, first cast of three, 300 x 500 x 300 cm

This outdoor sculpture consists of two parts. One cube is tipped up to rest on an angle so that it attains greater overall height but also needs the support of its neighbour. The result is a sculpture in which an alteration in the expected arrangement focuses attention on the relationship of order and mass, adhesion and balance. Fundamantal architectonic and sculptural principles are implicit in the use of the non-solid cube as a new basic form. GL

XIV Sculpture in the City

Duisburg already had a reputation as a centre for art in the 1950s on account of its independently active Art and Architecture Commission and the many projects undertaken to promote 'Art in Public Spaces'. In the following decades, however, there was very little state-funded new building, and sculptors sought alternative means of exhibiting their work in the city. In the 1980s it was therefore recognized that a certain amount of rethinking was in order.

It was in the 1960s that the Wilhelm Lehmbruck Museum started using its own park, in addition to public spaces in the city, for the display of sculpture. In 1979 there took place on the neighbouring Lake Berta the 'happening' recorded in Marta Pan's *Floating Sculpture*. Other artists taking part in this event included Plessi, Uecker and Schmaltz. A group of trees by Menashe Kadishman recalls a lakeside sculptors' symposium. Numerous large-scale sculptures from the museum collection have found suitable places within the city.

With the *Rhine Orange* created by Lutz Fritsch and located at the confluence of the Ruhr and the Rhine, Duisburg has acquired an internationally recognized city symbol. This is equally true of the fountain devised by Niki de Saint-Phalle and Jean Tinguely, which stands in the city centre. This forms part of a fountain mile, the most significant artistic symbols of which are located where side streets run into the main street. The other fountains are by Alt, Hegenwald, Marjanov, Virnich and Volten. A corresponding programme was pursued during the 1980s with new underground stations for which architects collaborated with artists. New perspectives came *(cont. next page)*

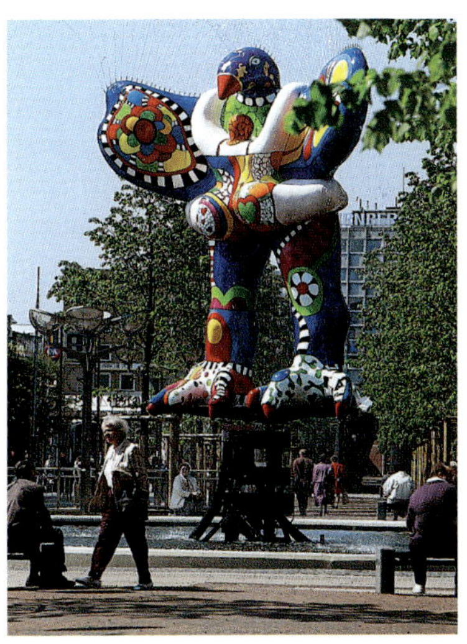

Niki de Saint Phalle and **Jean Tinguely**
(b. 1930; 1925–1991)
Life-saver, 1989/93, Königstrasse
Painted polyester on a steel base, basin in concrete, h 720 cm

This last joint work by these two artists, of which the Wilhelm Lehmbruck Museum displays the 'model', sparkles joyfully in the space of the city as a mythical mother and child in the form of birds. As water streams from the head and wings of the figure, this turns from left to right through 180 degrees. ChB

(cont. from previous page) into play during preparations for the International Architecture Exhibition held in Emscher Park in 1989. In collaboration with sculptors, old industrial plants were adapted for use as cultural spaces, specifically as spaces for avant-garde and multi-media art. At the centre of one of these newly created centres of cultural activity we find Dani Karavan's *Garden of Memories.*

ChB

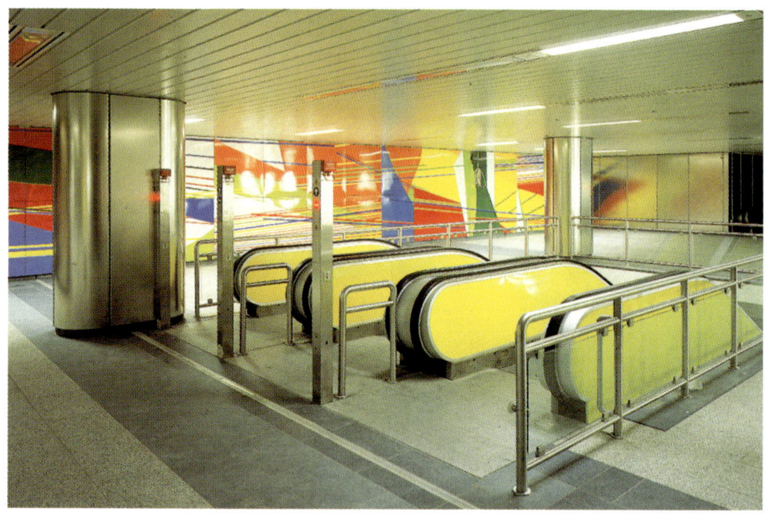

Gerhard Richter (b. 1932)/
Isa Genzken (b. 1948)
Design of the Duisburg Underground Station König-Heinrich-Platz, Königstrasse
Designs from 1981, station opened 1992

Planned under the architectural leadership of H. U. Zigan, this underground station consists of two spacious concourses linked by a system of tunnels running below Königstrasse and around 150 metres in length. The station also extends vertically, embracing access to two depths of platforms and train tunnels, each with its own design. The western concourse is decorated with an abstract mural of 23 by 2.5 metres, rendering a chronicle of the city in 24 enamel panels. All of the wall facings and pillars of the tunnels themselves are in silver-grey, high-grade steel and monochrome coloured panels. Especially notable is the design of the platforms and train tunnels. The upper level, with a total length of 116 metres, features exaggerated renderings of four different types of curvature. As a whole, this gives the impression of glowing, curved planes that 'entirely embrace' the surrounding space. On the walls of the lower level monochrome panels alternate with mirrors of equal size.

GL

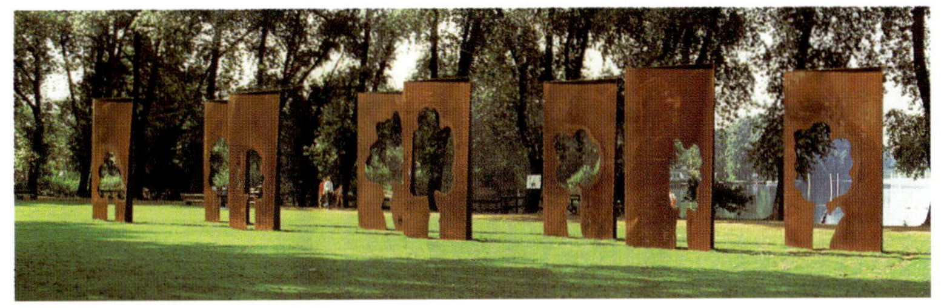

Menashe Kadishman (b. 1932)
Negative Trees, 1974, Lake Berta
Steel, eight sections,
each 505 x 258 x 42 cm

In 1999 Dani Karavan integrated into his *Garden of Memories* by the inner harbour the steel sculpture *Floating* (1968/81) by Menashe Kadishman, as the work of a colleague and an item already in the collection of the museum. By 1974 Kadishman had already exhibited his eight-part steel sculpture *Negative Trees* on the shore of Lake Berta. These upright vertical rectangles with their cut-out tree and cloud forms take up a position, like the parts of a stage-set, against the background of a line of real trees. As always, Kadishman here works with planar forms, but the view through the steel shapes allows the visible tree trunks and the lake to become a three-dimensional component of the sculpture. ChB

Marta Pan (b. 1923)
Floating Sculpture 7, 1979, Lake Berta
White-painted polyester, two parts,
dia 113 cm and 225 cm

Among the chief works produced by this artist are those numerous 'floating sculptures' in which the element of water enters into a synthesis with the shell-shaped bodies that are one of the artist's leitmotifs. Marta Pan made her first *sculptures flottantes* in 1961 for the park of the Kröller-Müller-Museum in Otterlo. Since then similar works have been installed in Lausanne (no. 2, 1966), at the Japanese Hakone Open Air Museum (no. 3, 1969), in Montreal (no. 4, 1970), in Bobigny near St Denis (no. 5, 1971) and in front of City Hall in Dallas, Texas (no. 6, 1977), in addition to that at Lake Berta in Duisburg (no. 7). Marta Pan has said of her work in this series: 'Sculpture and its movement, a movement it shares with the water and the wind, become a link between the lifeless world and the world of life. [Sculpture] is the point where one finds movement that embraces nature, the city and humanity, [it is] a connection and a transition, an event and a sign'. GL

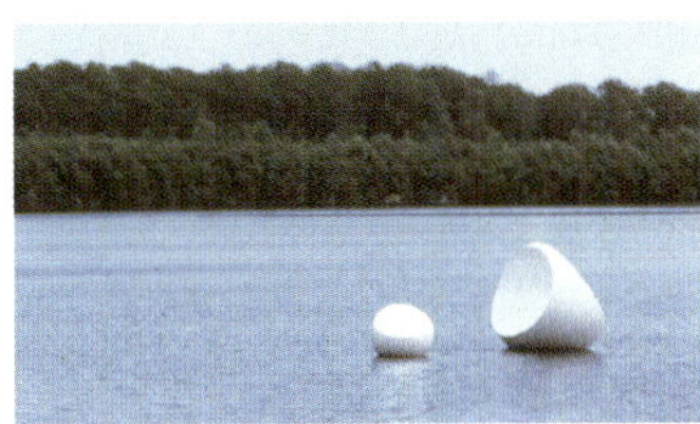

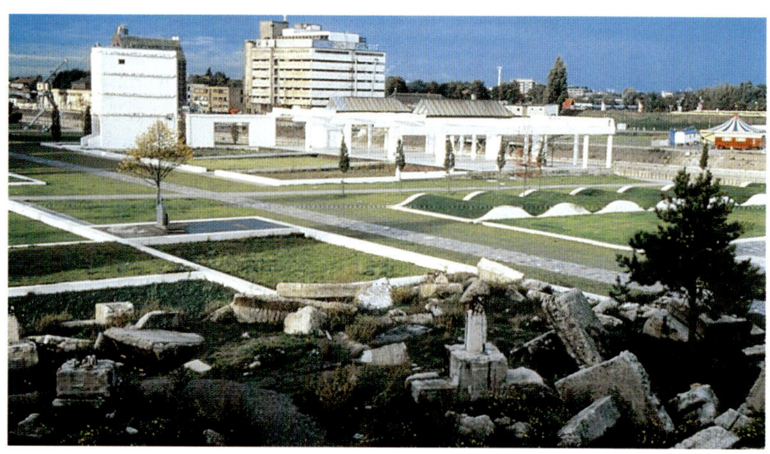

Dani Karavan (b. 1930)
Garden of Memories (detail),
1995–2000, inner harbour
Found architectural elements, pair of scales, steel, concrete, plants and trees, water, artificial light (Büro Belzner), c 3000 x 1800 cm

By the inner harbour, bordered by water, the street running along it (Uferstrasse), the Medieval city wall, the Jewish Community Centre (by Zvi Hecker) and a new Old Peoples' Home (by Helmut Kohl), the Israeli sculptor Dani Karavan has created a *Garden of Memories* out of seven pre-exisitng industrial and office buildings from recent decades to serve as a forum for the activities of the 'culture of industry'. Only one building has remained in its place, though it has been extensively altered: this provides studios for the composers Gerhard Stäbler and Kunsu Shim and also houses the DKM Foundation, which will organize exhibitions and multi-media happenings in collaboration with the museum.

In the case of all the other buildings, Dani Karavan has stripped the existing functional structure down to open spaces and intervening towers and has created a ground relief out of undulating mounds and a stone garden out of scrap and green spaces. He has also laid paths made of building materials. The former ground plans of the buildings are marked out in white concrete beams which also serve as seats. The garden is planted

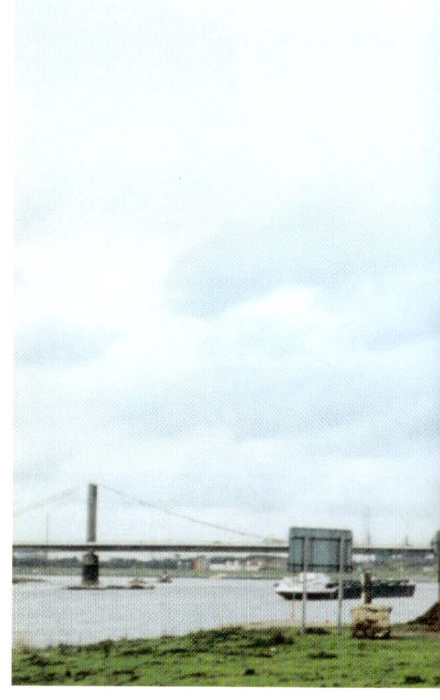

in accordance with artistic principles and develops the possibilities of a culture of industry, alluding in its selection to the city's former domestic gardens. ChB

Lutz Fritsch (b. 1955)
Rhine Orange, 1989–1992
Painted steel, 2500 x 700 x 100 cm

The history of the city of Duisburg, of which there is now over a thousand years, has its beginings in the geographical fact of the confluence of the Ruhr and the Rhine. But where exactly – amongst the dense coexistence of canals and harbours – is the point where these two rivers meet? This question led to the realization of *Rhine Orange*. As no state support was available for the project, a group of younger representatives of local industry not only assumed responsibility for the financing but also for the entire organization of the production of this symbol of the city (in both cases at the instigation of the museum). Altogether, more than 200 people and institutions were involved.

For weeks and months the artist circled the city in order to establish the appropriate scale and colouring for his sculpture. In every context he intended that it be distinguished both by autonomous qualities and by its reflection of the essential architectonic or functional characteristics of its surroundings at the edge of the world's largest internal harbour. As completed, *Rhine Orange* rears up as an architectonic structure 25 metres in height, defining the confluence of the two rivers and also taking into account its setting: the harbour buildings and the hotels as well as the slender chimneys and other manifestations of the presence of industry. ChB

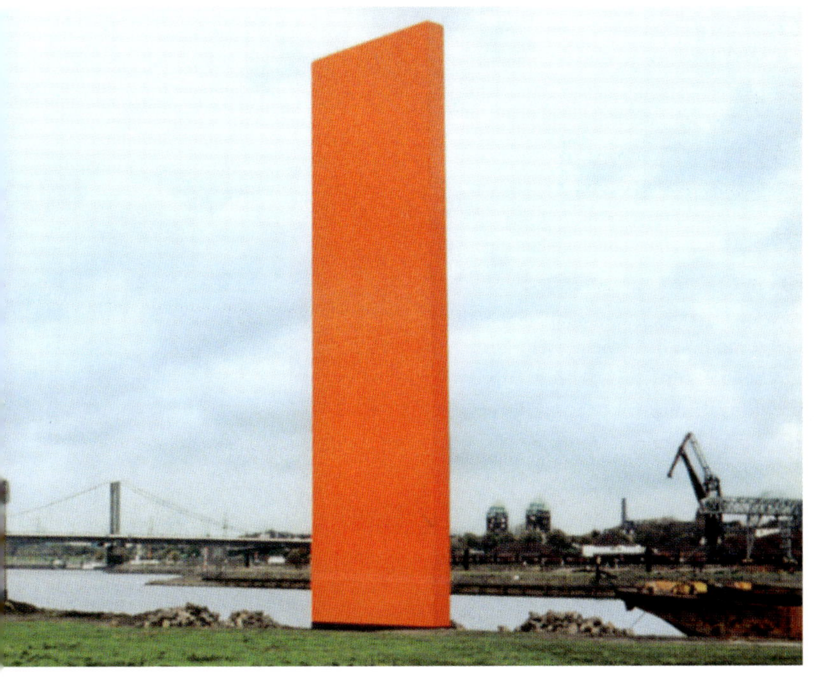

Ulrich Rückriem (b. 1938)
Untitled, 1986
Split and partially polished granite, 360 x 110 x 110 cm

Since 1963 stone has been Ulrich Rückriem's favoured material (he calls it 'the first nature'). In his view it is essential that all the working processes used to achieve the division, splitting and perforation of the volume of the stone be fully respectful of the material and clearly traceable in the end result. The dividing and splitting of the stone block, partially left 'rough' and partially polished, here issues in a monolithic 'tower' that is positioned in the landscape to secure an unobtrusive dominance there. GL

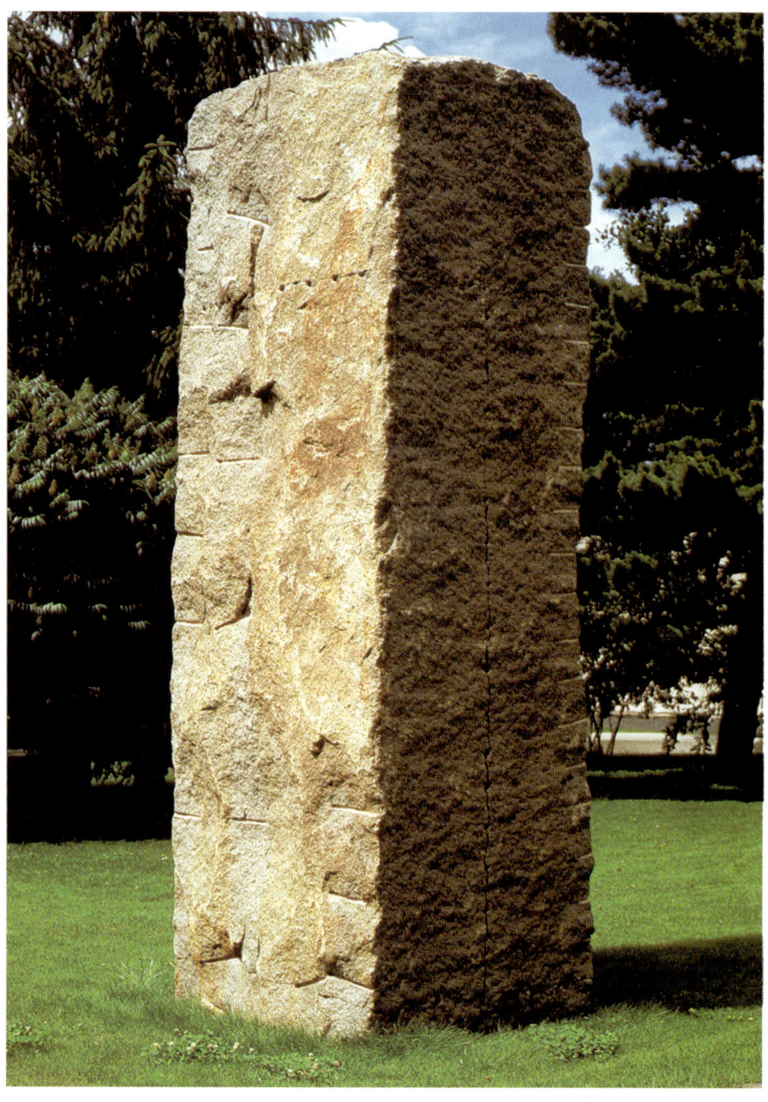

Bibliography

for the Wilhelm Lehmbruck Museum and its collections

Museum architecture

Frank Hovenbitzer, 'Die Museumsarchitektur Manfred Lehmbrucks', in: *Stadtbild Duisburg. Identität, Wandel und Vision*, ed. by Christoph Brockhaus, Wilhelm Lehmbruck Museum, Duisburg 1999, pp. 47–66

Collection and exhibtiton catalogues and other volumes on the work of Wilhelm Lehmbruck

Erwin Petermann, *Die Druckgrafik von Wilhelm Lehmbruck*, Stuttgart 1964 (out of print)
Wilhelm Lehmbruck Museum Duisburg, Vol. III: Wilhelm Lehmbruck, Frühwerk: Plastiken und Zeichnungen, Recklinghausen 1969 (out of print)
Lehmbruck und Italien. Zeichnung, Grafik, Plastik, exhib. cat., Duisburg 1978
Siegfried Salzmann, *Das Wilhelm Lehmbruck Museum Duisburg*, Recklinghausen 1981
Gerhard Händler, *Wilhelm Lehmbruck. Die Zeichnungen der Reifezeit*, Stuttgart 1985
Wilhelm Lehmbruck, *Plastik, Malerei, Graphik aus den Sammlungen des Wilhelm Lehmbruck Museums der Stadt Duisburg*, exhib. cat., Leipzig 1987/1988 (out of print)
Dietrich Schubert, *Die Kunst Wilhelm Lehmbrucks*, Worms, Dresden 1990 (2nd revised ed., out of print)
Wilhelm Lehmbruck, *Zeichnungen aus dem Wilhelm Lehmbruck Museum Duisburg*, Duisburg 1991
Margarita C. Lahusen, *Wilhelm Lehmbruck, Gemälde und großformatige Zeichnungen*, Munich 1997
Wilhelm Lehmbruck, exhib. cat., Bremen 2000

Collections catalogues on casts, sculpture and objects

'Meisterwerke moderner Kunst', Information sheets nos. I–VI, ed. by Ch. Brockhaus, Duisburg 1991
Internationale Plastik des 20. Jahrhunderts aus dem Wilhelm Lehmbruck Museum Duisburg, Duisburg 1988
Meisterwerke internationaler Plastik des 20. Jahrhunderts aus dem Wilhelm Lehmbruck Museum Duisburg in conjunction with the Kunstsammlung zu Weimar, Weimar, Duisburg 1988
Sculptures du XXe. Siècle. Collection du Wilhelm Lehmbruck Museum Ville de Duisburg, Musée des Beaux-Arts de Calais 1989
Sculptures of the 20th Century from the Wilhelm Lehmbruck Museum Duisburg, Portsmouth, City Museum and Art Gallery, Sheffield, Graves Gallery, Cardiff, National Museum of Wales 1989/90
Dani Karavan. Dialog Düsseldorf-Duisburg, Kunstsammlung Nordrhein-Westfalen, Düsseldorf, Wilhelm Lehmbruck Museum Duisburg 1989, Düsseldorf 1989
German Sculpture from 1949–1989, Vilnus, Minsk, St. Petersburg, Kiev 1990 (Russian edition)
Skulpturen, ed. by Christoph Brockhaus and Gottlieb Leinz, Wilhelm Lehmbruck Museum Duisburg, Duisburg 1992
Lutz Fritsch, *Rheinorange*, Munich1993
Wilhelm Lehmbruck Preis Duisburg 1966–1996, Laudatories and speeches, ed. by Christoph Brockhaus, Cologne 1997
Christel Blömecke, Peter Güllenstern, Servet Kocyigit und das Wilhelm Lehmbruck Stipendium seit 1966, Duisburg 2000

Collections catalogues on painting, graphics and photography

Stiftung Welker, *Gemälde aus drei Jahrhunderten*, Duisburg 1986
Henry Moore, Druckgrafik 1931–1980 aus dem Wilhelm Lehmbruck Museum, Galerie Jahrhunderthalle Hoechst, Duisburg 1988
Dr. G. Deneke und E. Deneke-Gerth, *Schenkung. Verzeichnis des Bestandes*, Duisburg 1990/91
Bildhauergrafik des Wilhelm Lehmbruck Museums Duisburg, Duisburg 1991
Franz Bernhard, Radierungen (1966–1992), Duisburg 1992
Sammlung Wilhelm Houben. Europäische Malerei und Zeichnung des 16.–19. Jahrhunderts, Duisburg 1995
Rolf Sackenheim, *Werke im Wilhelm Lehmbruck Museum Duisburg*, Duisburg 1996
Schön wie Blumen. Japanische Farbholzschnitte des 19. Jahrhunderts aus dem Wilhelm Lehmbruck Museum Duisburg, Duisburg 1997
Britta Lauer, *Das lebendige Museum, Wilhelm Lehmbruck Museum*, Duisburg 1997
Die Fotosammlung des Wilhelm Lehmbruck Museums, Duisburg 1997
Zeichnungen. Wilhelm Lehmbruck Museum Duisburg, Duisburg 1998
Gemälde. Wilhelm Lehmbruck Museum Duisburg, Duisburg 1999

List of Artists